URBAN AND REGIONAL POLICY AND ITS EFFECTS

VOLUME THREE

URBAN AND REGIONAL POLICY AND ITS EFFECTS

NANCY PINDUS

HOWARD WIAL

HAROLD WOLMAN

editors

BROOKINGS INSTITUTION PRESS
Washington, D.C.

Copyright © 2010
THE BROOKINGS INSTITUTION
1775 Massachusetts Avenue, N.W., Washington, D.C. 20036
www.brookings.edu

Library of Congress Cataloging-in-Publication data

Urban and regional policy and its effects / Margery Austin Turner, Howard Wial, and
Harold Wolman, editors.
      p.   cm.
  Summary: "Brings policymakers, practitioners, and scholars up to speed on the state of
knowledge on urban and regional policy issues. Conceptualizes fresh thinking of different
aspects (economic development, education, land use), presenting main themes and
implications and identifying gaps to fill for successful formulation and implementation of
urban and regional policy"—Provided by publisher.

  Includes bibliographical references and index.
  ISBN 978-0-8157-0406-5 (pbk. : alk. paper)
  1. Urban policy—Congresses. 2. Urban economics—Congresses. 3. Urban renewal—
Congresses. 4. Regional planning—Congresses. 5. City planning—Congresses. I.
Turner, Margery Austin, 1955– II. Wial, Howard. III. Wolman, Harold. IV. Title.

  HT151.U65 2008
  338.973009173'2—dc22   2008016030

9 8 7 6 5 4 3 2 1

The paper used in this publication meets minimum requirements of the
American National Standard for Information Sciences—Permanence of Paper for
Printed Library Materials: ANSI Z39.48-1992.

Typeset in Adobe Garamond

Composition by R. Lynn Rivenbark
Macon, Georgia

Printed by Versa Press
East Peoria, Illinois

Contents

Urban and Regional Policy and Its Effects, volume three, is the third in a series of publications that provide scholars, policymakers, and practitioners with accessible summaries of what is known about the effectiveness of selected urban and regional policies. This volume contains edited versions of the papers presented at a conference arranged by the editors and held at the George Washington University, May 21–22, 2009. The conference and this volume are products of a collaboration between the Brookings Institution's Metropolitan Policy Program, the George Washington University's George Washington Institute of Public Policy and Trachtenberg School of Public Policy and Public Administration, and the Urban Institute. All the papers represent the views of the authors and not necessarily the views of the staff members, officers, or trustees of the Brookings Institution, the George Washington University, or the Urban Institute.

Coeditors	Nancy Pindus, *Urban Institute*
	Howard Wial, *Brookings Institution*
	Harold Wolman, *George Washington University*

| Staff | Sean Hardgrove, *staff assistant* |
| | Richard Shearer, *intern* |

| Advisers | Alan Berube, *Brookings Institution* |
| | Margery Austin Turner, *Urban Institute* |

Contributors	Ajay Agarwal, *Queen's University*
	Robert A. Baade, *Lake Forest College*
	Richard Buddin, *RAND Corporation*
	Genevieve Giuliano, *University of Southern California*
	Cassandra Guarino, *Michigan State University*
	G. Thomas Kingsley, *Urban Institute*
	Robert W. Wassmer, *California State University, Sacramento*
	Ron Zimmer, *Vanderbilt University*

Discussants	Alan Berube, *Brookings Institution*
	David Brunori, *George Washington University*
	Kelly Clifton, *University of Maryland*
	Dennis Coates, *University of Maryland, Baltimore County*
	Dylan Conger, *George Washington University*
	Arlee Reno, *Cambridge Systematics*
	Andrea Sarzynski, *George Washington University*
	Gregory Squires, *George Washington University*
	Kenneth Temkin, *Temkin Associates*
	Margery Austin Turner, *Urban Institute*
	Robert W. Wassmer, *California State University, Sacramento*

Conference Participants

Gregory Acs, *Urban Institute*
Pamela Blumenthal, *George Washington University*
Leonard Burman, *Urban Institute*
Stephanie Cellini, *George Washington University*
Alec Friedhoff, *Brookings Institution*
Emily Garr, *Brookings Institution*
Charlotte Kirschner, *George Washington University*
Elizabeth Kneebone, *Brookings Institution*
Robert Lerman, *Urban Institute*
Alice Levy, *George Washington University*
Mark Muro, *Brookings Institution*
Robert Puentes, *Brookings Institution*
Margaret Simms, *Urban Institute*
Travis St. Clair, *George Washington University*
Brett Theodos, *Urban Institute*

Preface

The *Urban and Regional Policy and Its Effects* series is designed to present evidence about the impacts of urban and regional policies in a format that is accessible to policymakers and practitioners as well as scholars. The series and the conferences on which the series is based are the products of a collaboration between the Brookings Institution's Metropolitan Policy Program, George Washington University's George Washington Institute of Public Policy and Trachtenberg School of Public Policy and Public Administration, and the Urban Institute.

This volume and the 2009 Conference on Urban and Regional Policy and Its Effects came about with the support of several people at the sponsoring institutions. At Brookings, Bruce Katz, director of the Metropolitan Policy Program, provided the program's support for this project. Alan Berube provided essential intellectual advice. At the George Washington University, Joe Cordes, associate director of the Trachtenberg School of Public Policy and Public Administration, provided useful advice throughout. At the Urban Institute, Robert Reischauer, president, provided institutional support for this project. Margery Turner, one of the founding editors of the *Urban and Regional Policy and Its Effects* series, continued to be a source of sage advice.

A number of other people were instrumental in making the conference and this volume a reality. Katie Bruder of George Washington University managed the conference logistics. Jamaine Fletcher of Brookings and Olive Cox and Kim Rycroft of the George Washington Institute of Public Policy provided administrative support for the conference and throughout the publication process. Pamela Blumenthal, Alice Levy, and Travis St. Clair of George Washington University took notes on the conference sessions. Chad Shearer of Brookings helped prepare the conference papers for publication. Larry Converse, Eileen Hughes, and Janet Walker of the Brookings Institution Press expertly and gracefully managed the editing and production of the conference volume.

We are grateful to the John D. and Catherine T. MacArthur Foundation, whose generous support of the Brookings Institution's Metropolitan Economy Initiative made Brookings's cosponsorship of the conference and editorial work on this volume possible. We also thank the Fannie Mae Foundation, George Gund Foundation, Heinz Endowments, and Rockefeller Foundation for providing general support to the Brookings Metropolitan Policy Program. We thank the George Washington University for providing funding for the conference through its Selective Excellence Program.

1

Introduction

NANCY PINDUS, HOWARD WIAL, AND HAROLD WOLMAN

U rban and regional policy debates often are long on rhetoric but short on evidence about policy impacts. To redress that imbalance, the Brookings Institution, the George Washington University Institute of Public Policy and the Trachtenberg School of Public Policy and Public Administration, and the Urban Institute held the third in the annual conference series "Urban and Regional Policy and Its Effects" at the George Washington University in Washington, D.C., May 21–22, 2009. Papers were commissioned for the conference from distinguished social scientists and practitioners. The conference sought to engage authors and discussants in a cross-disciplinary dialogue focused on the central theme—evidence of policy effects. The chapters in this volume are revised versions of the commissioned papers.

Our examination of urban and regional policy and its effects is organized around five key policy challenges that most metropolitan areas and local communities face. Each of the chapters in this volume deals with a specific policy topic representing one of these challenges:

—*Creating quality neighborhoods for families*, represented in this volume by "Policies to Cope with Foreclosures and Their Effects on Neighborhoods," by G. Thomas Kingsley.

—*Building human capital*, represented by "School Choice: Options and Outcomes," by Ron Zimmer, Cassandra Guarino, and Richard Buddin.

—*Governing effectively*, represented by "Commuter Taxes in U.S. Metropolitan Areas," by Robert W. Wassmer.

—*Growing a competitive economy through industry-based strategies*, represented by "Getting into the Game: Is the Gamble on Sports as a Stimulus for Urban Economic Development a Good Bet?" by Robert A. Baade.

—*Managing the spatial pattern of metropolitan growth and development*, represented by "Public Transit as a Metropolitan Growth and Development Strategy," by Genevieve Giuliano and Ajay Agarwal.

The goal of this volume is to inform scholars, policymakers, and practitioners of the state of knowledge regarding the effectiveness of the policy approaches, reforms, or experiments listed above in addressing key social and economic problems facing central cities, suburbs, and metropolitan areas. Authors were not required to conduct original research, although some did so. Rather, their task was to take a fresh and unfettered look at the area and conceptualize (or reconceptualize) the issue and the questions that should be asked to inform intelligent public debate. Given that conceptualization, the authors were to summarize extant research on the topic and, on the basis of that research and their own knowledge, to set forth what is known about the effects of the public policy approach under discussion and the public policy implications of what is known. They also were asked to identify what is still not known but is important to find out.

Summary of Chapters

As the conference was being held, the United States was in the middle of a major economic crisis that had its most immediate origins in the collapse of a housing bubble that resulted in the decline of housing values and a vast increase in foreclosures, affecting low- and moderate-income families in particular. Tom Kingsley's chapter discusses how the collapse has affected neighborhoods and communities and examines the policies that have been employed to address the problems associated with it.

Kingsley begins by summarizing the causes of the foreclosure crisis, which he attributes to the relaxation of safeguards governing mortgage lending institutions. He also notes that while the foreclosure problem is national in scope, the extent of the problem varies by metropolitan region and by type of neighborhood. The greatest problems occurred in states where the density of subprime mortgages was highest, including Florida (Miami and Orlando), Arizona (Phoenix), Nevada (Las Vegas), and California (Riverside–San Bernardino). Problems varied by neighborhood as well, with subprime mortgage densities highest in neighborhoods where minority residents were predominant.

Kingsley identifies foreclosure's three major impacts on communities—physical deterioration and declining property values, crime and social disorder, and local government fiscal stress and service deterioration—and cites research findings that corroborate those impacts.

In terms of policies to respond to the adverse impact of foreclosures on neighborhoods, Kingsley says that most experts agree that the central objective is to restore a healthy private real estate market in neighborhoods experiencing foreclosures. He cites six programmatic elements as a means of accomplishing that objective:

—organizing, mobilizing support, and building capacity

—securing and maintaining vacant foreclosed properties

—expediting the private sale of foreclosed properties

—directly acquiring and managing foreclosed properties

—maintaining and upgrading the neighborhood environment

—developing a neighborhood-based strategy that includes various mixes of intervention types and investment priorities.

Kingsley observes that much of the federal government's response has been directed at efforts to *prevent* foreclosure and eviction; however, it did include a community-impact response through the establishment of the $3.9 billion Neighborhood Stabilization Program as part of the 2008 Housing and Economic Recovery Act. This program provides funds to states and communities for five eligible uses that are broadly consistent with the programmatic elements of neighborhood stabilization set forth above. The American Recovery and Reinvestment Act provided an additional $2 billion for the program in 2009. Although it is far too early to evaluate the program's effects, Kingsley cites skeptical observers who are concerned that many of the jurisdictions receiving the funds lack the capacity or experience to make wise use of them.

With respect to local policy, Kingsley reviews existing literature for lessons related to each of the six programmatic elements. He notes, for example, that because a good relationship with the servicers who are responsible for at-risk properties in neighborhoods with high foreclosure densities may prove beneficial in all phases of the neighborhood stabilization process, an important step in organizing is to identify and collaborate with those servicers.

Kingsley observes that experts agree that to secure and maintain vacant and foreclosed properties in weak markets where servicers may not have adequate incentives to do so, the local government should step in to encourage responsible behavior through some combination of incentives, sanctions, and standard setting and enforcement. He also cites researchers who argue that efforts should be made to prevent vacancies or minimize the period of vacancy by encouraging servicers to promote rental occupancy of the property, most likely by the prior owner-occupant, until a new purchaser can be found.

In neighborhoods where market conditions are weak and there are no prospective purchasers, it may be desirable as a last resort for local government agencies to acquire the foreclosed properties and get them back into use or hold them off the market for a time. In many municipalities that will require increased staff capacity and, in weaker areas, the creation of specialized land bank authorities, few of which currently exist. Kingsley also notes that maintaining and upgrading the neighborhood environment is critical in neighborhoods undergoing foreclosures so that the negative effects of foreclosed property on other neighborhood housing units is kept to a minimum. That suggests that local government should give priority to trash removal, street cleaning and repair, vacant lot cleaning, and targeted code enforcement in neighborhoods threatened by high foreclosure rates.

Kingsley emphasizes that both the extent and nature of problems resulting from foreclosure vary across neighborhoods and that public policy needs to be sensitive to those variations. He also notes that fiscally stressed local governments are not likely to have the resources to undertake the full range of activities in all neighborhoods experiencing foreclosure problems and that they must make use of an array of neighborhood data to allocate resources strategically. As a guide to resource allocation, Kingsley categorizes neighborhoods in terms of market strength and risk of foreclosure and recommends an appropriate investment strategy for each:

—In neighborhoods with low risk of foreclosures, regardless of market strength, little or no intervention is necessary.

—In strong-market neighborhoods, action should be directed toward prevention of foreclosures and minimization of vacancy should foreclosures occur.

—In neighborhoods with an intermediate level of market demand but only a moderate number of foreclosed properties, spending on prevention and on code enforcement and public maintenance should be a high priority.

—In neighborhoods with a weak market and a high risk of foreclosure—the most difficult cases—large-scale investments should be made to move the neighborhoods into the intermediate category when possible, although most cities will not have the resources to do so for many neighborhoods. Because large-scale rehabilitation that will not become economically self-sustaining could be a substantial waste of public funding, local governments may have to take the difficult step of acquiring foreclosed properties, demolishing the structures, and holding the parcels in a land bank until market conditions rebound sufficiently to justify further investment.

Kingsley concludes by stressing the importance of having good data and information to guide and evaluate neighborhood responses.

The poor performance of urban school systems has important implications for urban areas as well as for students, and it is drawing the attention of urban policymakers, parents, and academics alike. A number of reforms that expand schooling options in urban areas have been introduced to improve school performance, including school vouchers, charter schools, magnet schools, and inter- and intradistrict open enrollment policies. "School Choice: Options and Outcomes," by Ron Zimmer, Cassandra Guarino, and Richard Buddin, examines the evidence of the impact of such options. Their chapter updates prior studies of charter schools and voucher programs and adds a new and much-needed summary of studies on choice programs managed by school districts. An important contribution is their consideration of whether there is a difference between the effectiveness of district-managed choices, such as magnet schools and open enrollment programs, and that of independently or privately run forms of choice, such as charter schools and voucher programs.

The chapter describes the evolution of choice-based reform in the United States and discusses differences between the public's expectations of government forms of choice and its expectations of independently controlled forms. The authors note that theoretical arguments for choice identify the following elements of choice as promoting learning gains: better student-school matching, more innovative or higher-quality schools due to greater school autonomy, and a general increase in the quality of all schools in response to competition for student enrollments. The chapter examines the empirical evidence regarding the impact of voucher programs, charter schools, and government-managed school choice options—such as interdistrict choice and open enrollment programs and magnet schools—on student outcomes, the distribution of students, and competition among schools.

The authors distinguish between direct effects, the outcomes for students enrolling in schools of choice, and indirect effects, the impacts (mainly through competitive pressure) that a school of choice has on student outcomes in other schools. Reviewing the results of more than thirty studies of domestic school choice programs—including voucher programs, charter schools, and district-managed school choice programs—the authors find that, for those three types of school choice options, the evidence has been inconclusive, with no clear consensus that any of them are having strong effects on test scores. In terms of direct effects on student outcomes, then, there is no strong evidence of much difference between the effects of nondistrict and district-managed choice programs.

A major tenet of the school choice movement is that school choice should be able to create pressure on traditional public schools by creating competition for student enrollments. In reviewing the fairly limited research that has examined the competitive effects of vouchers and charter schools, the authors find that it has generally noted that although competitive effects are challenging to estimate, there is more consistent evidence of a competitive effect for voucher programs than for charter schools.

The authors also examine the effects of school choice on the distribution of students by race or ethnicity and ability. If schools of choice simply recruit the best students from traditional public schools, the success of choice programs might be illusory and school choice may further stratify an already ethnically or racially stratified system. On the other hand, schools of choice may improve racial integration by letting families choose schools outside of neighborhoods where housing is racially segregated.

The evidence on distributional effects has been somewhat mixed across the various school choice options. Research suggests that students who take advantage of vouchers are generally disadvantaged (as many of the programs are means tested) but tend to come from families with higher education levels and are less likely to be special education students. Research on charter schools has used stronger research designs and generally found that charter schools tended to attract students whose prior test scores were below the average for the schools that they exited. However, in some locations, black and white students were more likely to transfer to charter schools where there were higher concentrations of students from their own race than there were at the schools that they exited. The research on district-managed programs also is mixed.

The authors conclude that the mixed results concerning the efficacy, competitive impacts, and distributional effects of school choice are a consequence of methodological challenges, limited research, and excessive focus on test scores. The fact that selection is at the heart of school choice creates a challenge for research that attempts to find effects. For example, students choosing to attend schools of choice may be more motivated or have more involved parents than students who do not exercise choice, and any observed learning increases might result from those characteristics rather than from the quality of the schools themselves. The authors found no research that specifically examined the competitive effects of district-managed choice programs and scant research on the competitive effects of voucher programs or charter schools.

Zimmer, Guarino, and Buddin point out that research has focused primarily on test score outcomes and is only beginning to focus on other important outcomes, such as graduation rates and college enrollment. They recommend that researchers expand their analyses to understand what factors lead to positive and negative results. The authors find that the patterns that emerge in synthesizing the research highlight issues that warrant further exploration, including what operational features of school choice programs lead to differential effects and whether the programs are leading to widespread distributional effects.

The Great Recession, which began in late 2007, has strained municipal finances. In many large central cities the strain has exacerbated the fiscal problems resulting from the decades-long exodus of employers and middle- and high-income residents. In addition to cutting city services and laying off municipal employees, central cities have sought new sources of revenue. Commuter taxes, a revenue source whose use declined over the last half-century, have received renewed attention in New York, where Mayor Bloomberg suggested reinstating the city's commuter tax as an alternative to a steep property tax increase, and Philadelphia, where a long-term program to reduce the city wage tax was put on hold in 2010.

In "Commuter Taxes in U.S. Metropolitan Areas," Robert W. Wassmer examines whether commuter taxes are a desirable way for central cities to raise revenue. After reviewing the history and current use of commuter taxes, Wassmer considers whether commuters pay their fair share of the costs of central city services. It has been argued that central cities benefit commuters by providing public services to them during the work day, provide housing and services to a disproportionate share of the poor in their metropolitan areas, and, if economically healthy, increase property values throughout the metropolitan area. Commuters, it is claimed, do not fully pay for those benefits. Yet because commuters also benefit central city residents, theory provides no clear guide to whether commuters pay too much, too little, or the right amount for the benefits that they receive from central cities. Moreover, studies that attempt to measure the benefits and costs of commuters to central cities have not reached consensus on the issue.

Wassmer then considers the impact of commuter taxes on central city population, employment, and tax revenue. In theory, such taxes have the potential to discourage both residents and businesses from locating in the central city, and if the consequent reduction in the tax base is large enough, central city tax revenues may fall. However, the extent to which those effects occur, and whether they occur at all, depends on whether residents and businesses consider other suburban jurisdictions in the metropolitan to be good substitutes for the central city. In a metropolitan area such as Detroit, where the central city offers few inherent advantages to either residents or businesses, a central city commuter tax will induce more outmigration of people and jobs than in an area such as New York, where the central city offers distinctive amenities and opportunities for face-to-face business interaction that are less easily duplicated in the suburbs.

Wassmer reviews the evidence on the impact of commuter taxes, which uniformly shows that the taxes are associated with loss of population and employment in the central cities that impose them. Some evidence also suggests that after 1998 a reduction in Philadelphia's wage tax would have increased the city's tax revenues. Although most of the studies of commuter tax impacts do not take into account the cuts in city services that would be likely to accompany any serious effort to reduce or eliminate commuter taxes, the few that do take such cuts into account still find that the taxes reduce central city population and employment. However, the vast majority of those studies are about Philadelphia, which has the nation's highest municipal wage tax rate on commuters, so the studies' findings may not apply to the same extent, or at all, to other cities.

Wassmer also compares commuter taxes and alternative revenue sources. Citing Richard Bird, he lays out seven requirements of a local tax that economists generally consider desirable: the tax should be levied on an immobile base, should produce stable and predictable revenue, should not be easily exported to nonresidents, should be perceived as fair, should be levied on a base that promotes the accountability of the taxing authority to residents, should be easily administered, and should produce revenue adequate to meet local needs over time. Commuter taxes fail to meet all but the last two of those criteria. Wassmer considers alternatives that, in principle, are more desirable: annexation of suburban territory by the central city, a commuter tax with a credit toward the tax owed to the jurisdictions where commuters live, a reduction in central city government spending, increased assistance to the central city from the federal and state governments, interjurisdictional tax agreements, regionalization of local government at the metropolitan level, and replacement of the commuter tax with alternative central city taxes and fees.

Wassmer recognizes that completely eliminating commuter taxes and avoiding them in cities where they do not currently exist often is not politically feasible. He argues that central cities in need of additional revenue should pursue a multistep program that includes, in order of desirability, efforts to downsize city government to eliminate wasteful spending, regional funding of services whose benefits spill across jurisdictions, annexation in those parts of the country where it is possible, interjurisdictional tax agreements, state matching grants to fund city services whose benefits spill over to the suburbs, and, as a last resort, a commuter tax with a credit. Cities with commuter taxes, he argues, should try to phase out those taxes by pursuing the same steps.

The pursuit of professional sports teams and the construction of sports facilities to attract or retain teams has been a constant theme in local and regional economic development strategy for several decades. However, that strategy, particularly if there are public subsidies for construction, as there usually are, can be extremely expensive. Are the benefits worth it? Robert Baade examines that question in his chapter, "Getting into the Game: Is the Gamble on Sports as a Stimulus for Urban Economic Development a Good Bet?"

Baade begins by tracing the history of stadium construction. He finds that the cost of construction has increased since the mid-1980s and that most of the cost continues to be borne by the public sector, as it has since the end of World War II. He documents how new stadium construction has benefited owners of the new stadiums (through increases in the value of sports franchises) and players (through substantial increases in payroll after new stadium construction). Baade also observes that the public subsidies required to build new facilities can obviously be more easily borne by the public sector in larger cities or regions and that smaller cities (Green Bay in the National Football League is the iconic example) can afford to compete only in a league that engages in substantial redistribution of revenue from wealthy to less wealthy franchises.

Do the economic benefits derived from public subsidies of sports teams justify the costs of the subsidies? Baade first presents the theoretical argument on behalf of the subsidies, which holds that a major league team with a new stadium will increase attendance at the stadium from nonresidents who will not only purchase tickets to the game but also eat at local restaurants, stay at local hotels, and purchase other goods in the local area. In short, a stadium serves as part of the area's export base. The resulting increased income or a substantial portion of it will be spent locally (the multiplier effect) and will result in greater tax revenues to local government. Baade notes, however, that it is extremely difficult to accurately project benefits. Projections depend heavily on assumptions and often are undertaken by advocates whose objectivity is open to question. Their accuracy also depends on the economic condition of the region, not just the locality.

Baade questions whether the economic justifications provided are, in fact, theoretically accurate. He first notes that to the extent that owners and players are nonresident (for most of the year), most of the revenue earned by local sports teams is unlikely to be spent locally and therefore will generate low multiplier effects. In addition, the export base argument, while valid, relates only to fans attending games from outside the region. Attendees from within the region are simply rearranging their spending from one activity within the region to another. Baade argues that most attendees in most regions are local. The stadiums themselves usually accommodate only seasonal activity and do not integrate well with nearby commercial activity other than parking lots. In fact, new stadiums usually incorporate within them concessions that compete with neighborhood venues offering food, drink, and merchandise.

Baade compares projected returns from new sports stadium construction, which frequently are estimated by stadium boosters, with the more objective estimates of returns from stadiums that were actually built reported in studies by economists. He finds substantial divergence, with the former generally predicting positive returns and the latter finding little or no impact. Indeed, Baade argues that investment in new stadiums can have negative impacts for a community, since "[p]rofessional sports and stadiums divert economic development toward labor-intensive, relatively unskilled labor (low-wage) activities. To the extent that this developmental path diverges from less labor-intensive, more highly skilled labor (high-wage) activities characteristic of other economies within the region, it would be expected that the sports-minded area would experience a falling share of regional income." Baade does note, however, that sports facilities as a *component* of a downtown commercial development strategy, as in Cleveland and Indianapolis, may make sense.

The author then turns his attention to what are frequently viewed as "noneconomic" benefits of professional sports, including increased community visibility, improved community image, stimulation of other development, and the psychic value or income that residents derive from having a professional sports team in the region. Baade terms the first three of these benefits "economic signaling" and observes that if they have a positive impact on the regional economy, then that impact ought to be captured in an economic evaluation of actually built stadiums as increased economic output, income, or employment. However, as he shows, they are not.

Baade accepts that there is some psychic income associated with the presence of a professional sports team in a city but emphasizes that, while clearly difficult to estimate, the question is whether the value of that "income" exceeds the public subsidy paid. He reviews the literature and finds two methodologies for estimating psychic benefits. The first, the contingent valuation method, consists of surveying residents to determine how much money they would be willing to give up in a specific hypothetical scenario—for example, to construct a stadium and obtain or retain a professional sports team. The literature finds that there is willingness to pay nontrivial amounts, but those amounts, in aggregate, usually fall far short of the public subsidies provided.

The second method, compensating differentials, is based on the premise that if an area's amenities, such as professional sports teams and venues, provide value to its residents, then, in return for those amenities, residents will be willing to accept higher housing prices and lower wages to live there. Although one study does find compensating differentials that substantially exceed subsidies, other studies do not. Baade also notes that these studies incorporate all amenities (and disamenities) present in the region and thus the compensating differentials empirically estimated cannot all be attributed to the presence of a professional sports team.

Baade concludes that "[a] preponderance of evidence suggests that sport subsidies alone do not produce social value in excess of their social costs" and that there are adverse distributional consequences as income and wealth are transferred from taxpayers to owners and players. He observes that the only argument that might justify subsidizing sports teams is that the teams improve residents' quality of life (psychic income), and he calls for research to develop better methods for estimating any such benefit.

In "Public Transit as a Metropolitan Growth and Development Strategy," Genevieve Giuliano and Ajay Agarwal consider the theory and reality of public transit as a solution to the problem of urban sprawl. Urban sprawl—the decentralization of population and jobs—has been associated with congestion, air pollution, energy consumption, loss of open space, and more recently obesity and global climate change. Urban sprawl is also associated with problems such as loss of social capital and spatial segmentation by race and class.

Public transit, particularly rail transit, has been viewed as an essential component of reversing decentralization trends and supporting the revitalization and growth of cities. Public transit is also seen as an important means for restructuring the suburbs and guiding the growth of newer cities to transform them according to what are now accepted "smart growth" principles among urban planners: building cities with moderate to high population and employment densities, intermixed housing and jobs, heterogeneous neighborhoods, a high level of access to public transit and options for walking, and limited use of the private automobile.

The authors review the more than three decades of research on the influence of public transit—particularly rail transit—on urban form and find that while investment in public transit may in theory lead to a more compact urban form, the evidence is quite mixed. Their chapter presents a critical review of the influence of rail transit on travel behavior, land use, and urban form to answer the following questions: What are the theoretical expectations from transit investments? Under what conditions might transit investment lead to a more compact urban form? What is the evidence about the impact of transit on urban form? Finally, in view of the mixed evidence, why is transit investment still perceived as a critical policy tool for shaping cities?

Transportation infrastructure lowers transport cost by improving accessibility. Theoretically, economic activity should gravitate toward rail corridors, implying that rail transit has a redistributing/redirecting effect on future development, and that shift should be reflected in increased land values. That is, property values around transit stations should be higher, thereby stimulating higher densities around rail stations. However, the reality of metropolitan areas is far more complex than assumed in standard economic theory. Residential location choice is more than a simple trade-off between housing cost and commuting cost, and individual preferences play an important role.

Furthermore, basic assumptions about where people live and work have changed over time. In contrast to the standard assumption that all employment is located at the city center, most metropolitan employment is now located outside the center—some of it concentrated inside multiple "employment centers" and some dispersed more broadly. In addition, a substantial proportion of households now are dual-earner households, which implies that they must choose a residential location that can accommodate more than one job location.

With respect to a firm's location decision, the decline in manufacturing and increase in services and information processing implies that output costs (for example, the cost of shipping products to market) are becoming relatively less important. The decentralization of employment observed over the past several decades is consistent with labor force access becoming a relatively more important location consideration.

After reviewing the theory, Giuliano and Agarwal turn to the evidence. The authors maintain that the best measure of transit benefits is land values and that a second-best measure is land use changes. Other measurement issues considered include the appropriate spatial area for expected impact (for example, a quarter-mile radius, which is roughly the distance that can be covered on foot in five minutes), the appropriate time frame for measuring impacts, and the context of property values in the region as well as in similar transportation corridors.

The authors' review of the evidence finds that it does not establish unambiguously whether or not rail transit investments are capitalized in property values. The mixed results suggest that the impacts of any given rail investment depend on local circumstances, so the authors describe three illustrative cases: Portland, Oregon; the San Francisco Bay Area Rapid Transit (BART) system; and Metropolitan Atlanta Rapid Transit Authority (MARTA). Each case study addresses public transit, transportation and land use policies, impacts on travel behavior, impacts on land values and land use, and impacts on regional spatial trends.

The three cases describe very different efforts to use transit investment to influence metropolitan structure. Portland represents an ambitious, integrated transport and land use plan that has resulted in more transit use and possibly higher densities within its urban growth boundary (UGB). But there also is evidence of growth spreading beyond the UGB, and the overall structure of the metropolitan area is similar to that of other areas of its size. The BART system, the result of a consensus agreement among several counties in the San Francisco Bay area, was built in a mature, relatively dense metropolitan area that had a challenging geography and already had a high level of transit use. BART was not part of a comprehensive land use plan like Portland's, and, not surprisingly, BART outcomes have varied across the system. The MARTA system had neither a geographic nor policy advantage. Atlanta's urban form was and is dispersed and low density. As would be expected under such circumstances, the rail system has had no impact on accessibility and consequently no impact on land values or land use.

The authors conclude that rail transit does not consistently lead to significant land use changes and hence is not necessarily an effective growth management strategy. When impacts of rail transit are found, they are highly localized and tend to occur in fast-growing, heavily congested core areas; they also are likely to be small in magnitude. Furthermore, impacts depend on complementary land use policies and parking and traffic policies. The authors note that "[w]ithout changing our policies regarding private vehicles, transit investment will remain an inefficient strategy for influencing travel behavior and thereby location choices."

Giuliano and Agarwal suggest several options for addressing urban sprawl that would be more effective than rail transit investment, including more reliance on land use policy itself; providing incentives in the form of density off-sets, flexible parking requirements, or reduced fees; and using smart growth principles in designing new communities. They also recommend more serious consideration of bus transit, using busways to give buses the same travel time advantage as rail, typically at far less cost.

Policy Analysis Research and the Making of Public Policy

The chapters in this volume illustrate that in many urban and regional policy areas, policymakers are not guided by research that uses analytical techniques to determine whether policies achieve or are likely to achieve their goals. School choice programs are widely advocated despite the absence of clear and consistent evidence of their impact. Commuter taxes are used in some cities and advocated by some large city mayors despite evidence of their economic disadvantages. Stadiums are popular among local elected officials and economic developers despite strong evidence that they do not contribute to local economic development. Rail transit is popular among local elected officials and economic developers who think that it will create more compact and vibrant metropolitan areas, despite evidence that it does so only under circumstances that exist in just a few metropolitan areas. Policies to prevent foreclosure are not widespread despite evidence that there are effective practices to promote that widely shared goal.

Why do policymakers apparently pay so little attention to policy research? That question has been the subject of a substantial amount of both conjecture and systematic research. Indeed, there is an entire literature on research utilization, a subfield of knowledge utilization, and there are articles that address the question specifically.[1]

1. See, for example, Wolman (1988); Greenbaum and Landers (2009).

The literature makes an important distinction. Utilization can be viewed as either "concrete" (research is used to inform a specific program or policy) or "conceptual" (research influences the intellectual orientation of policymakers in the longer run).[2] In the first instance, policy research may or may not have an effect on a particular policy decision, while in the second it might affect the policy agenda (what gets considered in the policymaking process) and policy framing and design in the longer term. For example, there is probably more, and more sophisticated, public debate about stadiums than there was twenty years ago.

The literature makes clear that although policy research rarely has direct effects on policy design, it often plays an important role in the policy process in other ways. Policymakers use it to frame debates, to rationalize policy positions or decisions adopted for other reasons, and to support the legitimacy of their positions.[3] However, the questions with which we are concerned here are related to concrete utilization: Why do policymakers seem to ignore the findings of policy analysis research? What, if anything, can be done to increase the use of such research? We consider answers to those questions first in terms of the characteristics of research and researchers and then in terms of the characteristics of policymakers and the policy process.

Characteristics of Research and Researchers

Research often does not offer clear guidance to policymakers. Indeed, it frequently reaches inconclusive or contradictory results, and researchers may disagree both on research findings across multiple studies and on how they should be interpreted.[4] School choice research, in particular, is an area where the findings are quite diverse.[5] Contradictory findings often result in dueling experts, and the usual result is that policymakers ignore both or readily accept the findings that support their existing views.

There are many reasons for the lack of clear findings. Results often are sensitive to differences in assumptions, research design, methods, and data sources. (The chapters on sports and school choice illustrate that point especially clearly.) Research results also may be sensitive to context, including time and place. Results from a study of a program in one area may not be the same as those in another area because of differences in area characteristics. Some research may differ in quality from other research. Not all research or research findings should be treated as equal; some research is simply better than others.

2. Greenberg, Linksz, and Mandell (2003, pp. 48–50).
3. Shulock (1999).
4. Maynard (2006); Greenbaum and Landers, 2009; Hirasuna and Hansen (2009).
5. Henig (2008).

Research seemingly on the same topic may ask somewhat different questions. For example, consider two questions related to school choice: Do students who attend schools of choice through a lottery perform better than those who apply but aren't admitted? Do individual students who move between schools of choice and regular public schools perform better in schools of choice? They may sound like the same question, but, in fact, they are not. Or consider two other questions: Do schools of choice increase the performance of students who attend them? Do schools of choice narrow the performance gap between black and white students who attend them? Both are relevant questions, but they may yield different answers.

Policymakers often do not have easy access to research studies, and when studies are available, they often are presented in ways that make them unintelligible. They may, for example, be written in technical jargon, which researchers understand but policymakers are not likely to. The discussion may focus primarily on methodological considerations that condition the findings and that are important, indeed critical, to the research but that require a person to have a substantial technical background in order to understand them.

One reason why research findings are rarely presented in a way that makes them accessible to policymakers is that often researchers are not interested in the policy implications of their research or in the problems of policymakers. Many make little or no effort to draw policy implications or to do so in a way that makes their findings comprehensible to policymakers, nor do they try to disseminate their research to policymakers.[6] For example, many academic research articles about the impacts of public policies lack short and clear executive summaries that directly address findings and their policy implications, and the authors of the articles rarely produce such executive summaries as separate documents.

In particular, there is a lack of "overview policy research literature" that assesses the entire body of research in an area and comes to conclusions about the state of existing knowledge—what we know, what we think that we know but aren't sure of, and what we don't know.[7] The relative lack of such literature is readily explainable. Academic journals do not usually publish literature reviews, and academics seeking tenure and promotion do not receive much credit for writing and publishing them.[8]

Research questions and the way that they are formulated change over time, making research conducted in one period less useful for later policymakers and sometimes making it difficult for researchers to keep up with policy concerns.

---

6. Weisbrod (1997).

7. Greenbaum and Landers (2009); Henig (2008).

8. The *Journal of Economic Literature* and *Journal of Economic Perspective* are excellent exceptions, but of necessity they cover only a small number of areas, many not directly related to public policy.

For example, interest in transit as a densification policy is relatively new, so there are few studies of that topic per se. Moreover, research does not always address questions of the greatest relevance to policymakers. For example, most research on sports stadiums has analyzed economic development impacts, but policymakers and the public may be interested in the fiscal returns. (The evidence is clear that stadium construction does not yield net regional economic development benefits in terms of jobs or income, but it *may* yield a positive fiscal return for the specific locality in which it is located.) More generally, elected officials may see stadiums as a collective consumption good—that is, as a good that increases the overall psychic well-being of their residents. As Robert Baade's chapter indicates, research has only recently begun to consider such concerns. In addition, research is mostly about the behavioral impacts of policies (the impacts of school choice on student learning, for example, or the impacts of stadiums, rail transit, and commuter taxes on the location decisions of households and businesses), but behavioral impacts may be small and less important than other considerations in policymaking, such as distributional impacts or service provision.[9]

Researchers sometimes base their conclusions on statistical significance (the precision with which the impact of a policy is estimated) rather than substantive significance (the size and importance of the policy's impact). That may lead them to recommend policies whose impacts are trivial or to ignore policies whose impacts are potentially large or at least to fail to tell policymakers how large the impacts of policies are.[10]

Research and researchers often ignore political feasibility or produce "best" policies that are not politically feasible. (The commuter tax literature, for example, argues for abolition of the tax, but that is not feasible in a city like Philadelphia, which is highly dependent on it.) The policy process inevitably involves negotiation and compromise as a necessary means of aggregating majorities and the relevant question may not be what the optimal policy is but what the costs and benefits of various types of suboptimal policies are.

Characteristics of Policymakers and the Policy Process

Elected policymakers generally have a very strong interest in being reelected. (In fact, David Mayhew has famously characterized U.S. senators and representatives as motivated by a single-minded concern for reelection and argues that their behavior can best be understood through that lens.)[11] They may have electoral incentives to oversell policy solutions that bring short-term, visible benefits

9. Wyckoff (2009).
10. Ziliak and McCloskey (2008).
11. Mayhew (1974).

if the costs are mostly invisible or diffuse (that is, borne by others outside the jurisdiction). For its part, the public may want to believe that something can (and should) be done (build stadiums, offer a school choice program) but may be poorly informed about the options.[12]

Policymakers often lack the technical knowledge needed to understand research. For example, they usually are not trained in statistical analysis and often do not understand the difference between theory and evidence.[13] That lack could conceivably be compensated for if the policymaker has staff with sufficient knowledge to understand the research and to "translate" it for use in the policy process.

Policymakers make decisions in the face of time and resource limitations and with imperfect information. Therefore they consider only a limited menu of problems and policy solutions and may be impervious to others, and they often are satisfied with policies that appear to be working well enough even if they are not the best policies.[14]

Moreover, policymakers do not "think" like researchers. As summarized in table 1-1, they seek clear, timely answers that can be explained simply and embedded in a narrative that they and their nonacademic constituents will find credible. In contrast, researchers seek technically correct answers that are embedded in abstract theories, and they are willing to draw "messier" conclusions from multiple studies that use different methods and data sources.

As Henig suggests, policymakers, particularly elected policymakers, do not process "facts."[15] Instead, they use facts to fashion narratives and embed the facts in the narratives; it is the narratives that are meaningful. As Piore argues, there are two modes of policy analysis: interpretive and instrumental.[16] Policymakers need an interpretive framework within which to ask questions about the impacts of policies. But disagreement about policies often is disagreement about the interpretive framework as much as, or more than, it is disagreement about policy impacts, and evidence about policy impacts does not affect the framework itself. For example, if the controversies over school choice are mainly about the desirability of expanding the scope of markets—because of philosophical differences about whether markets improve freedom—then policymakers' views about choice will depend on their views on that question, not on whether choice programs raise test scores.

Evidence from policy research is only one source of substantive information that policymakers make use of in assessing policy. Information also comes from

---

12. Wyckoff (2009).
13. Wyckoff (2009).
14. Goodin, Rein, and Moran (2006).
15. Henig (2008).
16. Piore (1995).

Table 1-1. *"Researcher-Think" and "Policymaker-Think"*

Research dimension	Researchers	Policymakers
Time	Researchers take the time to get the research right.	Policymakers need answers now.
Multiple studies	Understanding emerges from the cumulation of findings from multiple studies.	Understanding emerges from the findings of the "right" study.
Causality	Establishing causality is problematic and requires a sophisticated research design.	Causality is straightforward: there is correlation plus a credible narrative.
Abstraction	Abstraction is required to find general patterns.	Abstraction (and generalization) denies the complexity of real life.
Simplification	Simplification is achieved through abstraction.	Simplification is achieved through "getting the gist" of research findings.

Source: Adapted from Henig (2008, p. 223).

non–social science experts or professionals in the policy area, from practitioners, from interest and advocacy groups, from peers, from trusted acquaintances, and from a policymaker's own experiences. The fact that such information often is nonsystematic and/or anecdotal does not make it less important or, indeed, less relevant, in affecting policymakers' decisions. In short, policymakers obtain information from many sources, of which policy research is only one, and research does not automatically displace understandings gained from other sources of information.[17]

Furthermore, information on potential policy impacts and their costs and benefits, whether from policy research or from other sources, is only one of many considerations that policymakers take into account in making policy decisions. Even if it is taken into account, it may be outweighed by one or more of the other considerations mentioned.[18] Thus, for example, elected policymakers take into account the views of their constituents, as they understand them; the views of important constituents as they are expressed to them (for example, views of bankers on issues related to finance); the need for the support of specific interest groups in campaigns; the need for campaign contributions; the views of the party leadership; opportunities for visibility, "credit-claiming," and

17. Weiss (1999).
18. Greenbaum and Landers (2009); Weiss (1999).

career advancement; and the fact that they are not considering an issue in isolation but as part of a larger set of decisions on which they will interact with their legislative colleagues.

Non-elected policymakers in the bureaucracy may take into account professional norms and operating routines related to their agencies' customary practices.[19] They also consider the views of clientele groups or other groups or individuals that can affect their resources, and, of course, they consider the views of their hierarchical superiors.

Policymakers (like all human beings) resist changing their core beliefs.[20] A policymaker may ignore or rationalize research findings if they conflict with his or her ideology, self-interest, values, or previous experience.[21] Policymakers may actively oppose research findings if they conflict with strongly held policy goals.[22]

How to Encourage Greater Substantive Use of Policy Research

The threshold problem in encouraging greater use of policy research is ensuring the accessibility of policy research results to policymakers. That requires researchers to make a greater effort to disseminate results and make them comprehensible and compelling to policymakers.

First, the policy research community should produce more current state-of-knowledge literature reviews, taking into account the best studies and discounting those that have methodological problems. The reviews should not simply be presentations of contradictory results. Instead, they should come to conclusions about what the preponderance of the results suggests.

If policy researchers expect their research to have direct substantive impact, they will have to make greater efforts to disseminate it so that they get it into the hands of policymakers. Possible means include writing op-ed pieces and articles in popular journals and giving research findings directly to knowledgeable staff or to others in networks that can affect policy debates, such as professional associations and interest groups.

Findings do not mean simply results. Sometimes the most important contribution that policy research can make to help policymakers understand an issue is to clarify the concepts involved. What are we trying to do? Does this policy really contribute to achieving that goal? With what should we compare the effects of a policy? To a policymaker, comparing a policy to what would occur in its absence is not always an obvious thing to do, but it can be very informative.

---

19. Weiss (1999).
20. Sabatier and Jenkins-Smith (1993).
21. Weiss (1999); Greenbaum and Landers (2009); Hirasuna and Hansen (2009).
22. Greenberg, Linksz, and Mandell (2003).

To increase the ability of policy research to affect policy, policy research and the policy research community should

—focus particularly on the impact (or lack thereof) of policy-manipulable variables in reporting research results.

—not just say that something does not work; suggest what might work better.

—explore the effects of politically feasible alternatives even if they are not the best possible policies.

—say how large a policy's impact is likely to be and interpret that in view of how important a precise estimate of impacts is to policymakers. Do not just report statistically significant results.

—pay attention to distributional and other impacts of policies as well as to behavioral impacts.

—accept interpretive, qualitative approaches as legitimate forms of policy research. Understand that policymakers are trying to answer questions that are different from the kinds of questions that large-scale quantitative research is trying to answer. Use such approaches when they are applicable to your topic.

—be aware of the ways in which policy research is actually used in policy-making and write up research results accordingly. Be satisfied to have research used in policy debates and do not expect it to trump other influences on policy-making.

Policy researchers and the policy research community can reasonably aspire to have their research considered by policymakers. However, it is neither reasonable nor desirable for policy research and its findings to dictate policy choices. In a democratic polity, policy research is part of the policymaking process broadly conceived, including public debate, interest group conflict over policies, and negotiating, bargaining, and compromising among policymakers. Its proper role is to inform policymakers and policymaking, not to determine it.

References

Goodin, Robert E., Martin Rein, and Michael Moran. 2006. "The Public and Its Policies." In *The Oxford Handbook of Public Policy*, edited by Michael Moran, Martin Rein, and Robert E. Goodin, pp. 3–35. Oxford University Press.

Greenbaum, Robert T., and Jim Landers. 2009. "Why Are State Policy Makers Still Proponents of Enterprise Zones? What Explains Their Action in the Face of a Preponderance of the Research?" *International Regional Science Review* 32: 466–79.

Greenberg, David, Donna Linksz, and Marvin Mandell. 2003. *Social Experimentation and Public Policymaking*. Washington: Urban Institute Press.

Henig, Jeffrey R. 2008. *Spin Cycle: How Research Is Used in Policy Debates: The Case of Charter Schools*. New York: Russell Sage Foundation.

Hirasuna, Donald P., and Susan B. Hansen. 2009. "Is Social Science Useful to State Legislators?" *International Regional Science Review* 32: 429–44.

Mayhew, David. 1974. *Congress: The Electoral Connection.* Yale University Press.

Maynard, Rebecca A. 2006. "Evidence-Based Decision Making: What Will It Take for the Decision Makers to Care?" *Journal of Policy Analysis and Management* 25: 249–65.

Piore, Michael. 1995. *Beyond Individualism.* Harvard University Press.

Sabatier, Paul, and Hank Jenkins-Smith. 1993. *Policy Change and Learning: An Advocacy Coalition Approach.* Boulder, Colo.: Westview.

Shulock, Nancy. 1999. "The Paradox of Policy Analysis: If It Is Not Used, Why Do We Produce So Much of It?" *Journal of Policy Analysis and Management* 18: 226–43.

Weisbrod, Burton A. 1997. "What Policy Makers Need from the Research Community." In *The Urban Crisis: Linking Research to Action*, edited by Burton A. Weisbrod and James C. Worthy. Northwestern University Press.

Weiss, Carol H. 1999. "The Interface between Evaluation and Public Policy," *Evaluation* 5: 468–86.

Wolman, Harold. 1988. "Local Economic Development Policy: What Explains the Divergence between Policy Analysis and Political Behavior?" *Journal of Urban Affairs* 10: 19–28.

Wyckoff, Paul Gary. 2009. *Policy and Evidence in a Partisan Age.* Washington: Urban Institute Press.

Ziliak, Stephen T., and Deirdre N. McCloskey. 2008. *The Cult of Statistical Significance.* University of Michigan Press.

2

Policies to Cope with Foreclosures and Their Effects on Neighborhoods

G. THOMAS KINGSLEY

Like the others in this book, this chapter examines policies designed to address an important national problem. The assignment is especially challenging in this case because the problem—the impacts of the foreclosure crisis on communities—is new and arguably unprecedented with respect to both its nature and its severity.

What happened in the Great Depression offers little guidance. In 1930, only 48 percent of U.S. households owned their own homes. The United States subsequently built what has been regarded as the world's most effective system of homeownership—the model to which the rest of the world has aspired. In 2005, the U.S. homeownership rate reached 69 percent.[1] The "American dream" had been made affordable for more than two-thirds of U.S. households, yielding what may be one of history's greatest success stories in terms of popular wealth accumulation. The current foreclosure crisis is the first nationwide trauma that this system has ever faced, and it is now having devastating effects on communities nationwide.

This chapter begins with a brief explanation of the foreclosure crisis—causes, magnitude, and differences in incidence across metropolitan areas and neighborhoods. It then looks more closely at the nature of community impacts—how foreclosures come to affect the overall well-being of neighborhoods and cities.

The rest of the chapter deals with policy. It first sets forth the elements of a policy framework to address community impacts, then presents a description of what federal and state governments have been doing about the crisis to this

---

1. Homeownership rates are from the U.S. Census Bureau. The 1930 rate is provided in U.S. Bureau of the Census (1975).

point. It continues with a more detailed review of ways to implement each of six elements of a proposed approach to neighborhood stabilization.

The elements were drawn from the writings of a number of specialists in the field, based largely on their own experiences. (No reports of formal evaluations of these elements were found.) Because there is considerable agreement in the literature about the basics of what should be done to stabilize neighborhoods, the approach can be thought of as something of an "experts' consensus." My review found no boldly differing alternatives being proposed.

The scant evidence that exists indicates that local governments and nonprofits in many areas are trying to implement elements of the suggested plan but, clearly, it is much too soon to assess results. Even where similar elements have been tried (for example, in neighborhoods where disinvestment was occurring before the current crisis), results have not been well documented. The chapter concludes, therefore, with my views on what needs to be done to evaluate these policies and priorities for implementing them effectively.

The Foreclosure Crisis: Underpinnings, Evolution, and Spatial Patterns

The U.S. mortgage market thrived in the late 1990s, paralleling the boom in the economy. By 2001, the economy had begun to falter but, unlike in almost all past periods of sluggish economic performance, the housing sector continued to surge upward.

Market Acceleration and Collapse

In the 2001–03 period, an average of 14.7 million mortgages was originated each year, almost double the 7.9 million average of the three previous years (table 2-1). The market was awash with credit and surprisingly low interest rates, and refinancing reached historic levels (71 percent of all originations). In the three years after that (2004–06), refinancing dropped off somewhat, but home purchase originations continued to expand, averaging 6.3 million a year, 70 percent higher than the level of the late 1990s. The growth in home prices far outpaced that of the economy overall, increasing at a rate of 5.3 percent a year between the first quarter of 2000 and the fourth quarter of 2006.[2]

The following year, however, marked the onset of the collapse. In 2007 a rising tide of foreclosures signaled that home prices had increased to unaffordable levels and that serious structural problems had developed in the market. Total

2. Based on the Federal Housing Finance Agency (FHFA) Index. For an explanation of the methodology, see HPI (www.fhfa.gov/Default.aspx?Page=81). Quarterly data were drawn from this site and adjusted for inflation.

Table 2-1. *Mortgage Originations, 1998–2007*

	All originations			Subprime originations
Measure	Total	Home purchase	Refinance	
Average per year (thousands)				
1998–2000	7,906	3,718	4,188	940
2001–2003	14,660	4,291	10,369	1,358
2004–2006	12,984	6,314	6,671	2,282
2007	8,789	4,213	4,575	. . .
Percent of total				
1998–2000	100	47	53	12
2001–2003	100	29	71	9
2004–2006	100	49	51	18
2007	100	48	52	. . .

Source: Home Mortgage Disclosure Act data set compiled by the Urban Institute; data on file with author.

originations dropped to 8.8 million, and home purchase originations dropped to 4.2 million (table 2-1). Between the fourth quarter of 2006 and the third quarter of 2008, home prices plummeted nationally, declining at a rate of 7.1 percent a year.[3]

What explains those dramatic changes?[4] Most important was the relaxation of a number of safeguards that had been inherent in the U.S. system of home-ownership since the 1940s. For most of that period, mortgages had been provided on fairly generous terms, typically at a fixed interest rate over 30 years. But borrowers had to make substantial down payments, and standards prevented the origination of loans when the amount to be borrowed was unreasonably high in relation to either the value of the home or the verified income of the borrower. The lending institutions usually were local, and because they were expected to hold and service a mortgage over its term, they had strong incentives to avoid mortgages likely to default.

In fact, the first change of importance had emerged in the 1980s: the securitization of mortgages to expand significantly the liquidity in the market. Many individual mortgages were purchased and pooled to create mortgage-backed securities (MBSs), which could then be sold to investors anywhere. The responsibility for servicing the individual mortgages was typically transferred to firms specializing in that activity, and the original lender was no longer involved.

3. Based on the Federal Housing Finance Agency (FHFA) Index.
4. What follows is a very short version of the story. For a more thorough explanation see Gramlich (2007); Herbert and Apgar (2009); and Carr (2008).

Although it took a while for the effects to work themselves out, that shift set the stage. There was substantial money to be made from the fees generated in mortgage origination, and the originators were increasingly separated from the pain associated with mortgage default. That created powerful incentives to expand lending.

Accordingly, the industry began to seek a broader class of borrowers. In the mid-1990s, well-intended new federal policies were designed to increase homeownership in general and among low-income and minority populations and neighborhoods in particular. The mortgage industry began to pay attention to the new incentives, and it also began to recognize that the new would-be borrowers represented real market opportunities that it had undervalued before. Whatever the mix of causes, the period was one of marked expansion that brought national homeownership rates to historic levels.

The growth of the subprime market was critical to that transformation. Subprime loans were offered to people with impaired or limited credit histories in return for higher rates and fees than were charged in the prime market. In the 2004–06 period, the subprime share of all originations reached 18 percent, double what it had been over 2001–03 (table 2-1).

Subprime lending allowed many low- and moderate-income families to become homeowners that never could have qualified for loans even in the early 1990s. But the downside is now well-known. The subprime market imposed requirements that were less stringent than those generally expected in the prime market. Down-payment and loan-to-income standards were relaxed. "Liar loans"—made under standards so lax that borrowers were implicitly encouraged to overstate their incomes—were so frequent that they became notorious. Unscrupulous brokers encouraged many families to take on loans that they ultimately could not afford, often for adjustable rate mortgages (ARMs) whose initially low monthly payments would automatically reset to unaffordably high levels after a year or two. While the problems were concentrated in the subprime sector, the degradation of standards spilled over into prime lending as well. That effect was exemplified by "Alt-A" loans—loans to people who would otherwise qualify for prime loans but who posed more risk, normally because their income or assets were inadequately documented.

The causes of the collapse, in the mortgage markets and credit markets more broadly, are complicated, but the failure of the subprime-laden MBSs certainly played a central role. And the problem continues to spread. Because of rapidly declining home values almost everywhere, many borrowers with properly underwritten prime mortgages are now threatened. Significant numbers of loans—prime as well as subprime—are now "upside down" or "under water," meaning that the amount still owed to the lender is now larger than the total market value of the home. Finally, the foreclosure threat inherent in the housing market problems that I have noted is now being exacerbated by the recession and the prospect of many additional homeowners losing their jobs.

Some have suggested that the central cause of the debacle was the effort to make homeownership affordable for lower-income families and neighborhoods. That argument, however, does not hold up. The share of subprime mortgages that were seriously delinquent was outrageously high—27 percent at the end of 2008.[5] But that means 73 percent were not delinquent at that point. If the stringency of down-payment, loan-to-income, and other standards had not been so relaxed, the market might well have denied loans to most would-be purchasers who would have turned out to be unable to meet the obligations of ownership. There is much to support the view that the basic goal was sound. It was just pushed too far.

On the other hand, the loosening of checks and balances that came with the introduction of mortgage-backed securities and the unleashing of the tremendous pressure to expand the volume of lending probably would have undermined the system even if the subprime sector had never existed.

Status and Prospects for the Next Few Years

The volume of mortgage delinquencies over the past decade has indeed been unprecedented. In the late 1990s, the share of all mortgages behind in payments for 90 days or more was consistently below 0.75 percent.[6] The rate then moved up gradually in the early years of this decade, hitting 1.0 percent for the first time in history in the last quarter of 2005. But an incredible acceleration set in after that. Over the next three years, the rate more than doubled, reaching 2.09 percent in the third quarter of 2008.

A more detailed account of defaults by type of mortgage at the end of 2008 (using 60-day delinquency rates) shows that subprime and Alt-A mortgages were in dramatically more serious straits than prime mortgages:[7]

—total mortgages: 55.9 million, 6.9 percent in default
—prime mortgages: 46.9 million, 3.5 percent in default
—Alt-A mortgages: 3.3 million, 20 percent in default
—subprime mortgages: 5.7 million, 27 percent in default.

Credit Suisse developed one of the few sets of estimates that link the recent past to the future.[8] Its figures indicate that 2008 was indeed a year of historic

5. Dina ElBoghdady and Sarah Cohen, "The Growing Foreclosure Crisis," *Washington Post*, January 17, 2009, p. A1. In these estimates, mortgages were considered delinquent when the borrower was at least 60 days behind in making mortgage payments.

6. Herbert and Apgar (2009, p. 3).

7. From ElBoghdady and Cohen, "The Growing Foreclosure Crisis."

8. Dubitsky and others (2008).

Table 2-2. *Credit-Suisse Estimates of Foreclosures through 2012*

Foreclosures and REOs	January– September 2008	October– December 2008	2009	2010	2011	2012
Total mortgages (millions)						
Number of foreclosures and REOs (end of period)	1.7	2.0	2.3	2.2	1.9	1.8
Number of new foreclosures	1.4	0.4	1.7	1.6	1.3	1.3
Subprime mortgages (millions)						
Number of foreclosures and REOs (end of period)	1.0	1.0	0.9	0.7	0.5	0.4
Number of new foreclosures	0.8	0.2	0.7	0.5	0.3	0.3
Subprime mortgages as percent of foreclosures and REOs (end of period)	59	50	39	32	26	22

Source: Dubitsky and others (2008).

proportions for foreclosures and that the problem was dominated by the foreclosure of subprime loans. The year saw a total of 1.8 million new foreclosures, 56 percent of which were on subprime loans. At year's end, there were 2 million total foreclosures—existing foreclosures plus real estate owned (REO) properties—half of which were on subprime loans (table 2-2).[9]

The company's estimates for the future indicate that a massive number of additional foreclosures is likely to occur over the next few years but that most of them will be on prime loans. The number of new foreclosures is expected to decline gradually, from 1.7 million in 2009 to 1.3 million in 2012. Total foreclosures should decline from 2.3 million in 2009 to 1.8 million in 2012. An important point is that the subprime share is projected to drop to 39 percent in 2009 and to only 22 percent in 2012.

Those figures imply that over the 2009–12 period, 8.1 million loans will be in the foreclosure/REO category, a number that amounts to roughly 15 percent of the 55.9 million total current outstanding mortgages noted above. Credit Suisse tested several alternative scenarios. It estimated that a severe recession, bringing unemployment to 10 percent in 2010, could raise the four-year foreclosure total through 2012 to 10.2 million. The combination of a milder recession and a more aggressive loan modification program (50 percent of loans expected to go into foreclosure are modified, but the default rate is 40 percent) would bring the total through 2012 down to 6.3 million.

9. An REO property is one whose title has been transferred to the lender after it fails to be sold for a sufficient price to a third party at a foreclosure sale.

Differences across Metropolitan Areas

While the U.S. housing market boomed on average through 2006, there were notable differences in performance across regions and metropolitan areas. According to the Federal Housing Finance Agency (FHFA) Index, the annual rate of home price appreciation for the 100 largest metropolitan areas between the first quarter of 2000 and the fourth quarter of 2006 ranged from only +0.5 percent (Detroit) to a phenomenal +13.8 percent (Miami).[10] The five lowest rates (ranging from +0.50 to +0.54 percent) were all in the Midwest (Detroit; Dayton, Warren, and Cleveland, Ohio; and Indianapolis). The five highest rates (ranging from +13.2 to +13.8 percent) were all in California or Florida (Miami, Riverside, Fort Lauderdale, Bakersfield, and Los Angeles).

Figure 2-1 shows the relationship between the rates of home price appreciation and the 2004–06 annual average densities of subprime (high-cost) mortgage originations in the 100 largest metro areas.[11] High-cost origination densities averaged 40 per 1,000 units throughout the nation over that period, reaching a high of 114 in Las Vegas. The top five were Las Vegas, Riverside–San Bernardino, Orlando, Miami, and Phoenix (ranging from 81 to 114). The five lowest were Buffalo, Wilmington, Syracuse, Pittsburgh, and Lancaster (ranging from 12 to 15).

In figure 2-1, the relationship between the density of high-cost loans and increases in home prices appears somewhat positive but fairly weak. Immergluck looked at the spatial determinants of subprime lending in more depth, conducting a regression analysis for 103 metropolitan areas where the subprime share of home purchase loans in 2003 was the dependent variable.[12] Explanatory variables with statistically significant impacts on the subprime share included the metropolitan area's 1997 subprime share, change in the median loan amount from 1997 to 2003, the income-to-loan-size ratio, and, interestingly, the proportion of residents with at least a college degree. The last two variables were negatively related to subprime share—that is, metro areas with low educational attainment and low income-to-loan-size ratios had higher shares of subprime lending.

---

10. Based on the Federal Housing Finance Agency (FHFA) Index.

11. Actually, figures 2-1 and 2-2 plot individual points for the twenty-nine major divisions of eleven large metropolitan areas (New York, Los Angeles, Chicago, Philadelphia, Washington, D.C., Miami, Detroit, Boston, San Francisco–Oakland, and Seattle) and additional points for the other eighty-nine metropolitan areas that make up the top 100.

12. Immergluck (2008b).

Figure 2-1. *Metro Density of High-Cost Loans (2004–06) by House Price Index (2000–06)*[a]

High-cost loans per 1,000 units (2004–06)

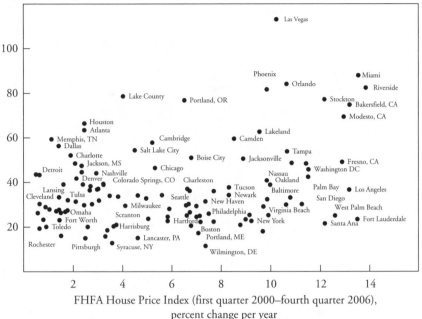

FHFA House Price Index (first quarter 2000–fourth quarter 2006),
percent change per year

Sources: Home Mortgage Disclosure Act data set compiled by the Urban Institute (data on file with author) and Federal Housing Finance Agency (FHFA).

a. *Density* is defined here as the number of high-cost loans per 1,000 units in one- to four-unit structures.

Figure 2-2 shows the collapse in home prices that occurred after 2006, comparing the home price changes earlier in the decade (first quarter of 2000 through fourth quarter of 2006) with what has happened since (fourth quarter of 2006 through third quarter of 2008). A metropolitan area would hope to be in the upper-right quadrant of this figure, showing solid price increases in both periods. The figure, however, is a picture of one of the most dramatic upsets in housing market performance in U.S. history. In the first part of the decade, all metropolitan areas saw growth in housing prices—outrageously high growth for most metropolitan areas in California and Florida. Since 2006, however, the picture has turned upside down. Only one metro area in the figure (Austin, Texas) experienced an increase; the rest faced losses, and the worst losses by far were for the California and Florida metropolitan areas that had done the best before. Clearly, these environments require very different kinds of policy.

Figure 2-2. Metro House Price Index, 2000–06 by 2006–08[a]

FHFA House Price Index (fourth quarter 2006–third quarter 2008),
percent change per year

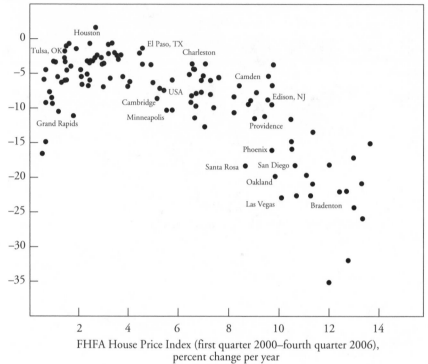

FHFA House Price Index (first quarter 2000–fourth quarter 2006),
percent change per year

Source: Federal Housing Finance Agency (FHFA).

Differences by Type of Neighborhood

All of the trends discussed above have also varied markedly by type of neighborhood. What follows is a summary of recent research by Kingsley and Pettit covering the 100 largest metropolitan areas.[13] It begins by noting that one of the most relevant ways to classify neighborhoods for this purpose is by poverty level. Four categories of neighborhoods are defined on the basis of their poverty rate in 2000: 0–10 percent (low poverty), 10–20 percent, 20–30 percent, and 30 percent or more (high poverty).

Figure 2-3 confirms the conditions that drove public policy to try to expand mortgage lending in poor neighborhoods in the 1990s. The density of mortgage activity (home purchase originations per 1,000 units in one- to four-unit struc-

13. Kingsley and Pettit (2009). Most of the data used in this report come from the Home Mortgage Disclosure Act (HMDA) data file. Under HMDA, lenders file reports on virtually all mortgage applica-

Figure 2-3. *Home Purchase Loans per 1,000 Units in One- to Four-Unit Structures, by Poverty Rate of Census Tract, 1997–2007*

Home purchase loans

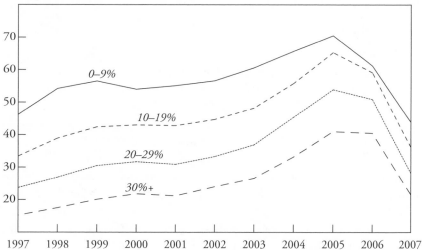

Source: Home Mortgage Disclosure Act data set compiled by the Urban Institute; data on file with author.

tures) stood at 15 in high-poverty neighborhoods in 1997, only one-third of the 46 figure for low-poverty neighborhoods; figures for the two other categories fell in between. For all categories, mortgage lending activity increased modestly over the following two years, leveled off through 2002, and then increased sharply between 2002 and 2005, before turmoil in the market led to declines over the next year. By 2005, the gaps were still significant (the rates were 71 for low-poverty and 41 for high-poverty neighborhoods), but they had grown smaller as the volume of mortgage activity in moderate- and high-poverty neighborhoods accelerated over the period. The density for high-poverty neighborhoods as a percent of density for low-poverty neighborhoods increased from 32 percent in 1997 to 58 percent in 2005 and to 66 percent a year later.

The pattern is similar for change in mortgage amounts. For low-poverty neighborhoods, the median amount increased from $141,000 in 1997 to

---

tions that they receive in metropolitan areas. The reports include data on the property's location (census tract), the borrower's race and income, and whether the mortgage was denied or originated. While the HMDA's purpose was to provide a basis for assessing discrimination in mortgage lending, the reports also provided, for the first time, a basis for monitoring key aspects of housing market activity year by year at the neighborhood level. Changes in volume of lending and in loan amounts are important indicators in this regard. Pettit and Droesch (2007) provides a comprehensive review of HMDA data and their uses.

$187,000 in 2006. The amounts for high-poverty neighborhoods were much lower ($74,000 in 1997 and $127,000 in 2006), but they had gone up faster. In 2006, the median mortgage amount in high-poverty tracts represented 68 percent of the median for the low-poverty group, up notably from 52 percent in 1997.

Neighborhood Variation in Subprime Lending

It would be ideal to be able to examine the neighborhood pattern of foreclosures directly, but complete and consistent national data on foreclosures are not available. However, subprime lending densities should serve as a reasonable proxy, at least for the first wave of foreclosures in the current crisis.[14] Some who have studied the crisis have looked at subprime loans as a share of total lending in an area, but that is not a good indicator of probable impact. An area could have a very high subprime share of a very low volume of total lending, making the number of properties with risky loans small in relation to the overall size of the housing stock.

A much better measure for this purpose is the "density" of subprime lending, since it is the density that generally heightens the risk of foreclosure and negative spillover effects such as declining property values and increasing crime rates. "Density" is defined as the number of "high-cost" conventional home purchase loans originated from 2004 through 2006 (the peak period of subprime lending) per 1,000 total housing units in one- to four-unit structures in the area as of the 2000 census.[15] Figures cited below refer to subprime (high-cost) densities for the 100 largest metropolitan areas. (In the rest of this chapter, the terms *subprime* and *high-cost* are used interchangeably.) The measure varies dramatically for different types of neighborhood.

First, there are major differences by predominant race in the neighborhood. For the large metropolitan areas, the average density nationwide was 40 across

14. Researchers have found strong relationships between subprime loans and foreclosure before 2008. The authors of one analysis state that "by far the strongest predictor of a loan foreclosing is its status as a high-cost subprime loan" (Coulton and others, 2008, p. 1).

15. The data on high-cost loans also come from the Home Mortgage Disclosure Act data set. High-cost loans are defined as those with an annual percentage rate 3 percentage points or more above the Treasury rate for first-lien mortgages with comparable maturities (or 5 points above in the case of junior liens). The denominator can be thought of as the number of housing units in 2000 that were "potential candidates" to serve as collateral for such mortgages. It includes all owner-occupied units (single-family homes and condominiums) and rental units in one- to four-unit structures. Data on high-cost loans were first provided in the 2004 HMDA data set. The indicator of subprime lending used before then was based on loans originated by lenders designated as "subprime" lenders by the U.S. Department of Housing and Urban Development (HUD). The high-cost measure is more comprehensive because it includes the nontrivial number of subprime loans originated by prime lenders as well as those originated by the lenders on HUD's list.

Figure 2-4. *Density of High-Cost Loans by Predominant Race and Poverty Rate of Census Tract, 100 Largest Metro Areas, 2004–06*[a]

Density

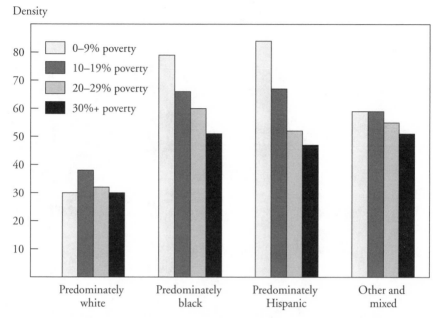

Source: Home Mortgage Disclosure Act data set compiled by the Urban Institute; data on file with author.

a. *Density* is defined here as the number of high-cost loans per 1,000 units in one- to four-unit structures.

all tracts and 32 where whites were the predominant race. (A racial group is considered predominant if it accounts for 60 percent or more of a tract's 2000 population.) The subprime density was much higher (61) where blacks predominated, 57 where Hispanics predominated, and 57 also for tracts where another race or no race predominated.

But there were major variations depending on the poverty rate of the tract as well. For the top 100 metropolitan areas, across all races, density was highest (51) for the groups with poverty rates in the 20–30 percent range and almost as high (48) for those in both the 10–20 percent and 30+ percent groups. It stood at only 34 for the low-poverty tracts.

Putting both variables together for the 100 largest metropolitan areas, figure 2-4 shows a strikingly disparate pattern. Within race categories, subprime densities are almost always highest in the census tracts with the lowest poverty rates and drop consistently as poverty rates increase. The highest densities occur where Hispanics are predominant, ranging from 84 per 1,000 units in low-poverty tracts down to 47 for the highest-poverty group. Predominantly black

Figure 2-5. *Density of High-Cost Loans by Census Tract Distance from Central Business District of Primary City, 100 Largest Metro Areas, by Region, 2004–06*[a]

Density

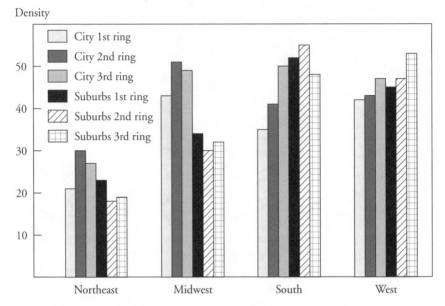

Source: Home Mortgage Disclosure Act data set compiled by the Urban Institute; data on file with author.

a. *Density* is defined here as the number of high-cost loans per 1,000 units in one- to four-unit structures.

tracts come next, with a density of 79 in the lowest-poverty group and 51 in the highest.

In short, the neighborhoods hardest hit by the subprime crisis have been those where minority residents predominate, but within those neighborhoods, the highest subprime densities are found in neighborhoods with higher-income residents, not moderate- or lower-income ones. That may seem surprising, but it occurs because of a point noted earlier. Subprime loans do account for a higher "share" of all loans in poorer neighborhoods, but because the overall volume of home lending (per 1,000 units) is so much lower in such neighborhoods, sub-prime densities are lower there.

Figure 2-5 tells the story of subprime (high-cost) density patterns in a different way. The tracts in the 100 largest metropolitan areas were divided into six geographical divisions on the basis of distance of their geographical center from the central business district (CBD) of the primary city.[16] All tracts in the pri-

16. This follows an approach developed by Berube and Forman (2002).

mary city were first ranked by that distance and then divided into three equal groups, thereby establishing, in effect, three rings. The same procedure was then followed for the suburbs, establishing three additional rings, again ranging from nearest to farthest from the primary city CBD. That approach permits understandable comparisons of spatial patterns between different metropolitan areas.[17]

Figure 2-5 shows subprime densities (again, high-cost loans per 1,000 units) in the six rings for the 100 metropolitan areas by region. In the Northeast (which had the lowest densities overall), the highest densities (27–30) are in the middle and outer rings of the central city. Densities are notably lower in the central portion of the city and in the outer two rings in the suburbs.

For the Midwest, densities are higher in all locations but the pattern is similar—the highest subprime densities (49–51) are in the middle and outer rings of the central city. Things are different in the South, where the highest density is in the middle ring of the suburbs (55) and the second-highest is in the city's outer ring and the suburbs' inner ring (50–52). In the West, densities are generally similar, but highest (53) is in the outer ring of the suburbs.

The Impacts of Foreclosures on Communities

The dramatic variations in mortgage market conditions—between metropolitan areas and between neighborhoods within metropolitan areas—are extremely important for the purposes of this chapter. The reason, as considerable research has now shown, is that metropolitan areas where subprime loans and the foreclosures that result from them are concentrated in particular neighborhoods are likely to suffer substantially more in negative spillover effects than they would if the same numbers of loans and foreclosures were spread out evenly across all neighborhoods. Similarly, neighborhoods with high concentrations of foreclosures will suffer much more than others. Thus, to be effective, policies and programs must be tailored to accommodate the differences.

Why that is the case can be better illustrated by describing the process whereby foreclosures affect individual properties and then neighborhoods and cities as a whole. Here I review that process in general and then summarize the research evidence on the magnitude of the various effects, starting with a description of the way the foreclosure process works.[18]

17. However, it must be kept in mind that the sizes of the rings can be quite different in different metropolitan areas. The three rings in Los Angeles, for example, are much larger than the three rings in Hartford, Connecticut.

18. Much of the material in this section is drawn from Kingsley, Smith, and Price (2009), a review prepared for the Open Society Institute.

The Foreclosure Process

Foreclosure allows a lender to realize value from a property after an owner defaults in making mortgage payments on it.[19] Two basic approaches are followed in different states. In the "judicial" approach, a lender in effect sues a borrower for failing to make payments as required by the loan agreement. The matter is heard before a judge, who, if the facts confirm default, sets a date when the property will be sold in order to compensate the lender with the proceeds from the sale. In states that have a "nonjudicial" foreclosure process, the lender simply sends a notice to the owner (normally filing a copy with the local government) and then sets a date for the sale in accordance with the mortgage terms. When a borrower contends that the lender's assertion of default is not valid, the borrower must bring suit to stop the process.

A foreclosure sale can be avoided under either approach, however, if the borrower either meets all outstanding obligations beforehand or enters into a new "workout agreement" with the lender. Notice is then filed with the local government to cancel the foreclosure. If the process is not stopped in that way, the property is offered for sale at a public auction and title is transferred to the highest bidder. Lenders normally set a minimum price, however, and if there are no bids at or above that price, title reverts to the lender and the property is classified as real estate owned. When title is transferred, the previous owner must move out and, generally, if the property has been rented out prior to foreclosure, the tenants are subject to eviction, even if they are up to date on their rent. Tenants do not have the legal protections against eviction that they would have had with the former owner.

Foreclosure has three major types of impact on neighborhoods and communities:
—physical deterioration of the property and declining property values
—crime and social disorder
—local government fiscal stress and deterioration of public services.

Physical Deterioration and Declining Property Values

Physical deterioration may begin even before the foreclosure sale if the original owner, trying to keep up with payments, begins to defer maintenance. There also are cases in which unscrupulous owners of rental properties in default stop paying for maintenance, even though they continue to collect tenants' rent payments. More often, however, deterioration sets in when a home remains vacant for a period of time without being maintained or kept secure, either before or after the transfer of title.

---

19. For more details on the process, see Pettit and others (2008).

That is most likely to happen when the property is in REO status and market conditions are weak. If the market in the neighborhood is strong, lenders can make a sizable profit by selling the property quickly, so they will keep it well maintained until the sale occurs. But if the property is in a neighborhood where prices are low and declining, those incentives disappear and the lender may try to avoid spending anything on security and maintenance.

A short period of vacancy and a modest lack of maintenance may not be too evident, but a prolonged vacancy will create problems. More visible signs of neglect (overgrown lawns and poor maintenance of the exterior) may invite other problems. Vandals may break in and gut the property, removing everything of value, including copper piping and hardwood floors as well as appliances. If the period of vacancy is extended and no one is paying for heat and electricity or maintenance, the building will begin to deteriorate physically. The likelihood of fire damage goes up, in some cases because indoor fires set by squatters to keep warm get out of control.[20]

Even one or two foreclosures represent a problem for a neighborhood. Real estate agents and neighborhood residents become aware of a foreclosure when the property is advertised for sale. Negative perceptions are enhanced the longer the period of vacancy and undermaintenance. The problem may not be too serious at that level in a strong market because of the natural self-correction processes. Owners of surrounding properties who have considerable equity in their homes are likely to exert great pressure on the owner of the affected property, the government, and anyone else who might be able to help correct the problem as soon as possible.

However, if the number of foreclosures increases notably, the problem becomes much more serious and harder to correct, even where the market has been strong. In a weak market, if property values already are declining, even a small number of foreclosures is likely to accelerate the trend. Depending in part on the metropolitan context, a continuation of such trends can ultimately lead to substantial decline in property values, abandonment, and neighborhood population losses.

Several studies have now been done to quantify the effect of foreclosures on property values. One of the earliest, by Immergluck and Smith, entailed hedonic regression analysis relating data on 3,750 foreclosures between 1997 and 1998 in Chicago to 9,600 single-family property sales in 1999.[21] The researchers found that each new foreclosure within one-eighth of a mile of a home resulted in a 0.9 percent decline in the value of the home. In low- and moderate-income

20. Kingsley, Smith and Price (2009). Hedonic regression analysis estimates the contribution that various characteristics of the home and its neighborhood make to the value of the home.

21. Immergluck and Smith (2006a).

neighborhoods, the drop in property value from each new foreclosure within the same radius was much higher: 1.8 percent.

Other research employing similar techniques has found varying results in different cities.[22] The most broad-based study to this point, by Harding, Rosenblatt, and Yao, was based on foreclosures and sales data for 140 zip codes in thirteen states (covering 628,000 repeat sales).[23] It found a negative effect of 1.3 percent on the value of homes within a 300-foot radius of a foreclosed home (probably one of the nearest two to three properties) but a drop of only 0.6 percent within a 660-foot (one-eighth-mile) radius of a foreclosure (probably one in the next block). That level is one-third lower than the level found by Immergluck and Smith in Chicago for the same distance.

Those studies make it clear that foreclosures do lead to reduced property values, but more research is needed before the relationship can be adequately understood. Results so far differ among cities, and there has been no satisfactory quantitative analysis of the determinants of the variations. Furthermore, the studies cited above assume a linear relationship between foreclosures and values, but there are good reasons to believe the relationship is curvilinear—that when foreclosure densities exceed some threshold, the deterioration in value accelerates. That possibility has yet to be adequately explored.[24]

Crime and Social Disorder

I noted above that vandals are likely to break into houses that are evidently vacant and poorly maintained; one explanation, the "broken windows theory," suggests that criminals feel that they have been "invited in" under such circumstances. Some unsecured homes may even become drug houses. As the word spreads and more criminals become aware of the disorder in a neighborhood, crimes of all types may increase, threatening residents in surrounding homes and apartments.

A study conducted by the Charlotte-Mecklenburg (North Carolina) police department demonstrates the phenomenon. The study began by identifying thirteen neighborhoods in the metropolitan area with high "clusters of foreclosure" from 2003 through 2007. Typically they were not the area's worst neighborhoods but places where home prices were considered to be in an "affordable" range ($90,000 to $150,000). The study then identified another twelve neighborhoods in the same price range that had not yet seen high levels of foreclosure. It found that violent and property crime rates had gone up in both types of

22. For example, Been (2008) cited a much lower 0.2 percent drop in values within a one-eighth-mile radius in the city of New York.

23. Harding, Rosenblatt, and Yao (2008).

24. The case for such research is made more completely in Kingsley, Smith, and Price (2009).

neighborhood but that they were significantly higher in the high-foreclosure clusters. In 2005 and 2006, there was an average of 1.7 incidents of violent crime per 100 houses in high-foreclosure clusters, almost three times the 0.6 average for the comparison group.[25]

Another study used regression analysis to relate crimes in all census tracts of Chicago in 2001 to track foreclosure rates and a host of other neighborhood characteristics.[26] The researchers found the relationship between foreclosures and violent crime to be statistically significant and sizable: "A one percentage point increase in the foreclosure rate (which has a standard deviation of 0.028) is expected to increase the number of violent crimes in a tract by 2.33 percent, all other things being equal. A full standard deviation increase in the foreclosure rate, all other things equal, is expected to increase violent crime by 6.68 percent." The effect on property crime was positive, although not statistically significant. As with the relationship between foreclosures and property values, it seems likely that the relationship between foreclosures and crime is curvilinear, but a statistical analysis of that possibility has yet to be done.

Local Government Fiscal Stress and Deterioration of Services

Foreclosures also have significant negative impacts on the finances of the local governments in the jurisdictions where they occur. First, foreclosures increase public expenditures, including for administrative and maintenance tasks related to the foreclosed properties themselves and for enhanced maintenance, code enforcement, and trash collection in the broader neighborhood to prevent the spread of problems. Increased outlays by the police and fire departments to address increased crime in the area also are sure to be required.[27] In addition, there will be costs to cover services to vulnerable residents who are displaced.

Second, to make matters worse, a reduction in neighborhood property values implies a corresponding reduction in municipal property tax revenues. Considering the weakening revenue position of most municipalities in the current environment, it seems likely that many of them will have cut back on services rather than expand outlays in response to foreclosures unless more federal or state assistance is forthcoming.

Another study for the city of Chicago explains why increases in spending due to foreclosures may have to be sizable.[28] The researchers estimated the direct costs to the city (as of 2005) of dealing with a foreclosure and its immediate effects under five different scenarios. In scenario A, the property is vacant but secured by

---

25. Bess (2008).
26. Immergluck and Smith (2006b, p. 863).
27. See Community Research Partners and Rebuild Ohio (2008).
28. Apgar and Duda (2005).

its owner, and only a few administrative processing tasks are required (cost of $430). If the current owner has not secured the property, however, the city has to step in and take action. When a decision is made to secure and conserve the property (scenario B), the processing costs jump to $5,400, but when a decision is made to demolish (scenario C), they go even higher, to more than $13,000. If the owner abandons the property (scenario D), the city's financial exposure is even steeper because of losses from unpaid property and utility taxes and the expense of new outlays to continue water service and provide lawn mowing and trash removal (almost $20,000). The city's exposure is highest by far if a fire occurs (scenario E). In that case there are the costs of fire suppression, eventually the costs of demolition and site clearance, and the costs of keeping the building from being a threat to safety in between (a total of more than $34,000).

It is also relevant to point out that the fiscal problems of U.S. local governments have become more severe of late. In an April–June 2008 survey of city finance officers by the National League of Cities (NLC), 64 percent of respondents reported that their cities were less able to meet fiscal needs in 2008 than in the previous year.[29]

These problems have many causes but foreclosures and the declining housing market certainly rank prominently among them. In another NLC survey, elected officials were asked what conditions had had the most severe impacts on their communities. "Increased foreclosures" came in third behind "decreased city revenues" and "decreased funding for other programs and projects."[30] Of the respondents, 62 percent said that foreclosures had increased "some or a lot" over the past year and one-third said the same about abandoned and vacant properties and other forms of blight. If foreclosure densities go up, there will be additional expenses in the other categories noted above (added maintenance and trash collection in the broader neighborhood and outlays by the police to address increased crime in the area).[31] And there will be the additional costs for services to displaced families: fifty-three percent of the officials said that the need for temporary assistance to families had increased some or a lot over the past year.[32]

Policy Framework

The foreclosure crisis is much too recent to expect researchers to have conducted studies to measure its effects. Still, anecdotal evidence is sufficient to conclude that its effects on many families and communities already have been devastating.

29. Pagano and Hoen (2008).
30. McFarland and McGahan (2008).
31. Community Research Partners and Rebuild Ohio (2008)
32. McFarland and McGahan (2008, p. 1).

And according to the estimates presented earlier, there is much more to come. What policies should be considered in response? The recent literature identifies four basic types as essential:

—policies to prevent further foreclosures on current mortgages

—policies to address the impacts of the crisis on communities

—policies to help displaced families recover

—policies to restructure the mortgage market to prevent a similar crisis from occurring in the future.[33]

This chapter was commissioned to deal only with the second type—policies to address the impacts of the crisis on communities—and indeed that is the only topic that it covers in any depth. It says just a few things about federal efforts to implement the first type, prevention policies, and it says nothing about the third and fourth types, although other policy researchers are paying increasing attention to them.[34]

As for the chapter's main focus, researchers must start by recognizing the lack of a solid research literature on policies intended to deal with the community impacts of foreclosures. There has been little time to design and initiate local response programs, let alone to formally evaluate them. Nonetheless, there is some relevant prior experience. As noted above, deleterious impacts are felt largely because properties become vacant and are sometimes abandoned, and those problems were extensive in older industrial cities in the United States well before the current crisis began. Lessons learned from efforts to address those issues as well as more recent foreclosure problems have been compiled by several authors, most notably Alan Mallach, Dan Immergluck, and a team from the Furman Center at New York University.[35] Most have offered ideas on how those lessons should be applied under the current circumstances, and their views are generally quite consistent. The suggestions offered here, then, represent an "experts' consensus" based on the views of these authors.

The foremost aspect of the current policy challenge is the diversity of community impacts across metropolitan areas and neighborhoods. To be effective, actions to mitigate the problems will have to differ from one community to

33. These types were derived from a review of a number of sources that look at the crisis from different angles: Baily, Elmendorf, and Litan (2008); Carr (2008); Gramlich (2007); Joint Center for Housing Studies (2008); Kingsley, Smith, and Price (2009); Lovell and Isaacs (2008); Mallach (2008b, 2009a).

34. These include several of the references cited in the previous note: Baily, Elmendorf, and Litan (2008); Carr (2008); Gramlich (2007); and Joint Center for Housing Studies (2008). In addition, the Mortgage Reform and Anti-Predatory Lending Act of 2009 (H.R. 1728), a comprehensive effort to reform the mortgage market by correcting the deficiencies that led to the current crisis, was introduced in Congress on March 26, 2009. See Kenneth R. Harney, "Congress Takes a Serious Look at Reforming the Mortgage Market," *Washington Post*, April 4, 2009.

35. Mallach (2006, 2008a, 2008c); Immergluck (2008a); and Madar, Been, and Armstrong (2008).

another, and that requirement underscores the need for local stakeholders to play the central role in making decisions and implementing programs. Direct federal or even state management would not make sense given the nature of the problem and the U.S. system of governance.

Over the past year, local efforts to address community impacts of the crisis have come to be labeled *neighborhood stabilization*. Experts recognize that the main goal of neighborhood stabilization in areas threatened by or already suffering from foreclosures is to restore a healthy private real estate market. A stabilization program needs to be able to perform six functions:

—organize the relevant local government agencies and build their capacity to undertake the program while mobilizing support for the program in the private and nonprofit sectors

—secure and maintain vacant foreclosed properties

—expedite the private resale of foreclosed properties

—directly acquire and manage foreclosed properties

—maintain and upgrade the neighborhood environment

—develop a neighborhood-based strategy that indicates the mix of interventions to be employed in different neighborhoods and sets priorities.[36]

The second and fourth functions on this list were adapted from a framework developed by Immergluck.[37] The first and sixth were added as a result of a literature review by the Urban Institute that suggested that they should be independent elements of a neighborhood stabilization agenda.[38]

Much of the remainder of this chapter is devoted to describing what the literature has to say about implementing each of these elements of neighborhood stabilization at the local level. Before that, however, I review some of the actions that the federal and state governments have taken to address the foreclosure crisis to this point.

The Federal and State Response

As noted, federal and state governments are not positioned to be direct actors in the effort to prevent foreclosures or stabilize neighborhoods, but they can perform extremely valuable supporting roles.

Federal Policies to Prevent Foreclosures on Current Mortgages

Policies to prevent foreclosures focus on providing counseling to borrowers and providing financial and other incentives to encourage lenders to modify mort-

---

36. More detailed information on the six elements is offered at www.Foreclosure-Response.org.
37. Immergluck (2008a).
38. Kingsley, Smith, and Price (2009).

gages as needed so borrowers can retain ownership.[39] Over the past two decades, the number of local homeownership counseling groups in the United States has grown substantially. These groups try to educate would-be owners on the purchase process and the ongoing responsibilities of ownership. They also advise existing owners on how to manage their finances so that they can avoid default and, if default occurs, on how to work with lenders to avoid foreclosure. The latter usually requires the lender to modify the terms of a mortgage (for example, to reduce the interest rate or lengthen the repayment period) to make it affordable over the long term.

Through 2008, the federal response to the crisis focused on counseling. In 2007, Congress funded NeighborWorks America to create the Hope Now Alliance, a consortium of banks and other groups charged with facilitating voluntary loan modifications, and to provide additional counseling through its $180 million National Foreclosure Mitigation Counseling Program (NFMC).[40] In addition, the Housing and Economic Recovery Act (HERA), enacted in July 2008, created a broader HOPE for Homeowners program in the Federal Housing Administration that supports the refinancing of loans at better terms for borrowers in or at risk of default.[41]

As of early 2009, however, no program had induced lenders to write down principal or reduce interest substantially, so results have been modest. The Comptroller of the Currency recently reported that more than half of owners whose mortgages were modified in the hope of achieving stability during the first half of 2008 ended up in default again within six months.[42] In December, the Department of Housing and Urban Development (HUD) reported that, due to high costs and difficult requirements, the HOPE for Homeowners program had hardly any takers.[43]

In February 2009, the Obama administration announced a more extensive ($75 billion) initiative that could make more of a difference: the Homeowner Affordability and Stability Plan (now called Making Home Affordable). The plan, designed to help up to 3 to 4 million owner-occupants who face hardships and cannot afford their current mortgage, offers a combination of interest rate

39. See, for example, NeighborWorks (2007); Hirad and Zorn (2002); Cutts and Green (2004); Hartarska and Gonzalez-Vega (2005); and Ergungor (2008).

40. Mayer and others (2008).

41. U. S. Department of Housing and Urban Development, "Housing and Economic Recovery Act of 2008 FAQ" (www.hud.gov/news/recoveryactfaq.cfm).

42. Binyamin Applebaum and Renae Merle, "Foreclosure Reduction Effort Yielding Mixed Results, Report Says," *Washington Post*, December 9, 2008. The finding was based on data from the Office of Thrift Supervision covering fourteen of the largest banks, which account for about 60 percent of the mortgage market.

43. Dina ElBoghdady, "HUD Chief Calls Aid on Mortgages a Failure," *Washington Post*, December 17, 2008, p. A1.

reductions and term extensions to bring monthly payments down to 31 percent of a household's income for five years, after which the rate gradually increases.[44] The additional resources needed for the modifications are coming in part from the government and in part from the lender.

As of July 2009, the program was not far into implementation so there was little basis for estimating its success; however, it would be unrealistic to expect it to result in any notable decrease in today's unprecedented foreclosure rates very soon. Addressing the community impacts of foreclosures will remain a high national priority for some time to come.

Federal Policies to Help Stabilize Neighborhoods

The federal government never had a coherent national program to address the problem of vacancies and abandonment that emerged in weak-market cities over the past few decades, although funds for the community development block grant (CDBG) program and other housing programs administered by HUD could be used for that purpose.[45] However, it has stepped up to address the community impacts of the foreclosure crisis more forcefully. The July 2008 HERA, noted earlier, also established a $3.9 billion neighborhood stabilization program (NSP).

The program is being administered by HUD with funds allocated by formula to states and localities (CDBG-eligible jurisdictions) to support just the kinds of local efforts to mitigate neighborhood impacts mentioned above.[46] More specifically, funds are provided for five eligible uses:

—establishing financing mechanisms for the purchase and redevelopment of foreclosed homes

—purchasing and rehabilitating properties that have been abandoned or foreclosed on

—establishing and operating land banks for homes and residential properties that have been foreclosed on

—demolishing blighted structures

—redeveloping demolished or vacant properties.

The first phase of NSP (NSP-1) moved to implementation very quickly. HUD promulgated the allocation formula and related regulations in September 2008. Jurisdictions receiving allocations had to complete action plans by December 1,

---

44. Another component of the plan is to allow up to 4 to 5 million owners who have loans owned or guaranteed by Fannie Mae or Freddie Mac and who can at present afford the payments to refinance through those institutions to enhance affordability over the longer term. White House, "Homeowners Affordability and Stability Plan: Fact Sheet," February 18, 2009.

45. Brophy and Burnett (2003).

46. For guidance on implementing this program locally, see Mallach (2008c).

and they were to receive their allocations by the end of the first quarter of 2009 if the plans were approved. The program requires all funds to be used within eighteen months of receipt.

Recognizing widespread concern that the original funding was woefully inadequate, the Obama administration approved a second phase of NSP (NSP-2) to provide an additional $2 billion as part of its recovery package, the American Recovery and Reinvestment Act (ARRA), passed in February 2009. The content of the second phase is similar to the first, but in the new program funding is being allocated through a competitive process. Nonprofits and consortiums of public and private actors, as well as individual state and local governments, are eligible to submit proposals. Also, unlike the earlier version, NSP-2 is accompanied by a substantial program of technical assistance to help local players design and implement their programs more effectively.

One early report summarized some characteristics of eighty-seven selected NSP-1 plans.[47] The plans ranged in size from just over $2 million (Montgomery County, Maryland) to $145 million (state of California). Across all plans, most of the funding was allocated to purchase and rehabilitation (56 percent), followed by 21 percent for homebuyer finance, 13 percent for property redevelopment, 6 percent for demolition, and 4 percent for land banking. Eighty-one percent of the grantees plan to leverage their NSP dollars, most frequently by linking additional private investment to NSP actions (41 percent). Information to support any comprehensive characterizations of implementation results is not yet available.

Although I have yet to find anything in print asserting that the federal NSP program should not have been attempted, there are qualified observers who doubt the likelihood of its success. First, there are doubts that many jurisdictions will be able to spend the funds wisely given the haste with which they must be spent, and there are concerns about the limited funding in relation to the formidable nature of the task.[48] Data presented earlier in this chapter show that the extent and nature of the foreclosure problem varies significantly across neighborhoods. Most local governments do not have the skills or information needed to target actions so that they are sensitive to market differences and many may not have the administrative capacity needed to implement programs adequately once targets have been set. Second, although no one has yet made a supportable estimate of the total amount of public funds needed to mitigate neighborhood impacts overall, advocates have generally considered that even with the additional $2 billion in ARRA, the funding provided so far will be not be nearly enough.

47. Sheldon and others (2009).
48. Mallach (2009a).

State Policy and the Legal and Regulatory Environment

Although direct actions have to be designed and implemented at the local level, state governments are extremely important in responding to the foreclosure crisis because they typically control many of the most relevant legal, regulatory, and budgetary levers. Mallach has developed a comprehensive set of recommendations for state action to respond to the foreclosure crisis, and two of his suggestions focus on neighborhood stabilization:

—*Establishing creditor responsibility to maintain vacant properties.* This may involve revamping state laws to strengthen nuisance abatement provisions and otherwise helping to build local capacity for enforcement. This means assuring that localities have the power to assure clear identification of the owners of foreclosed properties, compel owners to fulfill their responsibility for maintenance, enter the property to make repairs directly when necessary, and compel owners to forfeit the property after prolonged failure to respond.

—*Making the process of recycling the property as expeditious as possible.* This entails reforming laws as needed to make the process of foreclosure and judicial sale clear and less cumbersome and time consuming. This also includes tightening laws to prevent predatory and deceptive foreclosure "rescue" schemes, and other actions to support the creation of entities that can ensure that foreclosed properties will be conveyed to responsible owners.[49]

States also are encouraged to review their legal and regulatory environments to look for ways to help prevent foreclosure (for example, by using their leverage to encourage creditors to pursue alternatives other than foreclosure when possible) and to provide more funding and other support for local counseling and neighborhood stabilization efforts.

There has been no systematic review of what states have done to date, but there are indications that many are paying attention to these issues. In a number of states, public-private sector task forces have been organized, first to review the problems and then to recommend programs of legal and other actions by state governments.[50] According to one report, fourteen states had created foreclosure task forces by April 2008.[51]

---

49. Paraphrased from Mallach (2008b).

50. More complete descriptions of the task forces and their results are provided by the Center for Housing Policy, the Local Initiatives Support Corporation (LISC), and the Urban Institute at www. Foreclosure-Response.org.

51. Pew Charitable Trusts (2008).

Neighborhood Stabilization: Local Policies and Programs to Address Community Impacts

Below I present a more detailed review of what experienced specialists suggest about how to implement each element of the neighborhood stabilization program presented above.

Organizing for Neighborhood Stabilization

Primary responsibility for implementing the six elements of neighborhood stabilization inevitably rests with local governments—municipalities and counties—because they alone have the legal power to implement many of the program actions required. The first step is to get organized internally. Mallach recognizes that several different organizational units have to be involved—for example, planning, code enforcement, sanitation and street maintenance, and property acquisition and disposition.[52] That implies the need to mobilize a cross-department task force, probably directed by a deputy mayor or other official with enough power to ensure coordination of the efforts of the various agencies.

In most cases, officials will need to develop a program to rapidly build the local government's capacity to take on a much-expanded workload. That requires training staff in state-of-the-art practices in their existing disciplines and new ones as well—for example, more sophisticated approaches to real estate market analysis and performance management. In some cases, laws and regulations may have to be modified and new institutions created.

Generally, there is likely to be more emphasis on improving the process of contracting with the private sector and on contractor performance monitoring than on additional government hiring. Given the (hopefully) short-term nature of neighborhood stabilization, mobilizing private contractors to take on the many requisite tasks and giving them incentives to handle those tasks efficiently (ranging from property maintenance and rehabilitation to assistance in administrative processing) will make more sense than permanently expanding the public workforce.

Another high-priority recommendation by Mallach and the Furman Center team is to engage local community development corporations and other nonprofit housing and community development advocates in the planning process. Because they are likely to be called on to play direct roles in neighborhood maintenance and property acquisition, rehabilitation, and management, they

---

52. Mallach (2008c, p. 26); Mallach (2006, pp. 117–27).

should be involved early on so that they develop a feeling of ownership for the venture as a whole.[53]

Officials may not fully recognize the importance of the opportunity to develop new foreclosure response collaborations at the *metropolitan level*.[54] Such collaborations would examine how the nature of the problem varies across neighborhoods throughout the area, develop an overall foreclosure response strategy (offering guidance on where and how to target resources), mobilize local interest and participation, press higher levels of government to support needed reforms, and track the performance of all groups working on the issue. Those functions fill a real gap. Individual jurisdictions may face difficulties performing them because they cannot take advantage of economies of scale in mobilizing and coordinating the deployment of nonprofit resources.

Some areas already are moving in that direction. The Atlanta Regional Commission has taken the lead in analyzing the data on the incidence of foreclosure across the Atlanta region and is now working with the city of Atlanta, individual county governments, universities, and other local nongovernment partners on appropriate strategies.[55] In Baltimore, a number of local counseling and advocacy groups have come together to form the Baltimore Homeownership Preservation Coalition (BHPC), which has become the "central place" for those working on the issue (in and out of government) to meet to try to track the problems and discuss ideas for responding to them.[56] While the coalition initially focused on the city, it has been reaching out to work with metropolitan and state actors as well.

No one appears to be advocating any new government structures. The simplest approach would be to encourage the existing council of governments (COG) in a metropolitan area to exercise leadership on the issue and to do so in a way that stimulates the creation of a coalition of interested stakeholders (like BHPC) and partner relationships with individual local governments. Alternatively, a nongovernment coalition might form first and then play the central role in engaging the COG and other local players. In Memphis, for example, a metropolitan coalition that has formed outside of government sees its role in part as encouraging better performance by and accountability of government agencies in responding to the foreclosure crisis.

Another needed action noted by the Furman Center team is for local governments to identify neighborhoods with potentially high foreclosure densities to

---

53. Principle 11 in Mallach's "How to Spend $3.92 Billion" is "Form partnerships with other public, private and nonprofit entities to maximize capacity and resources" (Mallach, 2008c, p. 27). See also Madar, Been, and Armstrong (2008, p. 22).

54. Kingsley, Smith, and Price (2009, p. 46).

55. Rich, Carnathan, and Immergluck (2008).

56. Pierson (2008).

work out ways to collaborate with the servicers responsible for at-risk properties in those neighborhoods.[57] A large share of the threatened mortgages were securitized by financial institutions other than government-sponsored enterprises (that is, they were "non-agency" loans), and the parties now responsible for them day to day are the servicers who work for the investors in the mortgage pool, not the original lenders. If local governments can make contact and establish good working relationships with the servicers early on, they may have more influence on outcomes in all phases of neighborhood stabilization.

Securing and Maintaining Vacant Foreclosed Properties

I noted earlier that when a foreclosure occurs in a neighborhood where the market is strong, the issue may take care of itself without troubling impacts. If the property is likely to sell at a good price at auction, the servicer is likely to keep it secure and well maintained during any periods of vacancy before then. If it does not sell and instead becomes an REO, the servicer is still likely to be motivated to keep it up and perhaps to make improvements with the prospect of a profitable sale at a later time.

In a weak market, however, the servicer (or other owner of a vacant property) may not have that motivation. In that case, both Mallach and Immergluck outline several things that local governments can do to encourage responsible behavior.[58] First, they can apply various financial penalties and incentives by

—imposing differential property tax rates (Washington, D.C., for example, taxes vacant properties at $5 per $100 of assessed value rather than at the normal $1.85 rate).

—requiring owners of vacant properties to register them and pay an associated fee.

—placing a lien on a vacant property, justified by the additional costs incurred due to the vacancy.

—Providing financial incentives for the servicer to maintain and improve a vacant property (for example, grants and below-market loans, tax abatements, and forgiveness of liens).

Second, they can establish clear standards and hold the owner (or servicer) legally accountable for a vacant property, perhaps through creating and enforcing a "vacant property owner accountability ordinance." Third, state laws can be modified to make it more difficult for servicers simply to delay the process; that is, they can require creditors who initiate the foreclosure process to move forward within a specified period of time or relinquish the right to foreclose.

57. Madar, Been, and Armstrong (2008, pp. 25–28).
58. Mallach (2006, pp.144–47) and Immergluck (2008a, p. 11). See also Madar, Been, and Armstrong (2008).

Finally, the local government can step in and take direct action itself, still short of acquiring title to the property; this option is explained in most detail by Mallach.[59] He notes that normally such actions are taken under nuisance abatement provisions in state law. When nuisance conditions are documented, the municipality is allowed to abate or correct them, including by mowing lawns, removing trash, making various repairs, boarding up the building, and even demolishing the building. The municipality is usually able to place a lien on the property to cover the cost of abatement. State laws governing nuisance abatement make the process more difficult for local governments in some states than in others. The current crisis makes this an important time for all states to review and strengthen those statutes.

An alternative, although complementary, approach is to try to prevent or minimize any period of vacancy by renting a property until it is sold to a responsible new owner. First, Mallach recommends modifying state laws to eliminate foreclosure as legal grounds for evicting sitting tenants who are otherwise in compliance with their legal obligations as tenants. They would be allowed to stay "at least until the expiration of their lease (or, in the absence of a lease, some minimum period no less than twelve months from the sheriff's sale)."[60] He also recommends eliminating any barrier to allowing former owners to stay on as tenants in REO properties after foreclosure.

The Furman team recognizes that option and also that of encouraging servicers to rent properties to other parties after foreclosure. They note that these options should produce an attractive short-term revenue stream to help offset carrying costs and protect the property during a possibly long period of REO ownership; however, they also note that there are "obstacles preventing such strategies from gaining much traction." Most important is the possible difficulty of removing a tenant on short notice in states with strong tenant protections, thereby limiting flexibility in efforts to resell the property.[61] The answer to that problem may be to revise the law so that tenants are required to vacate when a new owner wants to occupy the property personally.[62]

Expediting the Private Resale of Foreclosed Properties

Even if a property has been stabilized in the interim, it is extremely important to move to the next stage as soon as possible: sale to a new owner capable of sustaining ownership and maintaining the property in good condition over the long term. The programs noted above that make it more expensive to hold a

59. Mallach (2006, pp. 40–48).
60. Mallach (2009b, p.17).
61. Madar, Been, and Armstrong (2008, p. 24).
62. Mallach (2009b, p.17).

vacant property are an obvious basis for policy in this area, but a municipality can go further. Sale to a responsible private buyer is preferred, however, and a municipality can follow up to make sure that the servicers are taking advantage of all that the local real estate industry has to offer to facilitate a sale, and if rehabilitation is essential to making the property marketable, that the servicers are aware of all programs that could help make that option feasible.

Alternatively, it may be more advantageous for many foreclosed properties to be sold to nonprofit housing groups that will not only maintain them but also keep them more affordable over the long term. That is where efforts by the municipality to establish good working relationships with servicers and the nonprofit sector ahead of time can be a substantial advantage.

Directly Acquiring and Managing Foreclosed Properties

Where neighborhood market conditions are weak to intermediate, it may be necessary for government agencies to take direct action by acquiring foreclosed properties and getting them back into use. Mallach, Immergluck, and the Furman team all offer advice on that approach.[63]

Municipalities need to make clear which agency will be responsible for this role, and staff capacity probably will have to be strengthened to handle it. For example, staff need to be skilled enough to enter into tough negotiations with REO servicers, many of whom may well be in denial about the extent to which the value of their properties has declined. There also may be a need for new state legislation that penalizes REO owners who turn down responsible offers by government but later sell the property for a lower price.

In some cases, it may make sense to negotiate with larger REO servicers to acquire property on a bulk-purchase basis rather than property by property, and negotiations obviously are more likely to succeed if collaborative relationships have been established with servicers ahead of time. Local governments should also actively take advantage of available methods of acquiring these properties at reduced cost—for example, through tax foreclosure or the FHA's 602 nonprofit disposition program.[64]

In metropolitan areas with weaker housing markets, the need for public property acquisition and management is likely to be substantial. Specialized land-banking authorities will be needed: public or quasi-public entities with the legal authority and capacity to handle the acquisition, management, and disposition of property in the public interest in an effective manner and to do so at

---

63. This subject is dealt with most completely in Mallach (2006, pp. 69–102). See also Immergluck (2008a, p. 12–17); Madar, Been, and Armstrong (2008, p. 15).

64. The 602 program allows local governments and nonprofits in specified "asset control areas" to purchase foreclosed FHA properties at a substantial discount. See Temkin and others (2006).

scale. Few such entities now exist. Probably the most successful, the land bank implemented in Genesee County, Michigan, would serve as a good model for development elsewhere.[65]

The Genesee Land Bank's achievements arose from changes to Michigan law in 2002 (allowing counties to foreclose if property taxes are delinquent and, through an efficient judicial proceeding, take ownership of unredeemed delinquent property) and in 2004 (authorizing the creation of land banks vested with broad redevelopment and financial powers). The land bank is able to retain income from delinquent tax interest and the resale of properties in more prosperous neighborhoods to cover the costs of maintaining and redeveloping properties in depressed neighborhoods. It can aggregate small properties to create large parcels that are more attractive for development, and it can use a negotiated sales process to dispose of property; in a negotiated sale a property has a much lower probability of re-foreclosure than it does with disposition by auction. The land bank has been aggressive since its founding; in 2008, it owned 12 percent of all land in the city of Flint.

When public agencies (land banks or otherwise) have acquired foreclosed properties, they must make sensible decisions about the future of each consistent with market realities. Mallach and the Furman Center team again offer guidance.[66] One option is for governments to rehabilitate a property and then market it to a private buyer. Another is to convey the property to a nonprofit housing group to implement the rehab and then manage the property as affordable rental housing over the long term. Alternatively, a community land trust model may make sense. The trust allows a family to purchase a physical unit at a below-market price but retains ownership of the land, and the unit's owners and the trust typically share profits from appreciation at resale.[67]

Any decision to rehab a property to try to bring it back into use must be carefully considered. Even with a reasonable subsidy, the market in the neighborhood (for either rental or for-sale properties) may not be strong enough to make rehab feasible in the short term. If so, the only reasonable course of action may be to board up or demolish the structure and then hold the property for a fairly prolonged period until the market improves again. To reduce maintenance costs after demolition, sometimes the practical thing to do is to landscape the cleared space and convert it into a public park. Another approach is to convey the land to owners of abutting properties; they obtain more expansive side lots, and the need for ongoing public outlays is eliminated altogether.

65. Guidance on the establishment and functioning of land banks can be found in Alexander (2005); Kildee (2008); and Shigley (2008).

66. Mallach (2006, pp. 103–16); Madar, Been, and Armstrong (2008, pp. 17–20).

67. Davis (2006).

Maintaining and Upgrading the Neighborhood Environment

Research cited earlier indicates that when the number of foreclosures in a neighborhood becomes noticeable, the value of other neighborhood properties is likely to decline.[68] Specialists recognize that local governments should move quickly at that point to prevent further deterioration and reestablish a positive market image of the neighborhood.[69] That implies giving priority to the neighborhood for government services like trash removal, street cleaning and repair, vacant lot cleaning, and targeted code enforcement. The effort is likely to be most successful if neighborhood residents are positively engaged. Neighborhood associations should encourage all owners to give special emphasis to property maintenance and improvements. Commercial establishments and other anchor institutions, such as schools and hospitals, also should be encouraged to participate and make visible improvements to their properties.

Baltimore's Healthy Neighborhoods Initiative (HNI) is an example of a program that took such an approach. It operated in neighborhoods "in the middle"—those that appear to be stable but are actually fragile, with weak but still functioning real estate markets. It provided below-market financing for the rehabilitation of some homes, but emphasized "small and varied block projects to help re-weave the social fabric among neighbors and lead to visible changes in the neighborhood."[70] It purposefully began by making improvements on the strongest block in the neighborhood.

Designing a Neighborhood Stabilization Strategy

The problem with all of this is that local governments do not have the resources to take all of the recommended actions in all neighborhoods at the same time. And it is clear that different neighborhoods have very different needs and opportunities. Program designers need to examine data on neighborhood conditions to determine how to allocate resources strategically. Many types of indicators on a host of social, economic, and physical neighborhood characteristics as well basic data on mortgages and foreclosure status could be useful. Such neighborhood data have seldom been available to local planners in the past, but with improvements in technology over the past few years, many cities should now be able to assemble the most important indicators needed at reasonable cost.[71]

68. Immergluck and Smith (2006a); Harding, Rosenblatt, and Yao (2008).

69. Immergluck (2008a, p. 11).

70. Boehlke (2001). See also Brophy and Burnett (2003).

71. University institutes and civic groups in a sizable number of metro areas already have obtained and are using much of the data needed. A rapidly growing network of such organizations in thirty-one cities—the National Neighborhood Indicators Partnership—works to advance techniques in this field and spread capacity to other cities. To learn more about NNIP, visit www.urban.org/nnip; see also Kingsley and Pettit (2007).

Table 2-3. *Foreclosure Response Strategy Framework*

| | Response strategy | | |
Market strength	A. Low risk of high foreclosure density	B. High risk of high foreclosure density	C. Actual high foreclosure density
1. Strong	Need for response is lower.	The priority is preventing displacement, foreclosures, and vacancies (low or no subsidy).	Facilitate rapid sales to responsible owners; rehabilitate as needed (low or no subsidy).
2. Intermediate	Need for response is lower, but market must be watched carefully to head off emerging problems early.	High priority is given to preventing displacement, foreclosures, and vacancies (increased subsidy and neighborhood maintenance).	High priority is given to rehabilitating and expediting rapid sales to responsible owners (targeted subsidies and neighborhood maintenance).
3. Weak	Need for response is lower, but market must be watched carefully to head off emerging problems early.	The priority is preventing displacement, foreclosures, and vacancies (low or modest subsidies justified).	Use targeted reinvestment and increase acquisition, demolition, and land banking of properties to hold until market rebounds.

Source: Author's illustration.

Which indicators are important? The need to focus resources on neighborhoods that have a high risk of foreclosure is generally understood, but Mallach emphasizes that in two neighborhoods with the same foreclosure risk, differences in the strength of their markets could imply the need for quite different strategies.[72] Starting from that basic idea, Kingsley, Smith and Price examined possible strategies that a local government could pursue under various conditions (see table 2-3).[73]

As noted earlier, the goals should be to recreate a healthy private market, to prevent foreclosures from destabilizing sound neighborhoods, and to revive neighborhoods already in decline. In a resource-scarce environment, that means investing time and resources in neighborhoods where the investments will have

72. Mallach (2008c, pp. 9–11).
73. Kingsley, Smith, and Price (2009). The framework is also presented at www.Foreclosure-Response.org.

the most significant payoff. At the simplest level, planners might apply guidelines like the following:

—Neighborhood stabilization teams should not have to invest much in neighborhoods where there is a low risk of many foreclosures, regardless of market strength (cells 1A, 2A, or 3A in table 2-3), although trends should be monitored so that low-cost interventions can be mounted in intermediate- and weak-market neighborhoods to head off problems quickly if risks start to increase.

—Similarly, strong-market neighborhoods generally should not warrant high levels of stabilization spending. However, where foreclosure risks are high (cells 1B and 1C), they should be a priority for action to prevent actual foreclosures and minimize vacancy in any properties where foreclosures do occur. If such actions are taken soon enough, the strength of the market should prevent serious further slippage without major public investment.

—Neighborhoods that have an intermediate level of market demand may be the highest priorities for stabilization. They could deteriorate swiftly if foreclosures are not prevented or foreclosed properties are not brought back into use rapidly. Where many properties are at risk but foreclosures have not yet occurred (cell 2B), the emphasis should be on prevention: outreach and counseling for troubled borrowers and help (sometimes financial) so that they can refinance on sustainable terms. Code enforcement, public maintenance, and neighborhood organizing also will be needed in such areas to prevent the broader neighborhood from declining.

—Intermediate markets where a sizable number of foreclosures already have occurred (cell 2C) also are likely to be high priorities for stabilization. The local team needs to continue all the types of actions suggested for the type of properties in cell 2B and also to take forceful, direct public action to restore foreclosed properties to use as soon as possible. Rehabilitation may be needed in many cases, and subsidies may be appropriate. Rehabilitation is warranted, however, only where the market is strong enough that the new owners (investors or owner-occupants), taking into account the full costs of rehab as well as available subsidies, can subsequently operate the property in an economically stable manner over the long term.

—The most difficult challenges are neighborhoods that have both weak market demand and high risk of foreclosure impacts (cells 3B and 3C). In those cases, large-scale public investments that would move such neighborhoods into the intermediate category would be ideal, but most cities are unlikely to have sufficient funding to do that for all such neighborhoods. Where the market is likely to remain weak for some time, it may be difficult to justify rehabilitation because the rent or price required to cover the cost will exceed what people are willing to pay. If communities rehabilitate many properties in such markets, they can quickly run through available funds and end up without enough to stabilize the neighborhoods successfully. In a worst-case scenario, much of the available funding could ultimately be lost. The alternative would be for government to acquire the foreclosed properties, demolish the structures, and hold the parcels in a land bank until market conditions rebound enough to justify further investment. Choosing this approach is always difficult and substantial discussion with many constituencies may be required to reach a level of community acceptance that allows this strategy to move forward successfully.

Again, the matrix in table 2-3 oversimplifies the alternatives. When neighborhoods fit between these categories, a blending of the actions suggested for the two is likely to be appropriate. Additional information that may modify ideas about strategy also should be considered. For example, some neighborhoods have a greater capacity to influence the trajectory of areas that surround them. Funds that target such areas would have more impact than funds for a neighborhood that is more economically and socially isolated. Also, some neighborhoods have stronger internal resources and assets than others, including anchor institutions or strong community groups that can leverage new public investments. Such factors need to be taken into account, too.

A good example of a strategic planning effort that followed the "different treatments for different types of neighborhoods" approach was developed in Columbus and Franklin County, Ohio. It explicitly sought to

—prevent neighborhood decline associated with foreclosure in traditionally stable markets

—address the issue of backsliding due to foreclosure in "tipping point" neighborhoods

—focus resources in neighborhoods traditionally targeted by revitalization efforts to prevent further disinvestment and decline.

Weak-market neighborhoods were identified and "comprehensive acquisition and holding plans" were devised for them.[74]

In cities with many weak-market neighborhoods, practitioners often have advocated the idea of targeting particular areas for investment in community development. One analysis demonstrates the benefits of that approach. In 1998, Richmond, Virginia, began concentrating its neighborhood improvement investments in just a few locations rather than spreading them evenly with the idea of achieving a critical mass that would leverage for-profit investment. The study entailed econometric analysis of data on property values and other relevant indicators through 2004.[75] It showed that the program, called Neighbor-

---

74. Columbus and Franklin County Foreclosure Working Group (2008).
75. Galster, Tatian, and Accordino (2006).

hoods in Bloom, "produced substantially greater appreciation in the market values of single-family homes in the targeted areas than in comparable homes in similarly distressed neighborhoods."[76]

Opportunities for Evaluation and Policy

Successful or not, efforts to stabilize neighborhoods in the wake of the current foreclosure crisis will have a significant impact on the quality of U.S. residential environments for decades to come. This chapter outlines a set of policy approaches and techniques advocated by a number of experts to mitigate community impacts. Nevertheless, there are doubts as to whether there is sufficient local capacity to implement them effectively, and there is uncertainty about how well they are likely to work.

It is important to recognize that the type of policy problem explored in this chapter is especially challenging. With some types of urban problems, the job of the public sector is to establish the rules of the game and provide incentives, setting the stage for the market to efficiently carry out the actual work of development, neighborhood by neighborhood. With this problem, success will require the local public sector to adapt its own direct actions in a quite sophisticated way across different types of neighborhoods—a much more difficult assignment. In spite of the magnitude of the challenge, I see reasons for some optimism:

—Remarkable improvements in information technology over the past decade mean that it may now be possible to improve significantly the capacity of local stakeholders to guide neighborhood change. Those improvements may make serious evaluation of programs a realistic possibility for the first time. The federal government should give high priority to helping practitioners and evaluators develop better data and the skills needed to apply those data.

—Given the improvements in information technology, high national priority should also be given to helping local stakeholders manage their way out of the current crisis in a manner that overcomes major housing market deficiencies that existed before the crisis began.

Information and the Capacity to Guide and Evaluate Neighborhood Change

What is known about how well the policies and techniques introduced in this chapter actually work? Surprisingly little. There have been very few write-ups of case experiences and hardly any formal statistical analyses.[77] A major reason is

---

76. Galster, Tatian, and Accordino (2006, p. 457)

77. A promising but still programmatically limited recent exception is Glass (2008). Temkin and others (2006) is one of the rare assessments of programs in this field that entailed some quantitative assessment. An early report documenting characteristics of a selection of local plans prepared under the first

that assessing such programs requires an extraordinary amount of data, and until very recently assembling such data has been prohibitively expensive. Evaluation requires documenting the amount of investment dollars (by date, program mechanism, and source of funds) going into specific properties along with describing the initial characteristics of the properties and how their characteristics (in particular, property values) change over time. But as discussed, documenting changes for specific properties is not the goal. The data needed would have to track changes in a host of conditions across a neighborhood and compare changes in the focus neighborhood with those in others in the city.

Even though the data requirements are formidable, in the last few years many cities have begun to assemble information systems that can support this sort of assessment.[78] For example, they have automated records on transfers of title that, with today's geographic information systems (GIS) technology, can be matched against a list of properties that have received notices of foreclosure. Monthly or quarterly reports could be produced for the city or county and for individual neighborhoods on changes in foreclosure activity as well as on neighborhood market trends.

Hard data on a wide range of program activities also are needed, but data collection is getting easier there, too. For example, for actions taken by the local government on specific foreclosed properties (demolition, boarding up, rehabilitation), all that may be needed is to link a brief description of what was done (type of action, dates, and dollar amounts) to the address; GIS technology then can be used to add up the results and produce reports for neighborhoods and the jurisdiction as a whole. In fact, HUD is requiring this form of electronic address-based reporting for funds spent under the neighborhood stabilization program.[79]

Some information in all these categories is now available in a number of cities, including Baltimore, Cleveland, Memphis, New York City, and Washington, D.C.[80] Some have done sophisticated analyses of the results of the process. One report available in Cleveland, for example, allows assessment of the probabilities of foreclosure given varying characteristics of the loan. Another report using the Cleveland data system analyzes how long institutional investors are

---

round of the NSP program has been prepared, but it is obviously too early to expect any assessment of results (Sheldon and others 2009).

78. Again, refer to information about members of the National Neighborhood Indicators Partnership (NNIP) at www.urban.org/nnip.

79. U.S. Department of Housing and Urban Development, "Disaster Recovery Grant Reporting System" (www.hud.gov/offices/cpd/communitydevelopment/programs/drsi/drgrs.cfm).

80. All are members of NNIP.

holding properties after foreclosure and the prices at which they are ultimately sold.[81] And methods recently developed by George Galster and others (used in the Richmond study cited earlier and relying on new and expanded databases) permit much more reliable assessment of program effects on neighborhoods than were feasible in the past.[82]

The federal government should provide funding and other forms of encouragement to help spread similar information system improvements to other cities in the near term. Such data will permit remarkable improvements in evaluation of the types of policies and programs discussed in this chapter—in fact, of all policies that attempt to improve conditions in U.S. neighborhoods. But federal support should not be motivated primarily by new opportunities for formal policy evaluation. The primary reason for enhancing local information systems is to improve the capacity of local stakeholders to design neighborhood-based foreclosure mitigation strategies, implement them, and monitor their performance.

The objective is not for the local public sector to take over the task of neighborhood development and revitalization from the private sector but to create conditions that help the market perform those tasks more effectively. The adequacy of what local governments do in neighborhoods (routine maintenance, code enforcement, rehabilitation assistance, dealing with hazardous conditions that emerge, regulating construction and property transfers) inevitably has a major effect on market performance. If local governments and nonprofits can develop the capacity to perform their own routine roles more effectively and improve the nature, timing, and scope of their special program interventions, healthier neighborhood markets should result.

Seeking More Comprehensive Improvement in Metropolitan Housing Markets

Policies and programs discussed in this chapter are directed at preventing or at least mitigating the devastating effects of high densities of foreclosures on neighborhoods: physical deterioration, social disorder, and the resulting decline in property values. These are indeed the most urgent matters to be dealt with at this point.

Addressing these issues, however, offers a broader opportunity. There were serious problems in U.S. metropolitan housing markets before the foreclosure crisis began. The concentration of poverty in particular neighborhoods reduced overall functional efficiency and economic competitiveness, and it has had disastrous

---

81. Coulton and others (2008); Coulton, Mikelbank, and Schramm (2008).
82. Galster and others (2004).

effects on the lives of the residents of those neighborhoods. The cost of housing was on an upward trajectory that was making decent housing and neighborhood environments increasingly unaffordable to lower-income groups long before 2000.

The manner in which immediate foreclosure mitigation efforts are carried out will inevitably have an effect on such longer-term issues. It might possibly work to change their course, and the opportunities to make that happen should be a focus of local and national strategic planning over the next few years. For example, the data show that many of neighborhoods with high foreclosure densities are low-poverty neighborhoods, often in the suburbs. Property values in those neighborhoods are suffering precipitous declines. A metropolitan-wide strategy could be adopted to facilitate the purchase of a number of those properties by nonprofit housing groups, which would then operate them as affordable housing over the long term. Such a strategy might involve innovative arrangements like community land trusts as well as traditional rental and ownership arrangements.

This approach would have to be managed carefully. Planners would probably try to avoid developing so large a quantity of affordable housing in any one neighborhood that the neighborhood's character would be markedly altered. But if affordable housing were developed even incrementally and modestly in a large number of neighborhoods, the aggregate effect in terms of deconcentrating poverty could be substantial.

Planners should also be on the lookout for opportunities to increase densities in selected locations in a way that will bring more workers closer to major employment locations—in short, to increase the efficiency of the overall use of geographical space. The time might be right (in the context of the "crisis") to push for more aggressive metropolitan-wide efforts to eliminate suburban regulatory barriers that unreasonably constrain the housing supply and drive up prices.

The federal government could do a number of things to promote the development of such strategies. Bruce Katz and Margery Turner have recommended, for example, that metropolitan planning organizations (which already exist throughout the country) be given funding and technical assistance to prepare regional housing strategies similar to the regional transportation plans that they already produce under federal law.[83] Such strategies would need to set specific targets for the households assisted and work to achieve those targets by deploying all forms of federal housing assistance, including low-income housing tax credits, HOME funds, and community development block grants as well as vouchers and traditional public housing. They might also include sensible neighborhood-based

83. Katz and Turner (2008).

foreclosure mitigation strategies, developed in collaboration with local governments and nonprofit housing providers, in line with the aims noted above.

References

Alexander, Frank. 2005. *Land Bank Authorities: A Guide for the Creation and Operation of Local Land Banks.* New York: Local Initiatives Support Corporation.

Apgar, William C., and Mark Duda. 2005. *Collateral Damage: The Municipal Impact of Today's Mortgage Foreclosure Boom.* Minneapolis: Homeownership Preservation Foundation.

Baily, Martin Neil, Douglas W. Elmendorf, and Robert E. Litan. 2008. "The Great Credit Squeeze: How it Happened, How to Prevent Another." Brookings.

Been, Vicki. 2008. "Testimony on 'External Effects of Concentrated Mortgage Foreclosures: Evidence from New York City.'" Subcommittee on Domestic Policy, Committee on Oversight and Government Reform, U.S. House of Representatives. May 21.

Berube, Alan, and Benjamin Forman. 2002. "Living on the Edge: Decentralization within Cities in the 1990s." Brookings.

Bess, Michael. 2008. "Assessing the Impact of Home Foreclosures in Charlotte Neighborhoods." *Geography and Public Safety* 1, no. 3: 2–5.

Boehlke, David. 2001. *Great Neighborhoods, Great City.* Baltimore: Goldseker Foundation.

Brophy, Paul, and Kim Burnett. 2003. *Building a New Framework for Community Development in Weak Market Cities.* Denver: Community Development Partnership Network.

Carr, James H. 2008. "Responding to the Foreclosure Crisis." *Housing Policy Debate* 18, no. 4: 837–60.

Columbus and Franklin County Foreclosure Working Group. 2008. *Prevention and Recovery Advisory Plan.* Columbus, Ohio: Community Research Partners.

Community Research Partners and Rebuild Ohio. 2008. "$60 Million and Counting: The Cost of Vacant and Abandoned Properties to Eight Ohio Cities." Columbus, Ohio.

Coulton, Claudia, Kristen Mikelbank, and Michael Schramm. 2008. *Foreclosure and Beyond: A Report on Ownership and Housing Value Following Sheriff's Sales, Cleveland and Cuyahoga County, 2000–07.* Center on Urban Poverty and Community Development, Case Western Reserve University.

Coulton, Claudia, and others. 2008. *Pathways to Foreclosure: A Longitudinal Study of Mortgage Loans, Cleveland and Cuyahoga County, 2005–2008.* Case Western Reserve University.

Cutts, Amy Crews, and Richard K. Green. 2004. "Innovative Servicing Technology: Smart Enough to Keep People in Their Houses?" Working Paper 04-03. McLean, Va.: Freddie Mac.

Davis, John E. 2006. *Shared Equity Homeownership: The Changing Landscape of Resale-Restricted, Owner-Occupied Housing.* Washington: National Housing Institute.

Dubitsky, Rod, and others. 2008. "Foreclosure Update: Over 8 Million Foreclosures Expected." New York: Credit Suisse.

Ergungor, O. Emre. 2008. "The Mortgage Debacle and Loan Modifications." Cleveland: Federal Reserve Bank of Cleveland.

Galster, George, Peter Tatian, and John Accordino. 2006. "Targeting Investments for Neighborhood Revitalization." *Journal of the American Planning Association* 72, no. 4: 457–74.

Galster, George, and others. 2004. "Measuring the Impacts of Community Development Initiatives: A New Application of the Adjusted Interrupted Time-Series Method." *Evaluation Review* 28, no. 6: 502–38.

Glass, Anne. 2008. *Post-Foreclosure Community Stabilization Strategies: Case Studies and Early Lessons*. Washington: NeighborWorks® America.

Gramlich, Edward M. 2007. *Subprime Mortgages: America's Latest Boom and Bust*. Washington: Urban Institute.

Harding, John P., Eric Rosenblatt, and Vincent Yao. 2008. "The Contagion Effect of Foreclosed Properties." University of Connecticut.

Hartarska, Valentina, and Claudio Gonzalez-Vega. 2005. "Credit Counseling and Mortgage Termination by Low-Income Households." *Journal of Real Estate Finance and Economics* 30, no. 3: 227–43.

Herbert, Christopher E., and William C. Apgar. 2009. *Interim Report to Congress on the Root Causes of the Foreclosure Crisis*. U.S. Department of Housing and Urban Development.

Hirad, Abdighani, and Peter M. Zorn. 2002. "Prepurchase Homeownership Counseling: A Little Knowledge Is a Good Thing." In *Low Income Homeownership: Examining the Unexamined Goal*, edited by Nicholas P. Retsinas and Eric S. Belsky, pp. 146–74. Brookings.

Immergluck, Dan. 2008a. "Community Response to the Foreclosure Crisis: Thoughts on Local Interventions." Discussion Paper 01-08. Atlanta: Federal Reserve Bank of Atlanta.

———. 2008b. "From the Subprime to the Exotic: Excessive Mortgage Market Risk and Foreclosure." *Journal of the American Planning Association* 74, no. 1: 59–76.

Immergluck, Dan, and Geoff Smith. 2006a. "The External Costs of Foreclosure: The Impact of Single-Family Mortgage Foreclosures on Property Values." *Housing Policy Debate* 17, no. 1: 57–79.

———. 2006b. "The Impact of Single-Family Mortgage Foreclosures on Neighborhood Crime." *Housing Studies* 21, no. 6: 851–66.

Joint Center for Housing Studies. 2008. *America's Rental Housing: The Key to a Balanced National Housing Policy*. Joint Center for Housing Studies, Harvard University.

Katz, Bruce, and Margery Austin Turner. 2008. "Rethinking U.S. Rental Housing Policy: A New Blueprint for Federal, State, and Local Action." In *Revisiting Rental Housing*, edited by Nicolas P. Retsinas and Eric S. Belsky, pp. 319–58. Brookings.

Kildee, Daniel T. 2008. "Testimony on 'Neighborhoods: The Blameless Victims of the Subprime Mortgage Crisis.'" Domestic Policy Subcommittee, Committee on Oversight and Government Reform, U.S. House of Representatives. May 21.

Kingsley, G. Thomas, and Kathryn L. S. Pettit. 2007. "Neighborhood Information Systems: We Need a Broader Effort to Build Local Capacity." Washington: Urban Institute (www.urban.org/url.cfm?ID=900755).

———. 2009. "High Cost and Investor Mortgages: Neighborhood Patterns." Washington: Urban Institute.

Kingsley, G. Thomas, Robin Smith, and David Price. 2009. "The Impacts of Foreclosures on Families and Communities." Washington: Urban Institute.

Lovell, Phillip, and Julia Isaacs. 2008. "The Impact of the Mortgage Crisis on Children and Their Education." Washington: First Focus.

Madar, Josiah, Vicki Been, and Amy Armstrong. 2008. "Transforming Foreclosed Properties into Community Assets." Furman Center White Paper. New York University.

Mallach, Alan. 2006. *Bringing Buildings Back: From Abandoned Properties to Community Assets: A Guidebook for Policymakers and Practitioners*. Montclair, N.J.: National Housing Institute.

———. 2008a. *Managing Neighborhood Change: A Framework for Sustainable and Equitable Revitalization*. Montclair, N.J.: National Housing Institute.

———. 2008b. "Tackling the Mortgage Crisis: Ten Action Steps for State Government." Brookings.

———. 2008c. "How to Spend $3.92 Billion: Stabilizing Neighborhoods by Addressing Fore-closed and Abandoned Properties." Philadelphia: Federal Reserve Bank of Philadelphia.

———. 2009a. "Stabilizing Communities: A Federal Response to the Secondary Impacts of the Foreclosure Crisis." Brookings.

———. 2009b. "Addressing Ohio's Foreclosure Crisis: Taking the Next Steps." Brookings.

Mayer, Neil, and others. 2008. "NeighborWorks America National Foreclosure Mitigation Counseling Program Evaluation: Interim Report 1." Washington: Urban Institute.

McFarland, Christina, and William McGahan. 2008. "Housing Finance and Foreclosure Cri-sis: Local Impacts and Responses." *Research Brief on America's Cities* 2008, no. 1: 1–2.

NeighborWorks® America. 2007. *Formula for Success: Questions and Answers for Local Leaders Designing a Foreclosure Intervention Program*. Washington.

Pagano, Michael, and Christopher W. Hoen. 2008. "City Fiscal Conditions in 2008." *Research Brief on America's Cities* 2008, no. 2: 1–12.

Pettit, Kathryn L. S., and Audrey E. Droesch. 2007. *A Guide to Home Mortgage Disclosure Act Data*. Washington: DataPlace, KnowledgePlex Inc.

Pettit, Kathryn L. S., and others. 2008. *Using Property Databases for Community Action*. Washington: Urban Institute.

Pew Charitable Trusts. 2008. *Defaulting on the Dream: States Respond to America's Foreclosure Crisis*. Washington.

Pierson, Julia. 2008. "Evaluation of the Baltimore Homeownership Preservation Coalition Activities in 2005, 2006, and 2007." Baltimore: Baltimore Homeownership Preservation Coalition.

Rich, Michael J., Michael Carnathan, and Dan Immergluck. 2008. "Addressing the Foreclo-sure Crisis in Three NNIP Cities: Atlanta Work Plan." Emory University and Atlanta Regional Commission.

Sheldon, Amanda, and others. 2009. "The Challenge of Foreclosed Properties: An Analysis of State and Local Plans to Use the Neighborhood Stabilization Program." Columbia, Md.: Enterprise Community Partners.

Shigley, Paul. 2008. "Fixing Foreclosure." *Planning* (June), pp. 6–10.

Temkin, Kenneth, and others. 2006. "Assessment of the 602 Non-Profit Disposition Pro-gram." U.S. Department of Housing and Urban Development.

U.S. Bureau of the Census. 1975. *Historical Statistics of the United States, Colonial Times to 1970*. U.S. Department of Commerce.

3

School Choice: Options and Outcomes

RON ZIMMER, CASSANDRA GUARINO, AND RICHARD BUDDIN

A major concern for policymakers, parents, and academics is the poor per-formance of central city school systems. Urban eighth-graders consistently perform at much lower levels than their counterparts in suburban schools.[1] In reading, 55 percent of all urban students but only 34 percent of suburban stu-dents are below basic skills; in math, the figures are 50 percent of urban students but only 20 percent of suburban students. Similarly, while 77 percent of students who attend suburban high schools graduate, only 59 percent of urban high school students do.[2] The dropout problem is especially severe in the largest ten urban districts, where only 49 percent of students graduate from high school.

In part, the performance of students reflects the background and preparation that they bring to the classroom. About 61 percent of urban but only 38 percent of nonurban students come from poor families that are eligible for the federally sponsored free and reduced-price lunch program. About 30 percent of urban students are black, and 39 percent are Hispanic; the figures for nonurban stu-dents are 14 percent and 17 percent respectively. English language learners con-stitute 12 percent of urban students but only 6 percent of nonurban students.

The problems of urban schools have important implications for students as well as for central cities themselves. Barrow and Rouse show that high school graduates earn 75 percent more than dropouts and that college graduates earn 130 percent more than high school graduates.[3] About 24 percent of dropouts live below the poverty level; the figure for high school graduates with no further education is half that, only 12 percent.[4] Low educational attainment and its cor-

1. National Center for Education Statistics (2005).
2. Swanson (2009).
3. Barrow and Rouse (2006).
4. Swanson (2009).

responding poverty put the next generation of students at increased risk of having difficulty in school. In contrast, educational achievement has positive spillovers—for example, on voting, community involvement, and crime.[5]

A number of reforms have been introduced to address the challenges in urban schools. Perhaps the most controversial is the introduction of greater schooling options through such programs as school vouchers, charter schools, magnet schools, and inter- and intradistrict open enrollment policies. Collectively, these "choice programs" have greatly expanded the schooling options of students and their families; however, it is unclear what impact the programs are having. Also, because some of the options are autonomous, operating beyond the district's control, it is important to understand whether there is a difference between the effectiveness of district-managed choices such as magnet schools and open enrollment programs and that of independently or privately run forms of choice such as charter schools and vouchers. This chapter reviews the evidence on the effectiveness of the various forms of school choice with a particular focus on the dichotomy between district-managed and independently run options in the United States.

We begin by describing the evolution of and rationale for choice-based reform in the United States. In so doing, we discuss the expectations that arise regarding differences between the impact of government and independently controlled forms of choice. We then review the recent evidence regarding the efficacy of various school choice options with regard to outcomes. We conclude with a discussion of the implications of the findings from our survey of the literature and of next steps for future research designs.

Evolution of School Choice in the United States

In colonial times, schooling, if it was provided, was often provided by a private tutor, a single teacher in a small school, or both. However, by the mid-1800s, Horace Mann and others were pushing for free public schools supported by local communities. Over time, two parallel systems evolved—one that used tax money to support free, government-run schools and the other a tuition-based system of private schools.

In the mid-twentieth century, with the two systems firmly entrenched, Milton Friedman wrote a provocative essay on the role of government in education, contending that public funding for a minimum level of education was justified because it provided benefits not only to individuals but also to society at large.[6]

5. Moretti (2004).
6. Friedman (1955).

However, he questioned whether it was necessary for government to be the predominant provider of educational services and argued that the private market might provide education more effectively and efficiently. He therefore advocated giving families publicly funded vouchers to be used to gain educational services through an array of providers. Forcing providers to compete for students, he claimed, would create more efficient and effective schools.

The early arguments in favor of school choice did not sway opinion until decades later, however. *A Nation at Risk*, a landmark publication that voiced broad concern that the United States was not providing education adequate to meet the needs of the twenty-first century, accelerated efforts to overhaul the educational system, and school choice was one among many reform efforts that gained wider acceptance.[7] The later advocates of choice echoed Friedman's efficiency arguments and maintained that the public education system could not reform itself because of the bureaucracy and political interests entrenched within it.[8] They argued that independently run schools would create new educational opportunities for students and lead to greater innovation, ultimately improving student achievement. In addition, they maintained that new schools would emerge offering alternative programs that could better match the various needs of families and children. Finally, they claimed that the use of vouchers and charter schools would exert pressure to improve traditional public schools.[9] Opponents, on the other hand, argued that school choice programs might create greater racial and ethnic stratification, skim the best students from traditional public schools, siphon much-needed resources away from traditional public schools, and fail to improve student achievement.[10]

Although vouchers sparked a great deal of debate, they were implemented in a limited number of locations in the United States, beginning in 1990 with the Milwaukee voucher experiment. Meanwhile, a somewhat less controversial reform—the charter school—arose as an alternative form of choice and became more widespread. Charter schools receive public funding under a contract, or "charter," with a public entity (for example, a school district, state, or university) and are given greater autonomy than other public schools with respect to curriculum, instruction, and operations in exchange for being held accountable for results. Since the first U.S. charter school opened in 1992, the charter movement has grown to include nearly 4,500 schools and more than 1.2 million students in forty states plus the District of Columbia.[11]

7. National Commission on Excellence in Education (1983).
8. Chubb and Moe (1990).
9. Kolderie (2004); Chubb and Moe (1990); Hill, Lawrence, and Gutherie (1997).
10. Wells (1993).
11. Center for Education Reform (2009).

However, some forms of choice evolved through district-managed schools, including magnet programs. Initially conceived as a mechanism for increasing racial integration during the 1960s and 1970s, magnet programs offer specialized courses and curricula in schools that draw students across standard school boundaries. Policymakers hoped that as students crossed those boundaries, magnet programs would reduce racial isolation.

As magnet programs evolved, so did a broader district-managed form of school choice known as open enrollment. Open enrollment allows parents to choose among existing government-run public schools and takes two forms—"intradistrict" and "interdistrict" choice.[12] Intradistrict open enrollment allows a student to transfer to another school within his or her school district. Interdistrict open enrollment allows students to transfer to schools outside their home district but often requires explicit consent from both the sending and the receiving district.[13] Open enrollment programs place less emphasis on integration goals than early magnet programs; they are motivated more by a desire to respond to parents' concerns. These programs became more widespread over time, most likely because of the rising popularity of charter schools. As of 2005, twenty-seven states had adopted intradistrict choice policies, while twenty had passed legislation mandating interdistrict school choice.[14]

Finally, as part of the No Child Left Behind (NCLB) Act, a new form of choice was introduced through the sanctions of schools failing to make "adequate yearly progress" for two consecutive years. Students could opt out of those schools and attend other schools within the district. It was hoped that by doing so, students would gain access to higher-quality education and improve their performance. However, across the nation, less than 1 percent of eligible students are taking advantage of this option.[15]

The theoretical arguments in favor of choice yield predictions regarding the performance of district-managed schools of choice, such as magnets and open enrollment schools, relative to that of independently run schools, such as charters and schools funded by vouchers.[16] The three factors that are claimed to promote learning gains in schools of choice are better matching of students with schools, more innovative or higher-quality schools resulting from the schools' greater autonomy, and a general increase in the quality of all schools in response

12. Technically, magnet programs are a form of intradistrict choice. However, for this chapter, we focus on open enrollment as the primary mode of intradistrict choice.

13. Education Commission of the States (2009).

14. Özek (2009).

15. Stullich, Eisner, and McCary (2006).

16. We do not discuss a fifth type of schooling choice operating in the United States—home schooling—because home-schooled pupils do not form schools such as those resulting from other forms of choice.

to a competitive market for student enrollments. Some critics of independently run schools of choice acknowledge the need for fresh ideas and greater educational opportunities for families, but they argue that those objectives can be achieved through magnet and inter- and intradistrict choice programs. But whether they are right may depend on the relative importance of the three factors in contributing to the success of schools of choice.

The potential for learning gains derived from better student-school matching is present in all forms of school choice. However, if greater autonomy can lead to higher-quality academics, then it is easy to infer that independently run schools have the potential to outperform government-managed schools. Furthermore, if districts strategically use magnet schools or even intradistrict open enrollment to minimize the outmigration of high-performing students, then the potential for overall learning gains due to competitive effects will be diminished. For instance, advocates argue that vouchers and charter schools can exert competitive pressure on traditional public schools by competing for students and their associated revenue. In theory, the loss of revenue motivates district-managed schools to improve. Intuitively, that may be less likely for government-managed choice programs. For example, because both magnet and traditional public schools are managed by a district, the district may introduce magnet programs as a way to minimize the pressure on traditional public schools (for example, it may create a magnet program within a traditional public school). Moreover, the transfer of students to a magnet program may have limited implications for the district's bottom line; in contrast, the financial implications when a student exits a district by using a voucher or enrolling in a charter school can be significant. In fact, magnet programs may help districts retain students and their associated revenue.[17]

Those considerations suggest that the different forms of choice may result in differences in efficacy. To address that question, we review the research regarding the effects of district-managed and independently managed school choice programs. We examine the empirical evidence regarding the impact of voucher programs, charter schools, and government-managed school choice options such as interdistrict choice programs, open enrollment, and magnet schools on student outcomes, the distribution of students, and competitive effects. We also include a discussion of the challenges of estimating these effects.

Student Outcomes

Synthesized here is the evidence on the direct and indirect effects of the various school choice programs. We use the term "direct effect" to describe the effect on

17. Engberg and others (2009).

outcomes for students enrolling in schools of choice—private schools (through use of a voucher), charter schools, magnet schools, or schools other than neighborhood schools (through an open enrollment program). We use the term "indirect effect" to describe the effect that a school of choice has on student outcomes (mainly through competitive pressure) in other schools. In other words, we examine the effects of a school choice program on the achievement of students who choose not to participate. It should be noted that indirect effects can influence an evaluation of direct effects. For instance, because schools of choice recruit students from traditional public schools, they may exert competitive pressure on traditional public schools, and the academic gains of students attending schools of choice may be biased downward if students attending traditional public schools improve their performance. However, researchers who have incorporated sensitivity analyses to see whether schools of choice are creating competitive effects have found little evidence that competitive effects are jeopardizing conclusions about direct effects.[18]

Direct Effects

Analyzing the direct effects of a school choice program is complicated by the fact that selection is at the heart of school choice reform. Many argue that students who choose to attend schools of choice are more motivated or have more involved parents than students who do not; observed learning increases therefore might result more from omitted characteristics relating to motivation than from the quality of the schools themselves. Because of that, a typical approach to comparing students attending choice schools and nonchoice schools could be biased by unobserved differences. That bias, often referred to as a "selection bias," can lead researchers and policymakers to invalid conclusions about the level of success of choice schools.

The research tools normally used to address selection bias are of questionable applicability in analyzing the impact of choice on achievement. Ideally, researchers would randomly assign students to different types of schools. However, that approach to evaluating reform would be inappropriate because the student-school match, which theoretically contributes to learning *through* the choice aspect of reform, would be undermined. In lieu of a pure randomized design, researchers have often used one of three approaches: lottery-based design; a fixed-effect approach; or an instrumental variable approach.

Many argue that lottery-based design, in which researchers rely on lottery assignment of oversubscribed schools or programs as a natural experiment proxying random assignment, is the strongest of the three approaches. However, this

---

18. Zimmer and others (2009); Bifulco and Ladd (2006); Sass (2006).

approach answers a narrower question: does learning improve for students who enroll in schools perceived to be of high quality if their choice is granted to them from a set of oversubscribed schools and programs? The efficacy of the lottery schools is found by comparing the subsequent test scores of lottery "winners," who attend the oversubscribed school, with those of "losers," who are denied admission and attend another school. In fact, one would expect schools with wait lists to be the best schools (as perceived by parents), so the results offer little insight into the performance of undersubscribed schools. Similarly, families applying for schools with wait lists may be more engaged in learning or have high aspirations for their children, so outcomes for those students may provide little information about outcomes for students from families with different motivations.

Other researchers have used a fixed-effect approach, in which databases track individual students over time in order to deal with selection bias. Fixed-effect approaches minimize the problem of selection bias by comparing over time the academic gains of individual students who switch between a traditional public school and a school of choice ("switchers"). An advantage of this method over the lottery approach is that it applies to schools with and without waiting lists for admission. However, some researchers have raised concerns with this approach too.[19] The critics note that it does not provide an estimate for students who remain in schools of choice or traditional public schools for the duration of the analysis ("non-switchers") and who do not contribute to the estimate because the method requires comparison of their results in both contexts. Switchers may differ from non-switchers in important ways, so the results may not be applicable for students who are continuously enrolled in traditional schools or schools of choice.

Researchers also wonder about the motivation of students switching to schools of choice midway through their educational careers. For instance, Hoxby and Murarka argue that a fixed-effect approach cannot account for the possibility that students who perform poorly on a standardized test may be especially likely to transfer to a school of choice the following year.[20] Poor performance could be caused by poor educational instruction, disruption in a student's life unrelated to school, or just measurement error in test scores.[21] Regardless of the reason, a fixed-effect approach could produce invalid estimates.

---

19. Hoxby and Murarka (2006); Ballou, Bettie, and Zeidner (2007).
20. Hoxby and Murarka (2006).
21. All tests have some level of noise in their measurement, and the score of some students will be lower or higher on a single administration of a test than the average score that they would receive if they took multiple similar tests. Therefore, a student could score poorly on a particular test one year and score higher the next year as the student bounces back to a score that better reflects his or her learning.

Studies that rely on student-level fixed effects therefore answer a different—but also narrow—question: does learning improve for children who switch from other schools to charter schools and decrease for those who make the opposite switch? Those studies do not investigate learning improvements for the bulk of students who do not make a switch unless they restrict their attention to grades in which most students are required to change schools, such as in the transition from elementary to middle school or from middle to high school.

An alternative to those two approaches is an instrumental variable (IV) approach. An IV approach uses an "instrument" to control for the choices that students and their families make and reduces selection bias in estimating the effects of any school of choice. An IV approach can have advantages over the lottery-based randomized design and fixed-effect approaches because it can include more students and schools. However, it often is difficult to find an "instrument" that is correlated with the choice that families make and uncorrelated with ultimate educational outcomes.[22] Another limitation of the IV approach is that the effect applies only to individuals who are at the margin on the instrument used.[23] For example, in the context of charter schools, distance to a charter school has often been used as an instrument. It may be a valid instrument, but the results apply only to individuals on the margin based on distance from a charter school. From a policy perspective, we would like to know the charter effect for the broader population. So this approach also answers the question of effectiveness for a narrow population. These methodological considerations, together with those above, suggest that differences in findings across studies could result from differences in research approaches in addition to—or in lieu of—differences in the choice programs themselves. We return to that point in synthesizing findings from our review of the literature.

While these three approaches have been used primarily to examine achievement effects measured by test scores, they have also been applied to other outcomes, such as school attendance and behavior, as well as to graduation and college attendance rates.[24] Below, we examine the literature evaluating the impact of vouchers, charter schools, magnet schools, and open enrollment programs, focusing primarily on these approaches.

22. An "instrument" must have these characteristics if the IV approach is to be valid.
23. Angrist, Imbens, and Rubin (1996).
24. One outcome that has been examined in limited cases is parental satisfaction, but evaluating it presents significant challenges. One could imagine surveying parents about their level of satisfaction with their children's attending a school of choice and traditional public schools. However, because families choose to send their children to a school of choice, they may rationalize their choice, which may influence their responses. In addition, it is also easy to imagine that there would be response bias because only those with strong opinions may respond to such a survey.

DIRECT EFFECTS OF VOUCHERS. While the concept of vouchers has been around for decades, publicly funded vouchers have been implemented and studied in only a few locations across the United States. However, privately funded vouchers have been established and evaluated in a few additional locations. While the scale and regulation of publicly and privately funded programs may differ, the programs are similar in that both provide a subsidy for students to attend private schools.

Publicly Funded Voucher Programs. Although a 2002 Supreme Court decision supported the constitutionality of Cleveland's voucher program, publicly funded voucher programs have not gotten much traction.[25] Laws have been passed to establish voucher programs in Arizona, Colorado, Georgia, Florida, Louisiana, Wisconsin (Milwaukee), Ohio, Utah, and the District of Columbia.[26] However, the Colorado and Florida programs were declared unconstitutional, Arizona defunded its program, and Utah voters repealed the voucher law.[27] At the time of writing, the District of Columbia's program, which was enacted in 2004 and includes about 1,900 students, was in jeopardy as Congress considered whether to discontinue the program. Nevertheless, programs in Milwaukee, Cleveland, Florida, and District of Columbia have been evaluated.

In 1990 Milwaukee started a voucher program in which low-income families were eligible for vouchers to attend private schools. The number of students receiving scholarships was capped at 1 percent of the total district population, and the scholarships could be used only at secular schools. Because of the restrictive nature of the program, by the fifth year only about a dozen schools and approximately 830 students participated in the program.[28] In 1995, the program was expanded to include religious schools and the percentage cap was lifted. The program has grown to include about 20,000 students using vouchers at more than 120 private schools in Milwaukee. While test score data were collected for the small set of students in the initial program, data for the larger program are just now becoming available. Therefore, initial analyses focused on the relatively small set of 830 students and a dozen or so private schools.

The first set of studies came from John Witte; Greene, Peterson, and Du; and Cecilia Rouse, each using different approaches with different results. Using observable controls in a regression analysis, Witte compared the performance of voucher students to that of all other students in the Milwaukee school system

25. Figlio and others (2009).

26. Ohio started a statewide program in 2005, but a voucher program has been operating in Cleveland since 1995.

27. Utah continues to manage a voucher program for disabled students, which was first enacted in 2004. Florida still has a voucher program for special education students and also has a tuition tax credit program, started in 2003.

28. Levin and Belfield (2003).

and found no differences in test scores.[29] However, Greene, Peterson, and Du found increases in reading and math test scores when they compared outcomes for voucher recipients who had stayed in voucher schools for multiple years with outcomes for a comparison group of students who had wanted to use the voucher but could not because of a lack of space.[30] In an attempt to resolve the conflicting findings from those studies, Rouse used statistical controls and took advantage of the randomization that occurred in a number of the voucher schools, finding slight positive significant effects in math test scores but none in reading.[31]

A team of researchers led by John Witte examined the effect of the voucher program after it was expanded to include more students.[32] Their research matched a random sample of voucher students to a sample of nonvoucher district students and used value-added models to compare the performance of the two. After one year of examining achievement growth, they found that students' achievement in math and reading were similar for the two groups. The authors noted that it may take time for the vouchers to attain full achievement effects and that more definitive conclusions can be drawn as they continue to collect data.

The second-oldest voucher program was established in Cleveland in 1995 through the Cleveland Scholarship and Tutoring Program. Cleveland's program also is a means-tested program, and currently more than 6,000 students use the vouchers. The primary evaluation of the program was carried out by Metcalf and others, who compared the academic achievement of voucher users to that of two other groups of students: students who were offered vouchers but did not use them and students who were not offered vouchers. For the second group, the researchers controlled for observable characteristics.[33] Because they controlled only for observable characteristics, some have argued that their analysis does not adequately control for student self-selection.[34] To address that issue, Clive Belfield compared the performance of voucher students with that of students who applied but were rejected because they did not meet the requirements, including for family income.[35] Belfield acknowledges the limitations of that comparison group but suggests that it is better than the alternatives. Overall, he finds that the voucher program had little effect on academic achievement.

Recently, a collection of researchers led by Patrick Wolf evaluated a federally funded voucher program that provides scholarships of up to $7,500 for low-income residents of the District of Columbia to send their children to participating

29. Witte (2000).
30. Greene, Peterson, and Du (1997); Greene, Peterson, and Du (1998).
31. Rouse (1998).
32. Witte (2000).
33. Metcalf and others (2003).
34. Gill and others (2001).
35. Belfield (2006).

local private schools. Because the scholarships were awarded by lottery, the researchers were able to use a random design approach in evaluating the program, which created an unbiased treatment-control group comparison, but they statistically adjusted for students who declined to use their scholarships. The researchers found that students who participated in the voucher program experienced improved test scores in reading but not in math.[36]

Privately Funded Voucher Programs. Over the last decade or so, a number of philanthropists and foundations have established privately funded voucher programs in an array of cities across the United States. Of those programs, the Children's Scholarship Fund, funded by the Walton Family Foundation, has received the most attention, from both the media and researchers. In many cases, the scholarships are in short supply, leading to long wait lists. The scholarships therefore have been distributed through lotteries, making the randomized design approach to evaluation feasible. Such studies have been carried out in Charlotte, Dayton, New York, and Washington, D.C., among other locations.

Scholarship recipients and applicants in the city programs completed questionnaires and took the Iowa Test of Basic Skills at baseline and at annual follow-up sessions. Although Greene found a positive overall effect in Charlotte, the studies have generally shown no effect for the overall student population.[37] However, some studies have shown some positive effects for black students.[38] The results are not without controversy, however. Krueger and Zhu found no statistically significant effect for any population when they reanalyzed the data using an alternative definition of black students and included students with missing baseline test scores.[39] In the end, the implications of the results suggest, at best, that the vouchers have had a positive effect on a limited population.

Finally, while most research has focused on student achievement, a major question in the debate on school choice is what effect if any the programs have on nonacademic outcomes, including safety and civic participation. One of the few examples of research focusing on such outcomes is a study by Bettinger and Slonim.[40] Using surveys and new methods from experimental economics, the authors attempted to measure the effects of a privately funded voucher program

36. Wolf and others (2009). While the researchers also looked for parental satisfaction, it is often difficult to disentangle the possibility of parents justifying their decision to use the voucher from their actual satisfaction.

37. Greene (2000).

38. Peterson and Howell (2002); Mayer and others (2002). Greene (2000) did not break out the effects by race.

39. While the original analysis used the student's mother's identified race for the student's race, Krueger and Zhu (2002) identify as black students those students whose mother or father is identified as black.

40. Bettinger and Slonim (2006).

in Toledo on nontraditional outcomes such as students' and parents' level of altruism. They found that voucher recipients were more likely to make charitable donations than nonvoucher students.

DIRECT EFFECTS OF CHARTER SCHOOLS. In the past decade, a number of researchers have examined how charter enrollment affects student achievement. A key component of that research has been access to large databases that allow researchers to track student progress from year to year and from school to school. The studies have generally used either fixed-effects or lottery approaches to estimate charter effects.

Hanushek, Kain, and Rivkin examined charter school performance in Texas by tracking student test scores over time.[41] They found that students who transferred to charter schools had smaller test score gains than they would have had if they had remained in traditional public schools. Those negative effects were largely attributable to charters that were newly established, however. If the charters had been in operation for three or more years, then achievement gains of charter and traditional public schools were comparable.[42] The study also found considerable variability in charter and traditional public school performance across the state.

Buddin and Zimmer examined student achievement in six California districts by using a fixed-effects approach to compare performance of elementary (grades 2–5) and secondary (grades 6–11) students in charter and traditional public schools.[43] The results showed that charter students kept pace with traditional school students but did not have larger achievement gains in either reading or math. In a separate study examining not only charter schools but other district-managed choice programs in San Diego, Betts and others, who also used a fixed-effects approach, found that charter schools were performing on par with traditional public schools.[44] However, the results differed by age, grades served, and type of charter schools. Elementary start-up charter schools typically underperformed in their first few years of operation but appeared to catch up with traditional schools after the third year. Conversion charters (schools converting from traditional public school to charter school format) had lower performance in elementary math and middle school reading than traditional public schools did, but conversions outperformed the traditional schools in middle school math.

41. Hanushek, Kain, and Rivkin (2002).
42. Booker and others (2007) found similar results in Texas.
43. Buddin and Zimmer (2003).
44. Betts and others (2006).

Bifulco and Ladd looked at the performance of North Carolina students in grades 3 through 8[45] using a fixed-effects approach. They found that students had *smaller* test score gains while attending charter schools than they had in the traditional public schools that they attended previously. They also found that new charter schools did worse than established charters, but their results indicated that charter effects remained negative and significant even for charters in operation for five years.

Also using a fixed approach, Sass focused on student achievement outcomes for Florida students in grades 3 through 10.[46] He found that students switching into new charter schools had smaller gains than they had in their previous traditional public schools and that charter students kept pace with traditional students in charters that had been in operation for at least five years. Charters that targeted special education or at-risk students had smaller student gains than charter schools that did not. Finally, he found that for-profit and nonprofit charters had comparable effects on student achievement.

Hoxby and Rockoff used charter school admission lotteries to examine how charter enrollment affected student achievement in three Chicago charter schools serving predominantly low-income black and Hispanic students.[47] Two of the schools served kindergarten through eighth grade, and the third served kindergarten through twelfth grade. Lotteries were held by grade in each school if applications exceeded vacancies. Most vacancies occurred in kindergarten classes; grade-level vacancies opened up when students left the charter school. The authors found different effects of charters for grades K through 3 than for higher grades. In the lower grades, lottery winners who attended charters had significantly higher test scores than did other students who applied to the charter, lost the admission lottery, and attended a traditional public school. Winners of the lottery in kindergarten and first grade scored about 8 percentile points higher in reading but no higher in math than did losers of the lottery. Winners in second and third grade averaged about 10 percentile points higher in math but no higher in reading than losers did. In contrast, the researchers found no significant effects of charter enrollment beyond grade 3.

In a similar lottery-based study, Hoxby and Murarka found large effects of charter enrollment on the achievement of charter students in grades 3 through 8.[48] Lottery winners who enrolled in charter schools had higher test scores in math than lottery losers who attended traditional public schools. The reading effect, though smaller, was positive and significant. The authors were unable to isolate

45. Bifulco and Ladd (2006).
46. Sass (2006).
47. Hoxby and Rockoff (2005).
48. Hoxby and Murarka (2007).

the specific charter school characteristics that were associated with the large gains, but they noted that many charters had longer school days and years than did traditional public schools.

Hanushek and others, using fixed-effects methods, estimated a wide range of statistical models and found that the average charter school and the average traditional public school were about the same with respect to improving test scores for Texas students in grades 4 through 8.[49] An interesting result in their study was that charter school parents were more sensitive to school quality (as measured by test score gains) than traditional school parents—that is, charter school parents were more likely to transfer their child if the school was not performing well.

Imberman examined how charter schools affected student attendance and discipline as well as achievement in a large urban district.[50] Using fixed-effects methods, he found that although charters had little effect on test scores, charter students did have better attendance and discipline and that those behaviors persisted even for students who left charters and returned to traditional public schools.

A recent study examined charter success in several states and urban areas. Zimmer and others used fixed-effects methods to assess student achievement gains in Chicago, San Diego, Philadelphia, Denver, and the states of Texas and Ohio.[51] The authors relied primarily on estimates from charter middle and high schools in which test scores from previous schools were available for nearly all students. Across locations, the researchers found that student achievement gains in charter schools generally kept pace with those of traditional public schools. However, middle school charter students in Chicago had smaller reading achievement gains than traditional public school students, and Texas test scores were lower in both reading and math for charter school students than for their counterparts in traditional public schools. The study also found that student performance across charter schools varied more than across traditional public schools, especially in Ohio.[52]

Zimmer and others also examined whether charter high school enrollment leads to higher educational attainment in the form of higher graduation and college attendance rates in Chicago and Florida.[53] Using a matching strategy as well as an instrumental variable approach, the authors found that students attending

49. Hanushek and others (2007).

50. Imberman (2009).

51. Zimmer and others (2009).

52. Zimmer and others (2009). This study, along with studies by Zimmer and Buddin (2006) and Bifulco and Ladd (2007), found that charter schools were not improving the achievement of minority students.

53. Booker and others (2008); Zimmer and Buddin (2006); Bifulco and Ladd (2007).

a charter school in the two locations were 7 to 15 percent more likely to graduate and attend college.[54]

Another recent study by Abdulkadiroglu and others examined the success of
Boston charter schools and autonomous district schools called pilot schools, which
we describe in greater detail in our discussion of district-managed schools.[55]
Because they were concerned about the lack of controls for baseline ability of elementary school students, the authors focused on middle and high school students,
using both covariate adjustment (for example, regression controls for observable
student baseline characteristics) and lottery methods. The lottery approach was
used for the subset of schools that were oversubscribed. The researchers found
large positive effects of middle and high school charter schools on student achievement with both methods.

In addition to estimating the effects of attending charter schools on test scores,
Abdulkadiroglu and others also estimated the impact on other schooling outcomes, such as time spent on homework in English and math, grade retention,
switching schools, and graduation probability. They found few statistically significant or large differences in those factors between charter and traditional public
schools. Using lottery-based design, they found that charter high school students
were more likely to report doing more than three hours of math and English
homework a week than were comparable students in traditional public high
schools. In contrast, they found no significant differences in time spent on homework in the larger sample of charter schools using the fixed-effects method.

Taken as a whole, the results regarding the direct effects of charter schools varied across locations and methods. The fixed-effects models found charter effects
that ranged from small positive effects to substantial negative effects, with many
studies finding no significant difference in test score performance between charter and traditional public schools. The lottery evidence on test scores for charters
was more positive, as was the evidence for educational attainment (that is, graduating from high school and attending college) in Chicago and Florida. In Boston,
Chicago, and New York City, lottery winners in charters did much better than
lottery losers who attended traditional public schools. The Boston and Chicago
results were incongruent, however. Whereas the Boston study found that charters
had strong positive effects for middle and high school students, the Chicago
study found positive effects only for kindergarten through third grade and no significant effects for higher grades. These lottery results provided strong evidence
of the efficacy of the oversubscribed charters, but they said nothing about the
broader class of charter schools that were not oversubscribed.

54. Zimmer and others (2009)
55. Abdulkadiroglu and others (2009).

DIRECT EFFECTS OF GOVERNMENT-MANAGED CHOICE SCHOOLS. Government-managed school choice programs include intradistrict programs (including magnet, open enrollment, and school choice options for students in schools identified for improvement under NCLB) and interdistrict choice programs. Among these programs, magnet programs have been the most heavily researched, but research is now emerging for open enrollment and NCLB school choice options as well. Very little research has examined interdistrict choice programs; in fact, to our knowledge, the only study that has is a study of interdistrict magnet schools in Connecticut.[56]

Some early studies of intradistrict choice programs, including magnet programs, found some promising results for student achievement.[57] However, more recent research using higher-quality data, a broader scope of schools, or better controls for selection bias has found less promising results.

Among the intradistrict choice studies most often cited are those by Cullen, Jacob, and Levitt that examined open enrollment programs in Chicago. The first of the published studies used distance from a student's residence to schools other than the assigned school as an instrument for attending a choice school.[58] They found that students had no more probability of graduating from high school than they had if they had remained at their initial high school. They did find that shifts to magnet schools known as career academies were associated with higher graduation rates, however.

A second study compared the performance of students attending magnet high schools to which they were assigned by lottery with that of students attending traditional public high schools.[59] They found that magnet school students did not have higher test scores or better results on other measures—such as graduation and attendance rates, type of courses taken, and accumulated credits—despite the fact that lottery winners attended magnet high schools with lower poverty levels and better overall test scores and gains and graduation rates than the schools that lottery losers attended. However, the authors did find that students attending magnet high schools had a lower number of self-reported disciplinary incidents and arrests.

In a third study, Cullen and Jacob examined the impact of open enrollment at the elementary level.[60] They also tracked students who had won and lost lotteries, but this time they studied students who applied to oversubscribed Chicago elementary schools in kindergarten and first grade. Tracking students

56. Bifulco, Cobb, and Bell (2008).
57. Gamoran (1996); Crain, Heeber, and Si (1992).
58. Cullen, Jacob, and Levitt (2005).
59. Cullen, Jacob, and Levitt (2006).
60. Cullen and Jacob (2007).

for up to five years, the authors found no evidence that opting out of default schools had a positive effect on educational outcomes. In all three studies, the authors noted that more than half of the district's students opted out of their assigned schools and that that had broad implications within the district. Nevertheless, because the studies focused on only one particular district, their generalizability is limited.

Ballou, Goldring, and Liu estimated the effect of magnet schools in a midsized district in Tennessee.[61] They relied on lottery assignment to compare the achievement of winners and losers, paying careful attention to the fact that not all winners actually went on to attend magnet schools and that several students were lost from the sample due to attrition. They found positive effects for magnets, particularly for math achievement, but those effects were not robust to the inclusion of different variables. They concluded that lottery assignment alone could not be relied on for unbiased estimates of the effects of magnets in the presence of assignment and attrition imbalances.

Recently, Zimmer and others examined whether the performance of students who took advantage of the NCLB school choice option in six large urban districts across the nation improved after they attended their new school.[62] To estimate the effect, the authors used two approaches. First they used a student fixed-effect approach. Second, to increase the validity of that approach, they took advantage of the fact that not all students became eligible for the school choice option at the same time. Because students became eligible only when their school was identified for improvement, the authors compared the performance of students who were "early choosers" with that of students defined as "eventual choosers." In other words, the authors compared the test score gains of early choosers (those who transferred earlier than eventual choosers primarily because their school was identified for the option earlier) in years in which they transferred to a new school with the gains of eventual choosers (those who had not yet transferred) in the same years. Both the treatment and control group were inclined to use the school choice option and therefore should have been similar in both observable and unobservable ways. The authors found that transferring did not improve student achievement under either approach.

A recent paper by Özek examined an open enrollment policy in Pinellas County, Florida.[63] To control for nonrandomness in students' choice to opt out of their assigned school, the author used proximity to public alternatives as an instrument for exiting an assigned public school. The author found that students opted for schools designated as higher-quality schools on a number of

61. Ballou, Goldring, and Liu (2006).
62. Zimmer and others (2007).
63. Özek (2009).

dimensions, including test scores, but that students did not experience significant benefits and often performed significantly worse.

A series of papers investigated the impact of a districtwide school choice program introduced by the Charlotte–Mecklenburg school district in North Carolina in 2002. All parents in the district were asked to name their top three school choices, and admission to oversubscribed schools was determined by lottery. Hastings, Kane, and Staiger found positive effects of enrolling in a school of choice on the number of hours spent doing homework but negative effects on retention.[64] Like Cullen and Jacob, they found no effect of open enrollment on academic achievement for the average student.[65] However, they divided students into subgroups on the basis of a preference for academics inferred by their parents' school selections. While they found no effect for the average student, these results were masked by offsetting underlying effects. Students of parents with stronger preferences for academics experienced significant gains in test scores as a result of attending a chosen school. The authors concluded that parents who wanted improved academic outcomes were able to get them and that the absence of an average treatment effect on achievement did not imply that choice was ineffective.

Hastings and Weinstein also investigated the impact of choice in Charlotte–Mecklenberg in a study highlighting the role of information on both the selection of schools and student achievement.[66] In July 2004, taking advantage of a natural experiment provided by the NCLB-mandated distribution of school-level test score information to parents of students in low-performing schools, they observed the school choices made by parents both before and after receiving the information. They found that after parents received information on school performance, they revised their choices and chose higher-performing schools for their children. In addition, they found positive effects on student achievement as a result of the revised choices.

Taken together, the two studies indicated that attending a higher-performing school of choice had a positive effect on test scores of students whose parents were either better informed or were actively seeking academics.

As noted previously, in 1995 the Boston public schools and the Boston Teachers' Union created their own version of an "autonomous school model" to compete with the growing number of charter schools. The new schools, termed pilot schools, were public schools that were allowed to determine their own budgets, staffing, curricula, and scheduling, thereby gaining many of the freedoms granted to charter schools. In addition, like the Massachusetts charters, they were mostly start-up schools; the difference lay in the fact that they remained under district

64. Hastings, Kane, and Staiger (2006).
65. Cullen and Jacob (2007).
66. Hastings and Weinstein (2007).

control. The 2009 study by Abdulkadiroglu and others compared student achievement in pilots with that of students in traditional public schools, first in an "observational" study using statistical controls for student characteristics and second in a study using a lottery-based approach restricted to the sample of applicants to oversubscribed schools.[67] The lottery results showed a positive effect of pilot schools on achievement in elementary math but no significant differences in any other analyses. The observational results, however, showed slightly negative effects for pilot middle schools and positive effects for pilot high schools. They also estimated the impact of pilots on other schooling outcomes, such as hours spent on homework in English and math, grade retention, switching schools, and graduation probability, and found only that students in pilot high schools were less likely to switch schools than students in conventional public schools.

Also, in their previously described 2006 study, Betts and others used lottery data to examine the effectiveness of district-managed school choice programs and found that the programs had little effect on test scores.[68] However, the researchers did find a positive math effect for students participating in the district's high school magnet program.

Finally, while the above analyses examined intradistrict choice programs, Bifulco, Cobb, and Bell recently examined an interdistrict magnet program established in Connecticut to increase integration of students across district boundaries.[69] The researchers also used two approaches to estimate the effectiveness of the program. For two magnet middle schools that had sufficient waiting lists, they compared lottery-based results to results obtained through nonexperimental approaches, including matching design. They found that results were similar for both approaches, which gave them greater confidence in estimating effects using the nonexperimental approach for twelve interdistrict magnet high schools and six additional interdistrict magnet middle schools. While the comparison of nonexperimental and experimental results in the two middle schools provided some confidence in the results for the rest of the magnet schools, it was assumed that the possible selection bias across all schools was similar. That might be a big assumption for the interdistrict magnet schools. Nevertheless, the authors found substantial positive effects from attending an interdistrict magnet school.

SUMMARY OF DIRECT EFFECTS. Table 3-1 summarizes the results for three domestic school choice programs, including voucher, charter, and district-managed school choice programs. Across the three programs, the evidence has

67. Abdulkadiroglu and others (2009).
68. Betts and others (2006).
69. Bifulco, Cobb, and Bell (2008).

been inconclusive, with no clear consensus that any of them are having strong effects on test scores. Interestingly, there seems to be more of a consensus that the programs may affect nonacademic outcomes. Nevertheless, there is not strong evidence that the effects of nondistrict and district-managed choice programs differ much with respect to direct effects on student outcomes.

Indirect Effects

The indirect effects that schools of choice have on outcomes for students in traditional public schools have received substantially less attention than the direct effects on outcomes for students attending schools of choice. However, a major tenet of the school choice movement is that schools of choice should be able to create pressure on traditional public schools by competing for student enrollment—if schools of choice succeed in attracting students from traditional public schools, traditional public schools may face pressure to improve the quality of the education that they offer. It should be noted, however, that it may be difficult for schools of choice to exert more pressure on traditional public schools than the latter already are feeling from the demand for increased accountability.

Schools of choice also could exert indirect effects through greater innovation, which is part of the motivation for school choice policies. To date, however, very little research has explored whether charter schools are in fact innovating, so there is very little evidence on whether innovation is spreading from charter schools to traditional public schools.

Examining the issue of competitive effects is a challenging task. Education is provided through multiple levels, including teachers within classrooms who are managed by a principal who is given resources and instructional and curriculum guidelines by a district. While actors on any single level may feel competitive pressure, that pressure may not ultimately affect the performance of students if the other levels are not equally motivated to improve. Alternatively, only that particular levels feel competitive pressure may matter. For instance, teachers' perception of a competitive threat may be the only thing that matters because teachers are on the front lines in providing education. Or it could be that the key to improving schoolwide performance is to motivate the principal. On the other hand, it might not matter whether either principals or teachers feel competitive pressure if many of the curriculum, instructional, and staffing decisions are made at the district level. In addition, each of the actors at the different levels may perceive competitive threats differently and their ability to react to those threats may be different.

Furthermore, it is not clear when competitive pressure is felt. For instance, in the context of charter schools, does competitive pressure arise when a single charter school appears on the landscape or only after charter schools constitute a

Table 3-1. *Summary of Direct Effects on Student Outcomes*

Authors	Location	Outcome variable	Research approach	Results
Voucher programs				
Witte (2000)	Milwaukee	Test scores	Observational design with controls	No substantial effect.
Greene and others (1997; 1998)	Milwaukee	Test scores	Quasi-experimental design	Significant effects in both reading and math.
Rouse (1998)	Milwaukee	Test scores	Quasi-experimental design with co-variate controls	Significant effects in math only; effects grew over time.
Metcalf and others (2003)	Cleveland	Test scores	Observational design with covariate controls	No effect.
Belfield (2006)	Cleveland	Test scores	Quasi-experimental design with co-variate controls	Little effect from the voucher program.
Greene (2000)	Charlotte	Test scores	Lottery assignment of vouchers with baseline controls	Positive effects.
Mayer and others (2002); Howell and Peterson (2002)	Charlotte (Children's Scholarship Fund)	Test scores	Lottery assignment of vouchers with baseline controls	Positive effects for black students only.
Kruger and Zhu (2004)	New York City (Children's Scholarship Fund)	Test scores	Lottery assignment of vouchers	No effect for any set of students, including black students.

Bettinger and Slonim (2006)	Toledo (Children's Scholarship Fund)	Test scores as well as non-academic outcomes	Lottery assignment of vouchers	Little effect of the voucher program on student test scores; increased altruism among voucher recipients.
Wolf and colleagues (2009)	Washington, D.C. (federally funded voucher program)	Test scores, school safety, parental satisfaction	Lottery assignment of vouchers	Positive effect on reading but not math test scores. Parents of participating students reported that their child's school was safer, and they had higher overall satisfaction.
Charter schools				
Hanushek and others (2002)	Texas (statewide)	Test scores	Fixed effect	New charter schools had negative effects; older charter schools had similar effects.
Buddin and Zimmer (2003)	California (six districts)	Test scores	Fixed effect	Similar scores for charter and traditional public schools.
Betts and others (2009)	San Diego	Test scores	Fixed effect	Results differed by type of school, age, and grades served, but overall, charter schools were performing on par with traditional public schools.
Bifulco and Ladd (2006)	North Carolina (statewide)	Test scores	Fixed effect	Negative effects.

(continued)

Table 3-1. *Summary of Direct Effects on Student Outcomes (Continued)*

Authors	Location	Outcome variable	Research approach	Results
Sass (2006)	Florida (statewide)	Test scores	Fixed effect	New charter schools had negative effects; older charter schools had similar effects.
Hoxby and Rockoff (2004)	Chicago	Test scores	Lottery assignment of oversubscribed charter schools	Positive effect for grades K-3 but no significant effect for higher grades.
Hoxby and Marurka (2007)	New York City	Test scores	Lottery assignment of oversubscribed charter school	Positive effect.
Hanushek and others (2007)	Texas (statewide)	Test scores	Fixed effect	Similar results.
Imberman (2009)	Anonymous district	Test scores along with non-academic outcomes	Fixed effect	No effect on test scores; positive effect on behavioral outcomes.
Zimmer and others (2009)	Texas (statewide), Ohio (statewide), Florida (statewide), Chicago, Denver, Milwaukee, Philadelphia, and San Diego	Test scores; graduation rates; college attendance rates	Fixed effect for test score analysis matching strategy; instrumental variable approach for graduation and college attendance analyses	Similar test score effects except in Chicago and Texas, where effects were negative for middle schools; positive graduation and college attendance effects for high schools in Chicago and Florida.
Abdulkadiroglu and others (2009)	Boston	Test scores	Lottery assignment of oversubscribed schools and observational study	Positive effects for test scores and amount of time spent on homework.

District-managed school choice programs

Cullen, Jacob, and Levitt (2005)	Chicago (magnet high schools)	Graduation rates	Instrumental variable approach	Similar rates except for career academies, which had high graduation rates.
Cullen, Jacob, and Levitt (2006)	Chicago (magnet high schools)	Test scores along with non-academic outcomes	Lottery assignment of oversubscribed schools	Similar test scores but improved behavioral outcomes.
Cullen and Jacob (2007)	Chicago (magnet elementary schools)	Test scores along with non-academic outcomes	Lottery assignment of oversubscribed schools	No effect.
Ballou, Goldring, and Liu (2006)	Anonymous district (magnet schools)	Test scores	Lottery assignment of oversubscribed schools	Positive effects, but they were not robust to model specification.
Zimmer and others (2007)	Nine large urban districts (NCLB school choice option)	Test scores	Fixed effects and matching strategy	No effect.
Özek (2009)	Pinellas County, Florida (open enrollment program)	Test scores	Instrumental variable approach	Negative effect.
Hastings, Kane, and Staiger (2006)	Charlotte-Mecklenburg (open enrollment program)	Test scores along with non-academic outcomes	Lottery assignment of oversubscribed schools	Positive effect on time spent on homework but no effect on test scores. However, students with stronger preference for academics did experience a positive gain when attending a chosen school.

(continued)

Table 3-1. *Summary of Direct Effects on Student Outcomes (Continued)*

Authors	Location	Outcome variable	Research approach	Results
Hastings and Wein-stein (2007)	Charlotte-Mecklenburg (open enrollment program)	Test scores	Natural experiment	Positive effects for students with better information about school quality.
Abdulkadiroglu and colleagues (2009)	Boston (pilot schools)	Test scores along with non-academic outcomes	Lottery assignment of oversubscribed schools and observational study	Positive effects for elementary math but no other positive effects.
Betts and colleagues (2009)	San Diego (district-managed choice programs)	Test scores	Lottery assignment of oversubscribed schools	Generally no effect except a positive math effect for high school magnet schools.
Bifulco, Cobb, and Bell (2008)	Connecticut (intradis-trict magnet program)	Test scores	Lottery assignment of oversubscribed schools and value-added models	Positive effects.

Source: Authors' compilation.

certain percentage of the market? In addition, although students transferring to charter schools reduce district budgets for traditional public schools, they also reduce enrollment. If the students who transfer have above-average educational expenses (not offset by categorical grants), then financially the district is relatively better off without them. That, however, also assumes that districts have the flexibility to reduce costs easily, which may be a strong assumption. If transfers have below-average costs, then lost funds from transfers would lead traditional public schools to disproportionately reduce programs. Also, competition may occur in a variety of dimensions, depending on the reasons why families prefer schools of choice. Pressure to improve test scores may be weak if parents are choosing charters for school environment or extracurricular activities. In addition, schools of choice may create little pressure if test score performance in those schools is not better than that of traditional public schools. Finally, it is not clear that magnet and open enrollment programs are designed to have competitive effects. However, interdistrict choice programs, along with sorting by families across schools and district boundaries, may have competitive effects at both the district and school levels.

To examine competitive effects, researchers ideally would use data that allow them to track student performance over time. By examining the same students in the same schools over time, an analysis can control for the possibility that the introduction of schools of choice may change the population of students in traditional public schools as schools of choice recruit students away from them. In contrast, if researchers examine competitive effects by examining school-level data, they do not know whether a change in performance of the traditional public schools is due to a changing population or a competitive threat. Data on the performance of individual students over time can also help control for both observable and unobservable differences of students and schools by using a combination of student and school fixed effects known as "spell effects," which compare the performance of the same students in the same school over time. However, many researchers have not had access to those types of data and have used school-level data instead.[70]

We examine next the evidence of competitive effects by examining the evidence produced by voucher programs and charter schools. Unfortunately, to our knowledge, no research has examined the competitive effects of district-managed choice programs; we therefore do not present any literature on this topic. However, as stated earlier, there may be theoretical reasons to believe that district-managed choice programs may exert less competitive pressure.

70. These researchers have, however, generally used quasi-experimental designs such as regression discontinuity and difference-in-differences approaches.

INDIRECT EFFECTS OF VOUCHER PROGRAMS. What we know about the indirect effects of voucher programs in the United States has come entirely from the programs in Milwaukee, Florida, and Washington, D.C. Of those, the Florida voucher program has been studied the most extensively. Florida's Opportunity Scholarship Program was established in the 1999–2000 school year and was launched as part of the state's accountability program, in which schools were graded "A" through "F." Students attending a school that received an "F" two years in a row were eligible for vouchers. But because very few schools have received an "F" for two consecutive years, very few students have been eligible for vouchers.

Nevertheless, using both school- and student-level data, researchers have examined whether implementation of Florida's voucher programs has created positive effects for traditional public schools.[71] They generally have found positive effects from the program, but it is not entirely clear whether the effects were from competition or whether schools were inspired to improve because of the threat of receiving low grades and other sanctions associated with the accountability program.[72] In fact, accountability pressures have made it more difficult to examine competitive pressures from schools of choice in general.

Researchers have also examined the voucher programs in Milwaukee and Washington, D.C. Separate studies by Chakrabarti and by Hoxby examining Milwaukee's voucher program using school-level data and a difference-in-differences approach found similar positive effects.[73] Greene and Winters, who examined the first-year indirect effects of the Washington, D.C., voucher program using school-level data with school-level test scores as the dependent variable and a lagged test score as the independent variable, found no effects.[74] However, because those analyses used school-level data, there is some concern that they did not fully account for the possibility of changing populations. Overall, while the results are promising, questions remain with regard to whether the Florida results stem from the threat of a voucher or from the accountability regime more generally.

INDIRECT EFFECTS OF CHARTER SCHOOLS. A few recent studies have used school-level data to examine whether competition from charter schools im-

---

71. Greene (2001); Figlio and Rouse (2004); West and Peterson (2006); Chakrabarti (2008).

72. For instance, while Figlio and Rouse found a positive effect for their measure of competition, they found a similar positive effect on the state accountability test when the state established "a low-performing school list" in 1996 and 1997, suggesting that any positive effect from the Florida program may be more attributable to the stigma effect of the accountability program than to a competitive effect from vouchers (Figlio and Rouse 2004).

73. Chakrabarti (2008); Hoxby (2003b, pp. 11–67).

74. Greene and Winters (2006).

proved test scores at traditional public schools. Hoxby examined whether the share of charter students in a district affects test scores in traditional schools and found that charter competition had a positive effect on district-managed schools in Michigan.[75] In another Michigan study, Bettinger used distance to the nearest charter school as an instrumental variable to estimate school-level competitive effects.[76] He found no evidence that competition from a nearby charter improved test scores in traditional public schools.

Several more recent studies have looked at charter competition using student-level data. Bifulco and Ladd used distance to a nearby charter school to measure effects of charter competition in North Carolina and found no evidence that charters were improving traditional schools.[77] Sass examined whether test scores in traditional public schools in Florida were affected by nearby charters.[78] Using the presence, number, and share of charter schools as measures of competition, he found a small positive relationship between competition from charters and test scores in the corresponding traditional public schools. A study by Booker and others that used similar approaches found positive competitive effects on traditional public schools in Texas.[79]

Using both principal surveys and student-level test score data, Buddin and Zimmer examined competitive effects in California.[80] The survey results showed that traditional school principals felt little pressure from charters to improve performance or modify school practices. The student achievement analysis used an array of alternative measures for school competition, including distance to charter, share of charters, and number of nearby charters. The research showed no evidence that charter competition was improving the test score performance of students in nearby traditional public schools.

Zimmer and colleagues examined charter competition across jurisdictions in seven different states.[81] Because states have different policies toward charter schools and the quality of both charter and traditional public schools might vary, charter effects might vary considerably from place to place. The study used distance to the nearest charter and the share of charter students within 2.5 miles of a traditional school as measures of competition. In separate analyses of schools in Chicago, Denver, Milwaukee, Philadelphia, San Diego, Ohio, and Texas, they found positive effects only in Texas.

---

75. Hoxby (2003b).
76. Bettinger (2005).
77. Bifulco and Ladd (2006).
78. Sass (2006).
79. Booker and others (2008).
80. Buddin and Zimmer (2009).
81. Zimmer and others (2009).

The current body of evidence on the competitive effects of charter schools therefore is mixed. However, because charter schools generally do not represent a large share of enrollment in districts, we may not expect them to exert much of a competitive effect yet.

SUMMARY OF INDIRECT EFFECTS. Table 3-2 summarizes the fairly limited research that has examined the competitive effects of vouchers and charter schools. Researchers generally have noted that competitive effects are challenging to estimate. While there is more consistent evidence of a competitive effect for vouchers than for charters, questions remain regarding whether the positive effects from the Florida studies are due to a voucher effect or an accountability effect.

Distribution of Students by Race, Ethnicity, and Ability

Because students choose to enroll in schools of choice, it is important to examine whether these schools serve all types of students or just a select few. Critics of school choice programs such as charter schools and vouchers argue that their success might be illusory if the schools of choice are simply recruiting the best students from traditional public schools; they also suggest that the schools may further stratify an already ethnically or racially stratified system.[82] In general, the critics fear not only that schools of choice may have negative consequences for the students who attend them but also that if the schools skim off high-achieving students, they may have negative social and academic effects for students who remain in traditional public schools.[83] However, proponents of choice programs argue that schools of choice will improve racial integration by letting families choose schools outside of neighborhoods that are racially segregated.[84]

When researchers have examined distributional effects, they often have compared the racial–ethnic makeup or socioeconomic status of participating students to that of statewide, districtwide, or nonparticipating students. That approach is less than ideal, because those groups of students and schools may not be strong counterfactuals for students using vouchers or attending charter schools. The best research examining distributional effects has used data that allow researchers to track students over time to compare the characteristics of the schools that the students left to the characteristics of the schools that they entered. Although we

---

82. Cobb and Glass (1999); Wells (1993).

83. The interaction of students having diverse backgrounds and ability levels can have positive social and academic effects for students. See, for example, Frankenberg and Lee (2003); Zimmer (2003); Zimmer and Toma (2000); Summers and Wolfe (1977).

84. Finn, Manno, and Vanourek (2000).

highlight both sets of studies, we emphasize the results from studies using data that track students over time. However, it should be noted that what is missing from the literature—and what we therefore cannot review—is the broader effect that schools of choice are having on the distribution of students across districts and states. But because in most cases schools of choice represent a small portion of students in districts and states, it is unlikely that choice programs are having broad distributional effects yet.

Distributional Effects of Vouchers

Again, much of the research on the effect of voucher programs on the distribution of students has come from the handful of publicly and privately funded voucher programs. For instance, research on the early years of the Milwaukee voucher program showed that the program generally attracted poorly performing students from low-income families having a racial makeup similar to that of the district as a whole.[85] A survey of voucher parents during the 1998–99 school year also showed that percentages were similar to those of the district population as a whole.[86] However, the surveys also showed that the voucher parents had a slightly higher educational level than other parents in Milwaukee and that compared with mothers of eligible nonapplicants, applicant mothers were more likely to be employed and to have a higher educational level.[87]

Researchers have found mixed results in Cleveland also. Metcalf found that vouchers there were used primarily by minority students and students from low-income families; that the mean income level of students using the vouchers was $18,750; and that those students were more likely to be black than were students in a random sample of Cleveland students.[88] However, parents of voucher applicants had slightly higher levels of education.[89] In a more recent study, Belfield examined students entering the program in second and fourth grade and found that prior test scores of voucher applicants were generally similar to those of a public school comparison group.[90] However, when compared with students who were offered a voucher but did not use it, voucher students had higher average test scores and were less likely to be black or eligible for the free and reduced-price lunch program.

---

85. The average family income of students participating in the program in the early 1990s was $11,600. The test scores of those students were below the district average and below the scores of a sample of low-income students within the district (Witte 2000).

86. Wisconsin Legislative Audit Bureau (2000). Sixty-two percent of voucher students were black and 13 percent were Hispanic.

87. Rouse (1998); Witte (1996); Witte and Thorn (1996).

88. Metcalf (1999).

89. Metcalf (1999); Peterson, Howell, and Greene (1999).

90. Belfield (2006).

Table 3-2. Summary of Indirect Effects on Student Outcomes

Authors	Location	Outcome variable	Research approach	Results
Voucher programs				
Greene (2001)	Florida	School-level test scores	Regression analysis with school-level data	Positive effects but not entirely clear whether they were from the competitive or the accountability threat.
Figlio and Rouse (2004)	Florida	Student-level test scores	Value-added model	Positive effect on state accountability test. Smaller positive effects on low-stakes test but unclear whether they were from the competitive or the accountability threat.
West and Peterson (2006)	Florida	Student-level test scores	Regression discontinuity design	Positive effects on state accountability test but no statistically significant effect on low-stakes test.
Chakrabarti (2008)	Florida and Milwaukee	School-level test scores	Difference-in-differences approach and regression discontinuity design	Positive effects.
Hoxby (2003a; 2003b)	Milwaukee	School-level test scores	Difference-in-differences approach	Positive effects.
Greene and Winters (2006)	Washington, D.C.	Student-level test scores	Regression design with lagged test scores	No effect.

Charter schools

Hoxby (2003a)	Michigan	School-level test scores	Instrumental-variable approach with school-level data	Positive effect.
Bettinger (2005)	Michigan	School-level test scores	Instrumental-variable approach with school-level data	No effect.
Bifulco and Ladd (2006)	North Carolina	Student-level test scores	Student and school fixed effects	No effect.
Sass (2006)	Texas	Student-level test scores	Student and school fixed effects	Small positive effect.
Booker and others (2007)	Texas	Student-level test scores	Student and school fixed effects	Positive effect.
Zimmer and others (2009)	Texas (statewide), Ohio (statewide), Chicago, Denver, Milwaukee, Philadelphia, San Diego	Student-level test scores	Student and school fixed effects	No effect except in Texas, where the effect was positive.
Buddin and Zimmer (2009)	California	Student-level test scores and school-level survey data	Descriptive examination of survey data; student-level test score data	No effect.

District-managed school choice programs (no study has specifically examined such programs)

Source: Authors' compilation.

In examining the impact of the voucher program in Washington, D.C., Howell and Peterson found that among students who were offered a voucher, the mothers of those who used the vouchers had higher education levels while a study by Wolf and others found that such students were more likely to be black than students not offered a voucher but less likely to be Hispanic.[91] They also examined the prior test scores of students using the vouchers and found that they had higher prior math and reading test scores than nonusers.

Florida's tax credit program, which is similar in effect to a voucher program, began providing scholarships to students in 2003 and has provided scholarships to as many as 20,000 students a year.[92] Figlio and others used data on individual students over time to track them as they moved from public schools to private schools. The authors found that on average, transfer students were relatively low-performing students who previously had attended lower-performing schools than had nonparticipants. The researchers also found that participants were more likely to be black and less likely to be Hispanic or white than nonpartici-pants. Students also tended to transfer to schools that had a higher proportion of white students than the public schools that they left.

As with the student achievement summary, we can turn for further insights to research that has examined privately funded voucher programs. These pro-grams have generally targeted impoverished students, so it is not surprising to find that participants had relatively low incomes. Peterson, for example, found that the average income of families of students participating in the New York scholarship program was only $10,000.[93] However, Howell found that New York voucher participants were more likely than voucher-eligible low-income students to have mothers who had at least some college education.[94]

In addition, research suggests that the programs served a low percentage of special education students. In New York, for example, only 9 percent of par-ticipating students had disabilities although the districtwide average enroll-ment of special education students was 14 percent.[95] In Charlotte, only 4 per-cent of participating students had disabilities while the district-wide average enrollment was 11 percent.[96] The situation differed somewhat in Washington, where 11 percent of students were disabled and the districtwide average was 11 percent.[97]

91. Peterson and Howell (2002); Wolf and others (2005).
92. Figlio and others (2009).
93. Peterson (1998).
94. Howell (2004).
95. Meyers and others (2000).
96. Greene (2000).
97. Wolf, Howell, and Peterson (2000).

Distributional Effects of Charter Schools

Weiher and Tedin used survey data from charter school parents to examine factors associated with charter school choice.[98] They found that parents reported similar values on school attributes irrespective of race, ethnicity, and socioeconomic status (SES). In practice, however, parents' choices often were at odds with their avowed preferences. While 60 percent of parents ranked high school test scores as a primary factor in choosing a school, the majority of those parents picked a charter school with lower average test scores than the traditional school that their student left. Similarly, few parents mentioned race or ethnicity as a factor in choosing a school, but parents tended to pick schools with a higher concentration of students in their racial-ethnic group than existed at their previous school.

Booker and others used student data to track students transferring from traditional to charter schools in California and Texas.[99] In both states, black charter students transferred to schools that had a higher concentration of black students than the school that they had attended previously. In Texas, white students also moved to schools with a higher concentration of whites than existed at their traditional public school, but in California the opposite was true. Hispanic charter students had fewer Hispanic peers than at their traditional public school in both states. In terms of measured ability, transfer students had lower test scores than the average student at their traditional public school. In both states, charters attracted a relatively higher share of students with low test scores than the traditional public schools that the students exited.

In North Carolina, Bifulco and Ladd found that charters increased the racial isolation of black and white students.[100] On average, black charter students left schools that were 53 percent black for charters that were 72 percent black; similarly, white charter students shifted from traditional schools that were 72 percent white to charters that were 82 percent white. Both black and white charter students had more peers with college-educated parents than there were at their previous traditional public school, but the percentage increase in college-educated parents was about 6 times larger for whites than for blacks. On net, black students transferred to charters whose test scores were lower than scores at their previous school, while white students transferred to charters with higher scores.

Zimmer and others examined how charters affected peer competition in five urban districts and two states.[101] They found modest effects of charters on the

98. Weiher and Tedin (2002).
99. Booker, Zimmer, and Buddin (2005).
100. Bifulco and Ladd (2006).
101. Zimmer and others (2009).

racial-ethnic mix of schools. In some locations, black and white students tended to attend charters with a higher concentration of students of their own race than at their previous traditional public school, but those differences generally were small. The study also looked at the ability distribution of students transferring to charter schools. In most cases, the charter students were near or slightly below the test score average for the traditional public school that they had previously attended.

Distributional Effects of District-Managed Choice Programs

Given that increasing racial-ethnic integration was the original intention of magnet programs and may be a benefit of inter- and intradistrict programs, it is important to examine the effects that the programs have had on the racial-ethnic distribution of students. What we find is that research has not always concluded that the programs are increasing integration.

In evaluating San Diego's district-managed choice programs, Betts and others noted that unlike previous studies, which typically examined attendance data, their study focused on students applying to the programs for the 2000–01 school year by using a probit analysis, which allowed them to examine a number of student and school characteristics simultaneously.[102] In examining test scores, grade point average (GPA), and parental education level, the researchers found that there was slight evidence that the programs were skimming off high-ability students but that the advantage was relatively small. In addition, the researchers found that non-white students were more likely to participate in the programs than white students. However, students generally transferred to schools that were "more white," had fewer English-language learners, and had higher test scores. From that perspective, such school choice programs may create greater segregation.

In recent studies, Bifulco, Cobb, and Bell and Özek examined the racial makeup of schools in which students chose to enroll through intra- and interdistrict choice programs.[103] In examining an interdistrict magnet program in Connecticut, Bifulco and others found that the magnet schools had a more balanced racial-ethnic mix of students than schools in major urban districts. Özek, examining an open enrollment program in Pinellas County, Florida, found that students opting out of their default schools had lower prior test scores than those who did not opt out and that they were more likely to be black and eligible for free and reduced-price lunches. However, neither of the studies directly compared the mix of students in the schools that the students left with the mix in the schools that they entered.

102. Betts and others (2006).
103. Bilfulco, Cobb, and Bell (2008); Özek (2009).

In a study of the eight-grade cohort of Chicago students in 2000 who advanced to high school in 2001, Lauen found (after adjusting for several other factors) that white students were more likely than black students to attend a selective school of choice through the intradistrict choice program, though there was no difference in their likelihood of attending a nonselective non-neighborhood school.[104] In addition, he found that contextual factors relating to feeder schools and neighborhoods were associated with the likelihood of exercising choice. Poor students were less likely to attend any type of school of choice than wealthier students, and students in affluent neighborhoods were more likely to attend a selective school of choice. Also, the probability that middle school students would enter a selective high school of choice was positively related to the propensity of students from their school to have done so in the past.

Finally, in a study of a large urban district's magnet program, Engberg and others examined data from a lottery for admission to magnet programs and found that students who won admission were much more likely to stay in the district than students who lost.[105] In addition, more affluent families were much more likely to leave the district if they lost a lottery than lower-income families were. That suggests that magnet programs may help districts retain students from families that can create a stronger tax base.

Summary of Distributional Effects

Across the types of school choice options, the evidence on distributional effects has been somewhat mixed. In addition, researchers have often used descriptive comparisons of demographic characteristics of students attending schools of choice to district means, which mask distributions at the prior schools attended by individual students. Nevertheless, some insights can be drawn.

Research suggests that students who take advantage of vouchers generally are disadvantaged (many voucher programs are means tested) but that they tend to come from families with higher education levels and to be less likely to be special education students than non-voucher students. In many cases, research on charter schools that has used stronger research designs than used previously generally found that charter schools tended to attract more students with below-average prior test scores than did the schools that students left. However, in some locations, black and white students were more likely to transfer to charter schools with higher concentrations of students of their own race than existed in the schools that they exited, but generally the differences were small.

Finally, the research on district-managed programs is mixed. An evaluation in San Diego found that students were more likely to take advantage of the district's

104. Lauen (2007).
105. Engberg and others (2009).

choice programs if they were non-white and if they showed higher ability (on some measures); they also tended to transfer to schools that were "more white" and that had higher test scores and fewer English language learners. A descriptive study in Connecticut found that magnet schools achieved a better racial mix than traditional schools in urban districts. Students transferring as a result of an open enrollment program in Florida were lower-achieving students and were more likely to be black and eligible for free and reduced-price lunches. However, a study that examined Chicago high schools found that whites were more likely to attend selective high schools and that poorer students were less likely than wealthier students to attend any type of school of choice.

Conclusion

Recent school choice reform has been motivated by the belief that the dual mechanisms of student selection of schools and school autonomy leads to an overall improvement in learning. Since school selection forms the core of reform, any direct school effects that we might expect to find should, in theory, result from both the quality of the school and the quality of the student-school match. Since vouchers, charters, and district-managed schools have different levels of autonomy, we might expect to find that effects vary along that dimension.

However, selection creates a conundrum for research that attempts to find effects. Many argue that students who attend schools of choice are more motivated or have more involved parents than students who do not and that therefore observed learning increases might result more from omitted characteristics related to motivation than from the quality of the schools themselves.

As described in this chapter, researchers have used a variety of analytical designs, each of which has certain advantages and disadvantages, to try to compensate for the selectivity issue in determining effects on achievement. The results of their research across the various types of school choice programs are somewhat mixed and often difficult to reconcile. In some cases, differences may be due to variations in the methodological strategies used to compensate for selection issues; in others, differences may be due to variations in context or policies.

In addition, research has focused primarily on test scores and is only beginning to focus on other important outcomes, such as graduation and college enrollment rates. It is difficult to draw strong conclusions regarding the broader effects of school choice programs when the research has focused narrowly on a small set of outcomes. Even if we were able to come to a consensus about the effects of the various types of school choice programs, we would not be able to determine what was driving those effects because researchers are not examining how the schools operate to see whether variations in operations and practice lead to different outcomes. If we want to learn from the school choice movement, which is designed to create schools with greater autonomy and innovation, researchers need to expand their analysis to understand what factors lead to positive and negative results.

In terms of indirect effects (competitive effects), estimating the impact of various choice programs is again challenging because the programs can alter the makeup and peer dynamics of the schools that students exit, which, in some cases, have been subject to accountability standards.[106] To our knowledge, there has been no research that has specifically examined the competitive effects of district-managed choice programs. The research on voucher programs, which is scant, has found some evidence of competitive effects, but in the case of the Florida studies, it is difficult to tease the competitive effect of vouchers from the effect of the accountability threat. The slim set of studies examining the competitive effects of charter schools has found mixed evidence of competitive effects.

Whether researchers are able to detect competitive effects may depend not only on the methodology used but also on how the programs were designed. So, for instance, intradistrict choice programs may have limited competitive effects because districts may design the programs to minimize competition among schools. In addition, charter schools and voucher programs in many locations may not have a sizable enough share of students to create a competitive effect.

Finally, there is mixed evidence regarding the distributional effects of various choice options. There has been some evidence that voucher programs have disproportionately attracted students from more educated families, but most voucher programs are means tested and therefore have attracted low-income families. Regarding charter schools, although evidence does suggest that in some locations, black and white students transferred to charter schools with slightly higher shares of students of their own race, there is little evidence that these schools are skimming off students of higher achievement levels. For district-managed choice programs, again, the results are somewhat mixed: some studies show that magnet schools are more racially or ethnically integrated while other studies suggest that white students are more likely to attend these schools.

What these studies have failed to examine is whether choice programs have distributional effects beyond the effects on students taking advantage of the programs. In other words, are choice programs creating new peer environments not only for participating students but also for nonparticipating students? Although choice programs are generally small in scale and are unlikely to have had effects on the overall distribution of students across schools in most locations, such

---

106. It is becoming increasingly difficult to tease out competitive effects from accountability effects as NCLB pressure for accountability has become more widespread.

effects may become more widespread as school choice programs continue to expand.

In sum, across the issues that we have considered—student achievement, other types of student outcomes, and the demographic distribution of students across schools—there is not strong evidence that nondistrict and district-managed choice programs lead to differential effects. However, almost no research has examined nondistrict and district-managed choice programs in a single location. The closest any studies have come to doing so is the study by Abdulkadiroglu and others in which they examined both charter schools and district-managed pilot schools in Boston and the study by Betts and others in which they examined various district-managed school choice programs and charter schools in San Diego.[107] However, even those studies compared the charter schools and the district-managed choice schools only with traditional public schools, not with each other.

The patterns that emerge in synthesizing the research findings raise issues regarding the relationship between methods and context. They also highlight issues that warrant further exploration—including what operational features of school choice programs lead to differential effects and whether the programs are leading to widespread distributional effects. In addition, further research is needed to examine the various forms of choice programs in the same location using a variety of methods. For instance, researchers could examine vouchers, charter schools, and district-managed programs in Cleveland, Milwaukee, and Washington, D.C., or possibly statewide programs in Ohio and Florida. Each of those locations has all three types of program, and one could examine which of the programs leads to stronger outcomes within the same environment. We hope that funders of school choice studies will push researchers to broaden the scope of their studies. Until then, it will be difficult to clarify whether one form of choice leads to better outcomes than another.

References

Abdulkadiroglu, Atila, and others. 2009. "Informing the Debate: Comparing Boston's Charter, Pilot and Traditional Schools." Boston: Boston Foundation.

Angrist, Joshua D., Guido W. Imbens, and Donald B. Rubin. 1996. "Identification of Causal Effects Using Instrumental Variables." *Journal of the American Statistical Association* 91, no. 213: 222–455.

Ballou, Dale, Teasley Bettie, and Tim Zeidner. 2007. "Charter Schools in Idaho." In *Charter School Outcomes*, edited by Mark Berends, Matthew G. Springer, and Herbert J. Walberg, pp. 221–241. New York: Lawrence Erlbaum Associates.

107. Abdulkadiroglu and others (2009); Betts and others (2006).

Ballou, Dale, Ellen Goldring, and Keke Liu. 2006. "Magnet Schools and Student Achievement." Working Paper 123. New York: National Center for the Study of Privatization in Education (www.ncspe.org/publications_files/OP123.pdf).

Barrow, Lisa, and Cecilia Elena Rouse. 2006. "The Economic Value of Education by Race and Ethnicity." *Economic Perspectives* 2Q: 14–27.

Belfield, Clive R. 2006. "The Evidence on Education Vouchers: An Application to the Cleveland Scholarship and Tutoring Program." New York: National Center for the Study of Privatization in Education (www.ncspe.org/publications_files/OP112.pdf).

Bettinger, Eric P. 2005. "The Effect of Charter Schools on Charter Students and Public Schools." *Economics of Education Review* 24, no. 2: 133–147.

Bettinger, Eric P., and Robert Slonim. 2006. "Using Experimental Economics to Measure the Effects of a Natural Educational Experiment on Altruism." *Journal of Public Economics* 90, no 8–9: 1625–1648.

Betts, Julian R., and others. 2006. *Does School Choice Work? Effects on Student Integration and Achievement.* San Francisco: Public Policy Institute of California.

Bifulco, Robert, Casey Cobb, and Courtney Bell. 2008. "Can Interdistrict Choice Boost Student Achievement? The Case of Connecticut's Interdistrict Magnet School Program." Working Paper 167. New York: National Center for the Study of Privatization in Education.

Bifulco, Robert, and Helen F. Ladd. 2006. "The Impacts of Charter Schools on Student Achievement: Evidence from North Carolina." *Journal of Education Finance and Policy* 1, no. 1: 50–90.

———. 2007. "School Choice, Racial Segregation, and Test-Score Gaps: Evidence from North Carolina's Charter School Program." *Journal of Policy Analysis and Management* 26, no. 1: 31–56.

Booker, Kevin, and others. 2007. "The Impact of Charter School Attendance on Student Performance." *Journal of Public Economics* 91, no. 5–6: 849–876.

———. 2008. "The Effect of Charter Schools on Traditional Public School Students in Texas: Are Children Who Stay Behind Left Behind?" *Journal of Urban Economics* 64, no. 1: 123–45.

Booker, Kevin, Ron Zimmer, and Richard Buddin. 2005. "The Effect of Charter Schools on School Peer Composition." Working Paper WR-306-EDU. Santa Monica, Calif.: RAND Corporation.

Buddin, Richard, and Ron Zimmer. 2003. "Academic Outcomes." In *Charter School Operations and Performance: Evidence from California*, pp. 37–63. Santa Monica, Calif.: RAND Corporation.

———. 2009. "Is Charter School Competition in California Improving the Performance of Traditional Public Schools?" *Public Administrative Review* 65, no. 5: 831–845.

Center for Education Reform. 2009. "All About Charter Schools." Washington (www.edreform.com/index.cfm?fuseAction=document&documentID=1964).

Chakrabarti, Rashid. 2008. "Impact of Voucher Design on Public School Performance: Evidence from Florida and Milwaukee Voucher Programs." Staff Report 315. Federal Reserve Bank of New York.

Chubb, John E., and Terry M. Moe. 1990. *Politics, Markets, and America's Schools.* Brookings.

Cobb, Casey D., and Gene V. Glass. 1999. "Ethnic Segregation in Arizona Charter Schools." *Education Policy Analysis Archives* 7, no. 1: 1–36 (http://epaa.asu.edu/epaa/v7n1/).

Crain, Robert L., Amy L. Heeber, and Yiu-Pong Si. 1992. *The Effectiveness of New York City's Career Magnet Schools: An Evaluation of Ninth-Grade Performance Using an Experimental Design.* Macomb, Ill.: National Center for Research in Vocational Education.

Cullen, Julie Berry, and Brian A. Jacob. 2007. "Is Gaining Access to Selective Elementary Schools Gaining Ground? Evidence from Randomized Lotteries." Working Paper 13443. Cambridge, Mass.: National Bureau of Economic Research.

Cullen, Julie Berry, Brian A. Jacob, and Steven D. Levitt. 2005. "The Impact of School Choice on Student Outcomes: An Analysis of the Chicago Public Schools," *Journal of Public Economics* 89, no. 5–6: 729–60.

———. 2006. "The Effect of School Choice on Participants: Evidence from Randomized Lotteries." *Econometrica* 74, no. 5: 1191–1230.

Education Commission of the States. 2009. *Open Enrollment: 50-State Report*. Denver, Colo. (www.ecs.org/html/educationissues/OpenEnrollment/OEDB_intro.asp).

Engberg, John, and others. 2009. "Identification of Causal Effects in Experiments with Multiple Sources of Noncompliance." Working Paper 14842. Cambridge, Mass.: National Bureau of Economic Research.

Figlio, David N., and Cecilia Elena Rouse. 2004. "Do Accountability and Voucher Threats Improve Low-Performing Schools?" Working Paper. Princeton University (www.ers.princeton.edu/workingpapers/14ers.pdf).

Figlio, David, and others. 2009. "Who Uses a Means-Tested Scholarship, and What Do They Choose?" Presented at meeting of American Education Finance Association, Nashville.

Finn, Chester E., Jr., Bruno V. Manno, and Gregg Vanourek. 2000. *Charter Schools in Action: Renewing Public Education*. Princeton University Press.

Frankenberg, Erica, and Chungmei Lee. 2003. "Charter Schools and Race: A Lost Opportunity for Integrated Education." *Education Policy Analysis Archives* 11, no. 32 (http://epaa.asu.edu/epaa/v11n32/).

Friedman, Milton. 1955. "The Role of Government in Education." In *Economics and the Public Interest*, edited by Robert A. Solo, pp. 123–144. Rutgers University Press.

Gamoran, Adam. 1996. "Student Achievement in Public Magnet, Public Comprehensive, and Private City Schools." *Educational Evaluation and Policy Analysis* 18, no. 1: 1–18.

Gill, Brian P., and others. 2001. *Rhetoric versus Reality: What We Need to Know about Vouchers and Charter Schools*. Santa Monica, Calif.: RAND Corporation.

Greene, Jay P. 2001. "An Evaluation of the Florida A-Plus Accountability and School Choice Program." Paper presented at the annual meeting of the Association of Public Policy and Management.

———. 2000. *The Effect of School Choice: An Evaluation of the Charlotte Children's Scholarship Fund*. New York: Manhattan Institute.

Greene, Jay P., Paul E. Peterson, and Jiangtao Du. 1997. *Effectiveness of School Choice: The Milwaukee Experiment*. Harvard University Program in Education Policy and Governance.

———. 1998. "School Choice in Milwaukee: A Randomized Experiment." In *Learning from School Choice*, edited by Paul E. Peterson and Bryan C. Hassel, pp. 335–356. Brookings.

Greene, Jay P., and Marcus A. Winters. 2006. "An Evaluation of the Effect of D.C.'s Voucher Program on Public School Achievement and Racial Integration after One Year." Working Paper 10. New York: Manhattan Institute.

Hanushek, Eric A., John F. Kain, and Steven G. Rivkin. 2002. "The Impact of Charter Schools on Academic Achievement." Stanford University.

Hanushek, Eric A., and others. 2007. "Charter School Quality and Parental Decision Making." *Journal of Public Economics* 91, no. 5–6: 823–848.

Hastings, Justine S., Thomas J. Kane, and Douglas O. Staiger. 2006. "Preferences and Heterogeneous Treatment of Effects in a Public School Choice Lottery." Working Paper 12145. Cambridge, Mass.: National Bureau of Economic Research.

Hastings, Justine S., and Jeffery M. Weinstein. 2007. "Information, School Choice, and Academic Achievement: Evidence from Two Experiments." Working Paper 13623. Cambridge, Mass.: National Bureau of Economic Research.

Hill, Paul T., Pierce C. Lawrence, and James W. Gutherie. 1997. *Reinventing Public Education: How Contracting Can Transform America's Schools*. University of Chicago Press.

Howell, William G. 2004. "Dynamic Selection Effects in Means-Tested, Urban School Voucher Programs." *Journal of Policy Analysis and Management* 23, no. 2: 225–250.

Hoxby, Caroline. 2003a. "School Choice and School Competition: Evidence from the United States." *Swedish Economic Policy Review* 10, no. 2: 11–65.

———. 2003b. "School Choice and School Productivity: Could School Choice Be a Tide That Lifts All Boats?" In *The Economics of School Choice*, edited by Caroline Hoxby, pp. 287–342. University of Chicago Press.

Hoxby, Caroline M., and Sonali Murarka. 2007. "Methods of Assessing the Achievement of Students in Charter Schools." In *Charter School Outcomes*, edited by Mark Berends, Matthew G. Springer, and Herbert J. Walberg, pp. 7–38. New York: Lawrence Erlbaum Associates.

———. 2009. "Charter Schools in New York City: Who Enrolls and How They Affect Their Students' Achievement." Working Paper No. 14852. Cambridge, Mass.: National Bureau of Economic Research.

Hoxby, Caroline M., and Jonah E. Rockoff. 2005. "The Truth about Charter Schools: Findings from the City of Big Shoulders." *Education Next* (www.wonderlandcharter.com/Findings%201.pdf).

Imberman, Scott. 2009. "Achievement and Behavior in Charter Schools: Drawing a More Complete Picture." Working Paper, University of Houston (www.class.uh.edu/faculty/simberman/imberman_2008_charter_submission_c.pdf).

Kolderie, Ted. 2004. *Creating the Capacity for Change: How and Why Governors and Legislatures Are Opening a New-Schools Sector in Public Education*. Bethesda, Md.: Education Week Press.

Krueger, Alan B., and Pei Zhu. 2002. "Another Look at the New York City School Voucher Experiment." Working Paper 9418. Cambridge, Mass.: National Bureau of Economic Research.

Lauen, Douglas. 2007. "Contextual Explanations of School Choice." *Sociology of Education* 80, no. 3: 179–209.

Levin, Henry M., and Clive R. Belfield. 2003. "The Marketplace in Education." *Review of Research in Education* 27, no. 1: 183–219.

Mayer, Daniel P., and others. 2002. *School Choice in New York City after Three Years: An Evaluation of the School Choice Scholarships Program*. Washington: Mathematica Policy Research.

Metcalf, Kim K. 1999. *Evaluation of the Cleveland Scholarship and Tutoring Grant Program: 1996–1999*. Indiana Center for Evaluation, Indiana University.

Metcalf, Kim K., and others. 2003. *Evaluation of the Cleveland Scholarship and Tutoring Program, Summary Report 1998–2002*. Indiana Center for Evaluation, Indiana University.

Myers, David, and others. 2000. *School Choice in New York City after Two Years: An Evaluation of the School Choice Scholarship Program*. Washington: Mathematica Policy Research.

Moretti, Enrico. 2004. "Human Capital Externalities in Cities." In *Handbook of Regional and Urban Economics*, vol. 4, edited by J. Vernon Henderson and Jacques F. Thisse, pp. 2243–2291. San Diego: Elsevier.

National Center for Education Statistics. 2005. *Condition of Education 2005*. Washington.

National Commission on Excellence in Education. 1983. *A Nation at Risk: The Imperative for Educational Reform*. Washington: U.S. Department of Education.

Özek, Umut. 2009. "The Effects of Open Enrollment on School Choice and Student Outcomes." CALDER Working Paper 26. Washington: Urban Institute.

Peterson, Paul E. 1998. *An Evaluation of the New York City School Choice Program: The First Year*. Harvard University Program on Education Policy and Governance.

Peterson, Paul E., and William G. Howell. 2002. *The Education Gap: Vouchers and Urban Schools*. Brookings.

Peterson, Paul E., William G. Howell, and Jay P. Greene. 1999. *An Evaluation of the Cleveland Voucher Program after Two Years*. Harvard University Program in Education Policy and Governance.

Rouse, Cecilia E. 1998. "Private School Vouchers and Student Achievement: An Evaluation of the Milwaukee Parental Choice Program." *Quarterly Journal of Economics* 113, no. 2: 553–602.

Sass, Tim R. 2006. "Charter Schools and Student Achievement in Florida." *Journal of Educational Finance and Policy* 1, no. 1: 91–122.

Stullich, Stephanie, Elizabeth Eisner, and Joseph McCary. 2006. *National Assessment of Title 1: Implementation*, vol. 1. U.S. Department of Education.

Summers, Anita A., and Barbara Wolfe. 1977. "Do Schools Make a Difference?" *American Economic Review*, 67, no. 4: 639–652.

Swanson, Christopher B. 2009. *Cities in Crisis 2009: Closing the Graduation Gap*. Bethesda, Md.: Editorial Projects in Education.

Weiher, Gregory R., and Kent L. Tedin. 2002. "Does Choice Lead to Racially Distinctive Schools? Charter Schools and Household Preferences." *Journal of Policy Analysis and Management* 21, no. 1: 79–92.

Wells, Amy S. 1993. *Time to Choose: America at the Crossroads of School Choice Policy*. Putnam University Press.

West, Martin R., and Paul E. Peterson. 2006. "The Efficacy of Choice Threats within School Accountability Systems: Results from Legislatively Induced Experiments." *Economic Journal* 116, no. 510: C46–C62.

Wisconsin Legislative Audit Bureau. 2000. *An Evaluation: Milwaukee Parental Choice Program*. Madison, Wis.

Witte, John F. 1996. "Who Benefits from the Milwaukee Choice Program?" In *Who Chooses, Who Loses? Culture, Institutions, and the Unequal Effects of School Choice*, edited by Bruce Fuller, Richard F. Elmore, and Gary Orfield, pp. 118–137. New York: Teachers College Press.

———. 2000. *The Market Approach to Education: An Analysis of America's First Voucher Program*. Princeton University Press.

Witte, John F., and Christopher A. Thorn. 1996. "Who Chooses? Voucher and Interdistrict Choice Programs in Milwaukee." *American Journal of Education* 104, no. 3: 187–217.

Wolf, Patrick, and others. 2005. *Evaluation of the DC Opportunity Scholarship Program: First Year Report on Participation*. U.S. Department of Education.

————. 2009. "Evaluation of the DC Opportunity Scholarship Program: Impacts after Three Years." Working Paper NCEE 2009-4050. U.S. Department of Education.

Wolf, Patrick J., William G. Howell, and Paul E. Peterson. 2000. *School Choice in Washington D.C.: An Evaluation after One Year.* Harvard University Program in Education Policy and Governance.

Zimmer, Ron. 2003. "A New Twist in the Educational Tracking Debate." *Economics of Education Review* 22, no. 3: 307–315.

Zimmer, Ron, and Richard Buddin. 2006. "Charter School Performance in Two Large Urban Districts." *Journal of Urban Economics* 60, no. 2: 307–326.

Zimmer, Ron, and Eugenia F. Toma. 2000. "Peer Effects in Private and Public Schools across Countries." *Journal of Policy Analysis and Management* 9 no. 1, pp 75–92.

Zimmer, Ron, and others. 2007. "State and Local Implementation of the No Child Left Behind Act: Title 1 Parental School Choice, Supplemental Educational Services, and Student Achievement." U.S. Department of Education.

————. 2009. *Charter Schools in Eight States: Effects of Achievement, Attainment, Integration, and Competition.* Santa Monica, Calif.: RAND Corporation.

4

Commuter Taxes in U.S. Metropolitan Areas

ROBERT W. WASSMER

Cities and even counties in the United States levy "commuter taxes" on employment, income, wages, or payroll generated within their jurisdiction by nonresidents. The locality imposing such a tax is usually a central city or central county within a metropolitan area. The intended payers are the suburban city or county residents who work in the central metropolitan location but do not live there. An appropriate justification for a commuter tax is that nonresidents working in a jurisdiction consume locally provided public services during their commute and workday; thus it is fair to ask them to pay for them. Commuter taxes may also appeal to central city residents and the politicians representing them because they offer a method by which a municipality's tax burden can be exported to those not living (and thus not voting for politicians) in the jurisdiction. A nonresident local income tax is also attractive to those seeking to reduce after-tax income inequality in a locality because the revenue it provides helps fund local services that benefit the disproportionate percentage of poor people living in central metropolitan locations. The economic arguments against commuter taxes include the claims that nonresident workers pay for local services or generate offsetting benefits to a locality in other ways and that the tax drives business away from central locations. Political arguments often used to rebuff the taxation of commuters include the claim that it represents "taxation without representation" and that local policymakers are likely to overuse the tax if allowed to do so. New York City's experience with commuter taxation over the last four decades illustrates that the debate over the use of this tax and its effects is far from settled.

I thank David Brunori, Arlee Reno, Richard Shearer, and Howard Wial for valuable comments that have improved this chapter and Eileen Hughes for superb copy editing.

As allowed by the New York State Legislature, New York City attempted but failed to institute a municipal income tax in both 1934 and 1952.[1] Encouraged by a wave of local income tax adoptions throughout the 1950s and 1960s in Kentucky, Michigan, Ohio, and Pennsylvania, New York City finally adopted such a tax in 1966, taxing income earned within its boundaries by both residents and nonresidents. Residents paid an amount based on graduated rates that topped out at 2 percent. Nonresidents paid a flat 0.4 percent on income earned in the city with graduated exclusions based on income level.[2] New York City's commuter tax remained in place for thirty-three years, with the flat rate levied on commuters eventually rising to 0.45 percent (0.65 percent for the self-employed). In 1999, over the protest of Mayor Giuliani, New York's legislature rescinded the commuter portion of the city's local income tax and Governor Pataki signed the new policy into law.[3] The sponsor of this legislation, a Republican state senator from Long Island, pointed to New York City's budget surplus at the time and defended elimination of the commuter tax as an appropriate way to lighten the tax burden on suburban commuters. Support came from upstate and suburban legislators of both parties, while Republican and Democratic representatives from New York City voted against it. When the tax was repealed, nearly 800,000 commuters paid the tax (of whom 58 percent lived in New York State), which amounted on average to $337.50 on an annual income of $75,000. The estimated loss in revenue to New York City from the elimination of the tax was approximately $360 million in 2000.

Following the devastation of 9/11, New York City faced a projected budget deficit of $4.4 billion in fiscal year 2003–04.[4] Mayor Bloomberg, with the support of some on the city council, floated a proposal to lower the highest local income tax rate from 3.65 to 2.75 percent but to apply it to both residents and commuters. He believed that such a change would raise an additional $1 billion in annual revenue. At the same time, former mayor Giuliani supported reinstatement of the old commuter tax. Both pointed to how New York City's public safety workers showed no discrimination on September 11, 2001; they responded to the needs of residents and nonresidents alike. In addition, commuter tax supporters argued that "New York City is the economic engine of the entire metropolitan region, and it seems reasonable for the beneficiaries of the engine to pay for some of the fuel."[5]

1. Sigafoos (1955).
2. Deran (1968).
3. Clifford A Levy, "Legislature Acts Quickly to Repeal Commuter Tax," *New York Times*, May 18, 1999, p. A1.
4. Gessing (2003).
5. Glenn Pasanen, "Bringing Back the Commuter Tax," *Gotham Gazzette.Com*, August 12, 2002 (www.gothamgazette.com/commentary/134.pasanen.shtml).

A chorus of others responded that the 1999 repeal of the commuter tax was not the reason for New York City's fiscal woes; other local tax cuts had followed the commuter tax reduction. Instead, they said, city expenditures had risen because of strong unions and "overgenerous" social programs.[6] Fast forward to late 2009: there is still no commuter tax, but there is a projected deficit of $2.3 billion for New York City in the upcoming fiscal year and more than double that in the following fiscal year.[7] Mayor Bloomberg proposed a 7 percent increase in local property taxes but pointed out that a simple reinstatement of the 0.45 percent rate on commuters would generate around $500 to $700 million a year and lower the need for such a steep property tax increase. The difficulty in reinstating New York City's commuter tax is that it requires majority support from a statewide legislative coalition and the governor.

Two other cities whose experiences with a commuter tax have gained national attention are Washington, D.C., and Philadelphia. Some D.C. policymakers have wanted a commuter tax since achieving limited home rule in the early 1970s.[8] Though nonresidents earn two-thirds of the income generated within the district's boundaries, permission to tax it must come from Congress. Some say Congress is reluctant to grant permission because of pressure exerted by its members from Virginia and Maryland, whose commuters directly benefit from the lack of a tax. Philadelphia's wage (earned-income) tax rate of 3.5 percent, levied on commuters in 2009, is the highest in the country.[9] Gessing has called the ongoing exodus of business from Philadelphia the nation's leading example of the harm that a commuter tax wreaks on a central city.[10]

The intent of this chapter is to propose and answer the questions that should be asked as a means of intelligently influencing public debate on the use of commuter taxes in the United States. The chapter continues with a further description of the history and current use of commuter taxes in the United States—and by necessity, the local employment, income, and payroll taxes from which they stem. The description includes both an account of their prevalence over time, specific nuances regarding current variations in their use, a summary of revenues currently generated by local taxes of this type, and revenue projections for their increased use. The chapter then reviews the theoretical arguments on whether suburban commuters pay their fair share for local government services consumed where they work but do not live and the statistical tests done to try to

6. McMahon and Siegel (2005, p. 97).

7. Benjamin Sarlin, "Budget Woes Beget Talk of Commuter Tax," *New York Sun*, September 26, 2008 (www.nysun.com/new-york/budget-woes-beget-talk-of-commuter-tax/86696).

8. O'Cleireacain and Rivlin (2002).

9. Gessing (2003).

10. Gessing (2003).

answer that question. The discussion continues with a summary of the economic theory and previous statistical work done to document the influence that local income and commuter taxes have exerted on local economic activity within metropolitan areas. Politics, which ultimately determines the institution and continuation of a commuter tax, also is explored, and possible alternatives are offered involving the efficient transfer of suburban resources to a central city. The chapter concludes with a list of pros and cons regarding commuter taxation for the policymaker and my own recommendations for its future in the United States.

History, Current Use, and Revenue from Commuter and Related Taxes

Since commuter taxes are an extension of local income taxation, understanding the history, use, and revenue raised from commuter taxes is not possible without examining local income taxation.

History

The first city in the United States to adopt a local income tax was Charleston, South Carolina, in the early 1800s.[11] Residents, but not commuters, paid a local tax on all forms of personal income. Citizen complaints regarding the increasingly unfair administration of the tax resulted in its elimination after only a few years. It was not until Philadelphia adopted a local wage tax in 1938, during the Great Depression, that a local tax of this type was able to remain in place up to the present in the United States.[12] Facing drastically reduced local property tax revenue at a time of increasing need for local social services (in an obvious parallel to the situation of large U.S. cities in 2010), Philadelphia exercised the option granted to it by Pennsylvania to tax local resident and nonresident income earned within its boundaries. The Ohio cities of Toledo and Columbus followed with their own local income taxes in 1946 and 1947. Two more cities in Ohio, seven in Pennsylvania, plus St. Louis, Missouri, and Lexington, Kentucky, chose the local income tax in 1948.[13] A continuing wave of adoptions occurred in the 1950s and 60s, which the Advisory Council on Intergovernmental Relations (ACIR) attributed not only to fiscal stringency but also to rising property tax burdens and a desire to extract revenue from nonresident workers.[14] By the late 1960s, twenty-two major central cities were levying a local income tax, and

11. Sigafoos (1955).
12. Deran (1968).
13. Smith (1972).
14. ACIR (1970).

another 150 smaller cities with populations greater than 10,000 were relying on them.[15] Of all U.S. cities levying a local income tax in the late 1960s, 85 percent were in Ohio and Pennsylvania.[16]

The ACIR noted that around 3,500 local jurisdictions in the United States taxed their residents' income in some form by 1970 "and [that] the vast majority of such taxes . . . [were] extended, where permitted by statute to nonresidents."[17] With the exception of Baltimore, all cities in the late 1960s with a population of more than 25,000 that imposed the local income tax also taxed nonresident income earned within their borders.[18] With the notable exception of New York City and cities in Michigan, most localities in the late 1960s with a local income tax applied the same rate to residents and nonresidents. The 1967 adoption of a local income tax in San Francisco, ruled unconstitutional by the California Supreme Court because it applied to nonresident income, demonstrated that the taxation of nonresident income in the late 1960s was not without controversy.[19]

Following the frenzied adoption of local income taxes by U.S. cities during the 1960s, far fewer adoptions followed in the 1970s and 1980s. In 1991, 636 cities, 126 counties, and 111 school districts in 12 states levied a local income tax—excluding the state of Pennsylvania, where 2,824 local governments used such a tax.[20] However, those figures amount to essentially the same number of localities that had a local income tax a decade earlier.

In addition, commuters can be taxed through a levy on the payroll or number of employees of a business operating in a jurisdiction. For the purposes of this chapter, I consider that a commuter tax because nonresidents are likely included in the local payroll or among the employees that make up a portion of the tax base. In the discussion that follows, I always distinguish between a payroll or employment tax and an income tax.

Current Use

Table 4-1 presents information available as of early 2009 on the allowed and actual use of income (wage) or occupational taxes at the county or city level within a state. The base of a local income tax is individual income, a locally defined variation of it, or taxable earnings for state or federal tax purposes. Only Pennsylvania restricts its localities to the taxing of wages (earned income) alone and not income from all sources. The base of a local occupational tax is business

---

15. Smith (1972).
16. Deran (1968).
17. ACIR (1970, p. 1).
18. Deran (1968).
19. Smith (1972, p. 173).
20. ACIR (1993).

payroll or employment. Table 4-1 divides those taxes into income (wage) and occupational categories and then by whether they are widely used, possible but not widely used, and possible but not used. Excluded states have not given their localities the ability to use these taxes. Differences between the rates levied on residents and nonresidents are included in the last two columns of the table.

As indicated in table 4-1 for 2009, twenty-six states and the District of Columbia allow some form of county or local taxation of payroll, employment, wages, or income (or some combination), whose ultimate burden can fall on the nonresident workers in a locality. However, in six of the states (Arkansas, Connecticut, Georgia, Kansas, Virginia, and Vermont) no city or county has yet exercised its right to put such a tax in place. The city of Fairbanks, Alaska, has approved a local occupation tax allowed by its state legislature, but implementation has been blocked by a local voter referendum. In nineteen states and the District of Columbia, some form of commuter taxation existed in 2009.

The income (wage) or occupational tax rate applied to residents is the same as that applied to nonresidents in Alabama, California, Colorado, Delaware, Illinois, Iowa, Kentucky, Maryland, New Jersey, Ohio, Oregon, Virginia, Washington, and West Virginia. In the District of Columbia, Indiana, Michigan, New York, and Pennsylvania, commuters pay a lower rate than residents do. In Indiana's counties, the commuter tax rate is about one-fourth that of a resident; in Michigan's municipalities, it is half. Commuters to New York City currently pay no local income tax with the exception of those who work in the special New York City Harbor Zone. In Pennsylvania, the city of Philadelphia gives only a slight break on its local earned-income (wage) tax rate to commuters, while other cities in the state tax commuters at less than half of the resident rate.

Revenue

Observing the limited presence of local income taxes in the United States, Brunori offers the opinion that the local "revenue raising potential of taxing personal income never materialized."[21] In fiscal year 2005–06, only about 3 percent of all own-sources revenue collected by all local governments in the United States came from local income taxation.[22] However, that aggregate value hides the concentrated use of local income taxation in some places. The highest reliance on local income taxes for own-source revenue at the state or district level occurs in Maryland (22.5 percent), the District of Columbia (18.2 percent), Kentucky (15.4 percent), and Ohio (12.9 percent). With the exception of D.C., local governments levying an income tax in those states tax commuters at the same rate as residents.

21. Brunori (2007, p. 83).
22. Tax Policy Center (2009).

Table 4-1. *2009 U.S. Local Income (Wage) and Occupational Taxes by Degree of Use and States Allowing Them*

Category	2009 Allowed local adoption	2009 Actual local use	2009 Actual residential rate	2009 Actual nonresidential rate
Income (wage) tax widely used				
Indiana	County income tax	Adjusted gross income tax (CAGIT): used by 56 out of 92 counties	0.5, 0.75, or 1.0 percent of state taxable income	0.25 percent
		Option income tax (COIT), only if no CAGIT: used by 28 out of 92 counties	Begins at 0.2 and increases 0.1 each year until 0.6 percent, then rises to maximum of 1.0 percent of state taxable income	Always one-fourth of the residential rate
		Economic development income tax (CEDIT), must supplement CAGIT or COIT: used by 70 out of 92 counties	0.1, 0.2, 0.25, 0.3, 0.35, 0.4, 0.45, or 0.5 percent of state taxable income	Not subject to tax if paying CAGIT, COIT, or CEDIT
Maryland	County income tax	All counties in state	Range of 1.25 percent (Worcester County) to 3.20 percent of federal taxable income (Howard, Montgomery, and Prince George's counties); Baltimore County at 3.05 percent	Applies to a commuter if commuter works in a Maryland county and lives outside the state
Michigan	City income tax	Detroit City	2.5 percent of compensation (excluding pensions, worker's comp, and job-related reimbursements)	1.25 percent of compensation (excluding pensions, worker's comp, and job-related reimbursements)

		21 cities in state	Maximum of 2.0 percent of compensation (Highland Park) to minimum of 1.0 percent of compensation (18 cities)	Maximum of 1.0 percent of compensation (Highland Park) to minimum of 0.5 percent of compensation (18 cities)
Ohio	City income tax	Used extensively (by nearly 600 cities in state)	0.5 to 2.75 percent of earnings (Columbus and Cleveland at 2.0 percent)	Same if city is primary place of employment
	School district income tax	Used extensively (by 170 school districts in state)	0.5 to 2.0 percent of earnings	Does not apply
Pennsylvania	City wage tax	Philadelphia City	3.93 percent of earnings	3.5 percent of earnings
		Pittsburgh City	3.0 percent of earnings	1.0 percent of earnings
		Scranton City	2.4 percent of earnings	1.0 percent of earnings
		Nearly all cities in the state	1.0 to 2.0 percent of earnings	0.0 to 1.1 percent of earnings
	School district wage tax	Nearly all school districts in state	0.5 to 1.1 percent of earnings	Does not apply
Income (wage) tax possible but not widely used				
Delaware	County income tax	None		
	City income tax	Wilmington City	1.25 percent of payroll	Same
District of Columbia	District income tax	Washington, D.C.	4 percent of first $40K, 6 percent of next $30K, and 8.5 percent on remaining federal taxable income	Same only if operating a taxable unincorporated business in the district

(*continued*)

Table 4-1. *2009 U.S. Local Income (Wage) and Occupational Taxes by Degree of Use and States Allowing Them (Continued)*

Category	2009 Allowed local adoption	2009 Actual local use	2009 Actual residential rate	2009 Actual nonresidential rate
Iowa	County income tax	Emergency medical services surtax only in Appanoose County	1.0 percent of federal taxable income	Same
	School district income tax	Used by 297 of 362 school districts in the state only for instructional support, educational improvement, and/or physical plant	Rates between 1 and 5 percent (58 districts), 6 and 10 percent (166 districts), and more than 10 percent (73 districts) of state taxable income	Same
Missouri	County income tax	None		
	City income tax	Kansas City	1.0 percent of earnings	Same
		St. Louis City	1.0 percent of earnings	Same
New York	County income tax			
	City income tax	New York City	2.907 percent to 3.648 percent of state taxable income	Does not apply
		New York City Harbor Zone	1.98 percent of payroll	Same
		Yonkers City	10 percent of state taxable income	0.5 percent of state tax income
Income (wage) tax possible but not used				
Arkansas	County income tax	None		
	City income tax	None		

Connecticut	County income tax	None		
	City income tax	None		
Georgia	County income tax	None		
	City income tax	None		
Virginia	County income tax	State legislation allows Arlington, Fairfax, Loudon, and Prince William counties to use (but not used)	0.25 to 1.0 percent of state taxable income allowed (but not used)	Same
	City income tax	State legislation allows cities of Alexandria, Fairfax, Falls Church, Manassas, Manassas Park, Norfolk, and Virginia Beach to use (but not used)	0.25 to 1.0 percent of state taxable income allowed (but not used)	Same
Occupational tax widely used				
Alabama	County occupational tax	Jefferson County (contains Birmingham City)	0.5 percent of payroll	Same
	City occupational tax	21 cities (including Birmingham City)	0.5 to 2.0 percent of payroll	Same
Kentucky	County occupational tax	Jefferson County (coextensive with Louisville City)	1.45 percent of payroll	Same
		Used extensively	Maximum of 1.25 percent of payroll	Same

(continued)

Table 4-1. 2009 U.S. Local Income (Wage) and Occupational Taxes by Degree of Use and States Allowing Them (Continued)

Category	2009 Allowed local adoption	2009 Actual local use	2009 Actual residential rate	2009 Actual nonresidential rate
	City occupational tax	Used extensively	Maximum of 1.25 percent of payroll	Same
Pennsylvania	City occupational tax	Local services tax used extensively by localities in state	$10 to $52 per employee, per year	Same
		Pittsburgh City nonresidential sports facility use	Does not apply	3.0 percent of income earned in facility
Occupational tax possible but not widely used				
California	County occupational tax	San Francisco City (coextensive with SF County)	1.5 percent of payroll	Same
	City occupational tax	San Francisco City (coextensive with SF County)	1.5 percent of payroll	Same
Colorado	County occupational tax	None		
	City occupational tax	Cities of Aurora, Denver, Glendale, Sheridan, and Greenwood Village	$4, $5.75, $5, $3, and $4 per employee, per month, respectively	Same
Illinois	County occupational tax	None		
	City occupational tax	Chicago City	$4 per employee, per month	Same
New Jersey	City occupational tax	Newark City	1.0 percent of payroll	Same
	City occupational tax	New York City Harbor Zone	1.98 percent of payroll	Same

Oregon	Transit occupational tax	Various city- and county-based transit districts including Washington, Clackamas, and Multnomah counties (Portland region)	0.6218 percent of payroll	Same
Washington	City occupational tax	Seattle City	$0.01302 per employee hour	Same
West Virginia	City occupational tax	Charleston City	$1 per employee, per week	Same
		Huntington City	$2 per employee, per week	Same
Occupational tax possible but not used				
Alaska	County occupational tax	None		
	City occupational tax	Fairbanks City approved, voter referendum blocked	$20 per employee, per month	Same
Kansas	County occupational tax	None		
	City occupational tax	None		
Vermont	County occupational tax	None		
	City occupational tax	None		

Source: Information gathered in spring 2009 from Thomson Reuters, which compiles it for a subscription-based Internet service described on the company's website (http://ria.thomsonreuters.com/About).

Furthermore, Brunori notes that personal income taxes in 2003 yielded nearly a quarter of all own-source revenue raised in U.S. cities with populations greater than 300,000.[23] Amazingly, that occurred with only thirteen of the fifty-seven cities using the local income tax. As reported in Von Ins (2001), municipal income tax revenue as a percentage of general revenue was 16 percent in Baltimore, 40 percent in St. Louis, 42 percent in Philadelphia, and 64 percent in Columbus, Ohio.[24] According to data from the U.S. Census Bureau, in fiscal year 2005–06, the city of Baltimore gained about $220.5 million from local income taxes, while Kansas City (Missouri) gained about $160.2 million and Cleveland gained about $290.5 million.[25] When divided by 2006 population in each place, those figures work out to approximately $350 dollars per person in Baltimore, $360 in Kansas City, and $650 in Cleveland. Philadelphia, whose local income tax rate on both residents and commuters is the highest in the country, raised $1,125.7 million in income taxes in 2006, or about $780 per resident. Even though most U.S. cities do not employ the local income tax, it is a key component of the public finance portfolio of the minority that do.

IssuesPA reports that in 2000 about 37 percent of the city of Philadelphia's local income tax revenue came from nonresidents.[26] Approximately two-thirds of the commuters into Philadelphia lived in Pennsylvania suburbs and the remaining one-third live in in New Jersey. O'Cleireacain and Rivlin estimate that if Washington, D.C., had taxed nonresident commuters in 2000 at the same local income tax rate as residents, the district would have gained $1.4 billion in addition to its existing $3.3 billion in local revenue;[27] about two-thirds of that revenue would have come from Maryland residents and one-third from Virginia residents. Restoration of New York City's commuter tax at the same rates as in 1999 would have raised about $715 million a year in 2008 in a city that spent about 78 times that amount in the same year.[28] The city of Baltimore estimated that it would have generated nearly $76 million dollars in additional revenue in 2009 if it had instituted a 1 percent tax on the wages of those who work but do not live there.[29] Such a revenue increase would have represented about 6 percent of Baltimore City's general fund spending in 2006. It would have allowed for a $0.24 reduction in the city's 2006 annual property tax rate of $2.28 per $1,000 of market value.

23. Brunori (2007).
24. Von Ins (2001).
25. U.S. Census Bureau (2009).
26. IssuesPA (2003).
27. O'Cleireacain and Rivlin (2002).
28. Marcia Kramer, *Warning Suburbanites: NYC Council Wants Your Money*, WCBS-TV, New York, November 17, 2008 (http://wcbstv.com/politics/commuter.tax.nyc.2.866907.html).
29. City of Baltimore (2007).

Do Commuters Pay Their Share for Services Consumed Where They Work?

Dispersion of residence in the United States occurred throughout the second half of the twentieth century and into the twenty-first century. The U.S. Census Bureau reports that 66 percent of the people living in U.S. metropolitan statistical areas in 1950 chose to reside in a central city.[30] By 2000, that figure had fallen to 38 percent. Economists have offered two broad theoretical reasons for the decline: "natural evolution" and "flight from blight."[31] The natural evolution view of growing suburbanization in the United States focuses on how rising real income, increasing demand for types of housing not available in central cities, private transportation innovations, and public transportation policies have influenced consumers' decision to work farther from their place of residence. The flight-from-blight view focuses instead on the various fiscal and social problems that often plague U.S. central cities more than the surrounding suburbs.

Though more Americans are choosing to reside in suburbia, economists point out that suburban residents still benefit from an economically and fiscally strong central city. A metropolitan area's central city (or even county) can provide benefits that spill over into the suburban municipalities (or counties) that surround it.[32] One of the spillover benefits is the greater employment and higher wage opportunities that exist for a suburban resident because of proximity to a central city. Another is the ability of central city firms to provide consumer services to suburban residents (and firms) at a lower price or of a higher quality, or both, than could be produced solely in the suburbs. Both of those benefits result from the higher density of firms and households in a central city. Central city firms also gain an advantage in innovative practices due to the greater likelihood of knowledge spillovers between similar firms. Finally, consumers may benefit from the economic advantages offered to retail and service firms, which are more likely to cluster together in a central city.

Low-quality public services and high local taxes work against the competitive advantages offered by central cities. Many central cities in the United States exhibit both problems because higher-income households are more likely to have left a central city for its suburbs for the natural evolution and flight-from-blight reasons previously described. That in turn generates a lower-income tax base and increases the difficulty of funding the provision of central city services to the larger proportion of the population that is poor. Either central city taxes need to increase to maintain the same level of services offered earlier, or central

30. U.S.Census Bureau (2002).
31. Mieszkowski and Mills (1993); Wassmer (2008).
32. Inman (2003).

city services need to decrease to maintain the same rate of taxation. Either choice generates greater fiscal blight, and the likelihood of even more flight by the more affluent households that remain in a central city. The relationships just described raise the important issue of whether suburbanites pay their fair share for central city services from which they benefit.

Reasons for Suburban Support of Central Cities

Haughwout and Inman summarize three arguments in favor of fiscal transfers from the suburbs to a central city in a metropolitan area.[33] The first is that equity and efficiency dictate that suburban residents pay for central city services that benefit them. If they do not, the central city must provide services at a less-than-optimal level for all who consume them. The second argument is that suburban households value the welfare of the poor in their metropolitan area. Altruistic suburbanites in a region may want to offer greater subsidies to the central city's poor than the city itself would provide in the absence of additional revenue from the suburbs. Self-interest alone is the third argument. The economic ties described earlier increase the value of living (reflected in higher land values) in a suburban area if the central city is fiscally and economically strong.

Because of the direct and indirect benefits that a central city can offer its suburbs, it is reasonable to question whether commuters from the suburbs pay their fair share for central city services consumed where they work. As early as 1955, Sigafoos raised concern about nonresident employees exerting a "considerable bearing" on a central city's finances and generating a "very challenging" problem.[34] Many of the early concerns were mistakenly rooted only in the costs that commuters impose on a city and not in the benefits that they can also offer. Ladd and Yinger, in an examination of eighty-six large U.S. central cities throughout the 1970s, found that the greater the presence of commuters (as approximated by greater employment), the greater a typical central city's expenditures on public safety and general services.[35] In a comparison of central cities that held constant other factors that cause differences in municipal spending, they found a 10 percent increase in a city's employment led on average to municipal spending that was 2.9 percent higher for general services and 3.9 percent higher for public safety.[36] Apart from this cost, however, Ladd and Yinger note that the presence of commuters increases the opportunity to export the sales tax burden imposed in a central city. Further benefits of commuters include commuters' paying central

33. Haughwout and Inman (2004).
34. Sigafoos (1955, p. 116).
35. Ladd and Yinger (1991).
36. Ladd and Yinger (1991, p. 87).

city user fees and/or tolls, investing time and money in central city organizations, and buying central city services.

Hawkins and Ihrke summarize seven studies that attempted to measure the benefits that suburban commuters bestowed on a central city and compared them with their costs.[37] Three of the studies found greater commuter costs than benefits; two found costs and benefits that were about equal; and the remaining two found more commuter benefits than burdens. Such mixed findings are by no means decisive and should not come as a surprise given the assumptions necessary to make them.

A study by Smith is a prime example of research that set out to determine whether commuters into San Francisco paid their fair share of city taxes.[38] Smith first divided the central city's expenditures between those that benefit business and those that do not. Next, he divided local government services between those benefiting residents and those benefiting nonresidents. That is possible only by making assumptions on forward and backward shifting and on the division of capital ownership between residents and nonresidents, and it requires accurate data on nonresident labor supply and consumer purchases in the city. Further conjectures were necessary to estimate the share of business taxes paid by nonresidents. After all those assumptions, Smith found that nonresident commuters in 1970 contributed about $20 to $54 million more in tax revenues than it cost the city to provide the services that they used.

Smith also estimated that in 1970 the city of San Francisco spent just over $108 million on public services that disproportionately benefited the city's poorer residents. Thus, he concludes that the commuters' overpayment may be justified as a fitting contribution to the disproportionate burden that the central city bears in the area of redistributive services. However, in a critique by Ziegler and Dyer of Smith's assumptions that substituted assumptions that they considered just as reasonable, commuters paid just about the right amount of taxes to San Francisco for the benefits that they received from city services.[39] According to Ziegler and Dyer's assumptions, commuters to San Francisco in 1970 would need to pay more only if they wished to help the central city cover a disproportionate level of expenditures for the poor.

A widely cited study by Greene, Neenan, and Scott, using 1970 data from the Washington, D.C., metropolitan area, also attempted to measure whether the surrounding suburbs exploited the central city.[40] Its methodology is noteworthy in at least two ways. First, it attempts to assess the incidence of local

37. Hawkins and Ihrke (1999).
38. Smith (1972).
39. Ziegler and Dyer (1975).
40. Greene, Neenan, and Scott (1974).

taxes, fees, and public services by geography (D.C., Maryland suburbs, and Virginia suburbs) and eight different income classes. Second, it attempts to value the benefits of publicly provided services using a cost-of-service method and a willingness-to-pay method. In this study, a suburban resident's willingness to pay for a service (say, the education of a low-income child in D.C.) may be greater than what the resident actually pays. However, the estimation of the demand curves required for those calculations is controversial.[41] Using the cost-of-service approach, a study by Greene and others found that the District was a net gainer. Suburban residents paid for more than the service benefits that they received from the central city as commuters and the service benefit spillovers that they received as residents. However, when applying the willingness-to-pay approach, the authors found that the suburbs received positive net gains from their fiscal interchange with the central city in this metropolitan area in 1970.

Two more recent studies also addressed the issue of whether commuters pay their fair share of central city taxes. Writing shortly after the state of New York repealed its largest city's right to tax nonresident income, Chernick and Tkacheva estimated what it cost the city to provide services at the time of the state-imposed revenue loss.[42] To do so, they used 1967 to 1997 panel data to regress city expenditures in twenty-four large cities throughout the United States against each of the cities' employment-to-population ratios. From that regression they estimated that one commuter into New York City increased the city's annual expenditures by $2,925 per resident. They compared that figure to the total tax revenue garnered from a typical commuter in 1997, which averaged $2,253. They found that expected tax collections from commuters did not fully cover the additional city expenditures that their study attributed to commuters. However, they did not attempt to estimate the benefits that a commuter offers to New York City besides tax payments.

Finally, Shields and Shideler used a two-city model to examine the theoretical effects of commuters on the recipient city's optimal provision of a locally provided good.[43] Such a model supports the institution of a commuter tax by the central city because of the "congestion" that commuters impose on central city residents' consumption of the city's public goods. Shields and Shideler then used 1990 data from fifty-six "workplace" communities (with substantial numbers of commuters) and more than 1,800 "bedroom" communities (without substantial numbers of commuters) in Pennsylvania to estimate regressions to explain differences in maintenance and operating expenses for expenditures on streets and highways, police, and libraries and parks in those cities. The authors chose those

41. Vincent (1975).
42. Chernick and Tkacheva (2002).
43. Shields and Shideler (2003).

particular local expenditures because they are most likely to rise in the presence of commuters. They estimated separate regressions for the workplace and bedroom samples that included the appropriate explanatory variables, and then compared the regression coefficients on the number of residents. For both the police and the libraries/parks categories, the marginal expenditure per resident was greater in the workplace (central city) than in the bedroom (suburban city) community ($54 and $39 for the police, and $23 and $9 for the libraries/parks categories respectively). Shield and Shideler took that evidence as support for use of a commuter tax in Pennsylvania's workplace communities. Nevertheless, they conceded that their method does nothing to indicate whether existing commuter taxes in Pennsylvania's workplace communities are too high or too low, nor does it measure the economic effects of such taxes.

Evidence on the Economic Effects of Local Income/Commuter Taxes

Economics teaches that the levying of a local income or occupational tax by a central city (or county) in a metropolitan area introduces a price distortion into the area's markets. The same is true if all local governments in the metropolitan area use the tax, but it is levied at a higher rate in the central city. Such a distortion and how it plays out in the metropolitan area's land, labor, and capital (machinery) markets ultimately determine the economic effects that such taxes have in a metropolitan area. Next I describe the possible cause-and-effect relationships that theoretically can develop when a central city levies a local income, wage, or occupation tax. Then I summarize the existing evidence on those relationships.

In the language that economists use to analyze the economic influence of a tax, the "statutory incidence" of a local income tax (or who, by law, pays it) falls on the employee. The law also states that the employer is the initial payer of a local occupational tax levied against a firm's payroll or number of employees. However, who ultimately bears the "economic incidence" of either of the two local taxes (or who actually pays them) depends on the ability and/or desire of the employee or employer to escape the tax. If the tax induces an employee or employer to change his or her behavior to avoid it, its incidence falls beyond the employee or employer required by law to pay it. That extended incidence can result in changes in the distribution of residences, employment, and land prices in a metropolitan area.

The Incidence of a Local Income/Commuter Tax

Consider first a local income tax levied only in a metropolitan area's central city and levied only on its resident workers (what exists now in New York City). An employee of a central city firm can escape the tax and still maintain his or her central city employment by moving to a suburban residence. Such a move is not costless; the central city resident will make it only if the resident views the net benefit of moving out of the central city (which includes not having to pay the present value of the stream of future local income tax payments) as greater than the direct and indirect costs of physically changing his or her residence. Therefore, such a tax could cause some, but definitely not all, residents to move out of the central city. The tax rate and how attractive the central city is as a residential location relative to the suburban alternatives both influence the degree of movement out of a central city due to a resident income tax.

A central city that levies a local income tax can discourage residents employed in the city from moving to a suburban residence if the city adds a commuter tax component to it.[44] The discouragement is greater the closer the commuter tax rate is to the resident rate—as in Philadelphia, where the resident rate is currently 3.93 and the commuter rate is 3.50, but not in Detroit, where the rates are 2.50 and 1.25 respectively. A commuter tax works to reduce the net benefit of a central city employee's move from her central city residence to a suburban one because at least a portion of the tax will still be due. When a central city commuter tax exists, the only way for the central city resident and employee to avoid it entirely is to move to a different community and take a job outside the central city. That will happen only if the net benefit of the change in residence is greater than both the direct and the indirect costs of changing both place of residence and employment. The possibility also exists for the central city resident to leave the metropolitan area because of a central city income and commuter tax, but that is unlikely due to the usual overriding consideration of having family and friends in the current metropolitan area and human capital specific to the local area.[45]

If a central city income and commuter tax exists and many employees of a firm in a central city are choosing (or threatening) to leave their jobs with the firm for a similar job in the suburbs that offers higher after-tax pay, the central city firm has two options. The first is to raise its employees' wages to compensate for the additional local income taxes that they pay. If the firm does so, then the burden of the income tax has been shifted from the employee to the employer (or eventually to the firm's customers, in the form of higher prices). Second, firms may choose instead to move their operations from the central city to a suburban location without a local income tax. A profit-maximizing firm will choose the less costly of the two alternatives. A central city income and

---

44. See Sasaki (1991) and Hettler (2004) for mathematical expositions of such an addition.
45. Ladd and Yinger (1991, p. 52).

commuter tax, by itself, could induce the firm to choose a suburban location. However, such a tax may also be a symptom of other flight-from-blight factors pushing the firm out. If the firm leaves the central city due to its use of a local income tax, the burden of the income tax shifts from the employee to immobile capital and land that must remain in the central city. That burden occurs through a reduction in the market value of immobile capital and land.

The Incidence of a Local Occupational Tax

A firm pays a central city occupational tax on the value of its payroll or number of employees. With such a tax, it makes no difference whether the employee generating the payroll resides in or outside the central city; thus, it is in part a tax on commuters. A firm can try to pass the economic incidence of the tax on to its employees in the form of lower wages, but it will succeed only if employees have limited or more costly employment options outside the central city. The employee will tolerate a reduction in wages equivalent to the tax only if the wage paid in the suburbs is less than the lower wage offered by the central city firm due to the occupation tax minus the additional cost of transportation to the suburban job. The firm may lose employees if they choose to take suburban jobs that offer higher wages because suburban firms have no occupational tax to pass on to them.

As with a local income tax, a firm could avoid paying a central city occupation tax if it moved to a location without the tax. It will choose that option only if it is unable to pass the tax on to its employees and if the discounted value of its expected future occupation tax payments is greater than the current cost of moving its operations outside the central city. If the firm moves out of the central city because of an occupation tax, the economic burden of the tax shifts from the employer to land and capital owners in the form of lower prices for their immobile central city assets.

Tests of the Incidence of Local Income/Commuter Taxation

The preceding explanations of the possible economic incidence of a central city's (or county's) adoption of an income, wage, and/or occupational tax illustrate that under certain conditions such taxes can induce both people and businesses to leave the central city. However, it is equally important to note that that does not necessarily have to occur. It really comes down to whether a local tax increase is enough to push a firm or individual to change the location in which it does business or lives. Thus, it is more likely that a place like New York City or perhaps Washington, D.C., could impose a higher resident or commuter income tax and induce less movement of residents and firms than a place like Detroit or Philadelphia. The benefits of central city amenities are more likely to outweigh the costs of a local tax in some places than in others where the amenities are less easily recognized. Accordingly, it is necessary to look to statistical evidence to determine the degree to which economic activity has left a city that has instituted such taxes.

Henchman, writing for the Tax Foundation, and Gessing, writing for the National Taxpayers Union, both state that local taxes on wages and income are more likely to be used in areas that exhibit the nation's poorest business climates and have experienced the greatest economic declines.[46] They both conclude that that is reason enough to believe that such taxes induce mobility and decline in the jurisdictions levying them. Nevertheless, just noting a simple correlation between a city's taxes and its decline is not enough to justify full confidence in a cause-and-effect relationship between them. Other studies, discussed below, have used regression and computable general equilibrium (CGE) analysis to better identify this cause-and-effect relationship.

Regression Studies

In a review of Scandinavian local income taxation, Gold observes that the mobility of the local tax base is the reason most commonly cited for not recommending greater use of a local income tax in the United States.[47] However, Gold could find no quantitative studies at the time that definitively showed mobility due to local income taxation. Grieson was one of the first to assess the influence of local income taxation on the ratio of employment in a central city (Philadelphia) to U.S. employment using multiple regression analysis.[48] Data for his study were from the period 1965 to 1975. The analysis comprises six regressions for an equal number of industrial sectors. Explanatory variables include only a set of variables to control for year and the key explanatory variable, a four-year average measure of the city's resident income tax rate. The regression coefficient on the key variable forecast that Philadelphia's 1976 local income tax rate increase of 1 percentage point—from 3.3125 to 4.3125 percent—would have led, four years later, to a 9.5 percent decrease in employment in manufacturing, services, and the finance, insurance, and real estate sectors. The study concludes that "[t]he decline in Philadelphia employment appears to be neither a state nor regional problem, but largely a function of the local income (and perhaps other) taxes."[49] As even Grieson notes, however, his study's relatively simple methodology does not fully control for other factors that could influence Philadelphia's

46. Henchman (2008); Gessing (2003).
47. Gold (1977, p. 473).
48. Grieson (1980).
49. Grieson (1980, p. 137).

employment besides its income tax.[50] For instance, the study leaves open the possibility that an income tax increase may be the result of another factor that caused an employment decrease. The local income tax increase may not itself be the cause of the employment decrease.

Mark, McGuire, and Papke used a model similar to Grieson's with data for 1964–94 from the Washington, D.C., metropolitan area. They found that local income taxation exerted no influence on local changes in population.[51] The two studies exhibit the extreme fluctuation in findings that can occur in a regression analysis when model specification is too simple. Thus, it is wise for the policy-maker to place greater faith in regression results derived from more fully specified models.

Philadelphia is also the subject of a regression study by Stull using data from 1980 for the 335 municipalities in Pennsylvania and New Jersey that made up the Philadelphia metropolitan statistical area at the time.[52] Stull ran a home price regression that specified the median value of owner-occupied homes as the dependent variable and included as explanatory variables the physical character-istics of homes, average neighborhood economic factors, average neighborhood social and demographic characteristics, and local fiscal characteristics. Relevant to the subject of this chapter, the local tax rate on earned income was included as a fiscal characteristic. Stull found that an increase of 1 percentage point in the municipal income tax rate lowered the estimated median home value by $1,600 to $1,800, which amounted to about a 4 percent decline in the metropolitan area's average median home value of $41,800 in 1980. Lower local home values are the expected capitalization effect if existing residents leave the community because of an increase in the local income tax rate and/or because the increase in the rate leads to a decline in demand for houses in the community by prospec-tive residents. Using an expanded data set, Stull and Stull offer an extension of the research just discussed and find essentially the same results.[53] These two regression-based studies do a good job of controlling for other factors that can influence home prices besides the local income tax. Thus, the influence of the local income tax in these models is likely more accurate than in a regression model that is less well specified.

50. Grieson (1980, p. 127–131). As Grieson points out, the time series of data that he used ends in a recession that was deeper in Philadelphia than in the national economy. Therefore, the decline in the city's share of national employment that his study attributed to the local income tax increase is probably exaggerated. In addition, multiplying coefficient estimates by "average 1965–1975 U.S. sectoral employ-ment loss" is unorthodox and distorts the relationship since those averages are likely to be highly skewed because of the recession.

51. Mark, McGuire, and Papke (2000).

52. Stull (1987).

53. Stull and Stull (1991).

A study by Haughwout and others also uses regression analysis to measure the effects of local income taxation on local economic activity in New York City and Philadelphia.[54] One set of regressions explains changes in the local income tax base in each city over time. A different set of regressions explains changes in the share of each city's total, manufacturing, and service employment as a result of the local income tax rate. The authors correctly account for the fact that a change in a city's income tax rate is likely to change the city's level of publicly provided services in the same direction. A city's local income tax base is modeled as a function of (1) the interest rate, (2) an alternate wage rate for those who commute, (3) a world price for city exports, (4) all of the city's tax rates, (5) a composite measure of local services provided by the city, and (6) measures of the attractiveness to firms or households of alternative locations. This represents a reasonable attempt at controlling for factors besides the local income tax rate that drive a city's local income tax base.

The study by Haughwout and others estimates that a 1 percent increase in New York City's local income tax rate would result in a 0.46 to 0.53 percent decrease in its local income tax base. The estimated response of Philadelphia's local wage tax base to a 1 percent increase in its tax rate was indistinguishable from zero. Importantly, the authors stress that the non-finding of a response for Philadelphia does not mean that the city's use of a local income tax is without economic effect. It occurred because the offsetting consequences of the city's jobs and residents falling equally leave the wage tax base per resident unchanged, but Philadelphia's economy smaller.

For both New York City and Philadelphia, Haughwout and others find that an increase in the local income or wage tax rate exerted a negative influence on local employment. Between 1970 and 2001, New York City's share of total U.S. employment fell from 5.3 to 2.9 percent. The study's statistical analysis indicates that New York City lost just over 330,000 jobs (roughly 8.7 percent of total city jobs in 2001, as the authors point out) over that period due to local income tax increases alone.[55] Over the same period, Philadelphia's share of total U.S. employment fell from 1.2 percent to 0.5 percent, and the regression results indicate that just over 202,000 jobs were lost over that period due to the increase in Philadelphia's local wage tax rate. The combined results of the two regressions indicate that the creation of a new job in New York City through a local income tax cut costs the city about $146,000 per job; the estimate for Philadelphia is about $134,000 per job. Nevertheless, a portion of those dollars returns to the residents of the cities when workers and residents spend some of their increased

---

54. Haughwout and others (2004).
55. Haughwout and others (2004, p. 579).

disposable income in the city's economy (thus generating a "multiplier" effect). As Inman notes, that results in a net economic gain for the central city and even the suburban communities that surround it.[56]

The Philadelphia Tax Reform Commission retained Econsult to use regression analysis to measure the impact of the city's local tax choices on its economic vitality between 1953 and 2002.[57] The study's regression methodology is very similar to that used by Haughwout and others in their study. On the basis of the extensive statistical analysis and simulations that it conducted, Econsult concluded that a reduction in Philadelphia's local income tax rate of 0.42 percent (or an initial decrease in $125 million in wage tax revenue, about 10 percent of the 2004 total) would eventually have the following effects:

—expand the base of taxable income in the city

—increase the property and gross-receipts tax base in the city

—increase city employment.

The Econsult forecast, based on an anticipated supply side stimulation of the city's economy caused by the wage tax cut, predicted that Philadelphia's wage tax base would grow by an additional $2.3 billion between 2004 and 2010 (or roughly 7.5 percent more than it would without the wage tax reduction). In addition, Econsult forecast that the wage tax reduction would result in higher property values (an additional $1.96 billion in citywide property value, or about 4.6 percent more than would have resulted otherwise).

Finally, Schmidheiny used a data set from Swiss municipalities in the canton Basel-Stadt to examine how the progressivity of local income tax rates influences the location choice of someone from the central city of Basel planning to move somewhere within the metropolitan area.[58] All municipalities in Switzerland rely on a local income tax. In the particular canton examined, rates varied from 6.2 to 27.0 percent in the central city of Basel to an average of 40 percent less in many of the suburban municipalities that surround it. The dependent variable in the regression analysis is the location choice of a household moving from a home in the central city to a choice of sixteen peripheral communities and nineteen boroughs within the central city. The study finds that rich households are substantially more likely to move to a low-tax municipality after controlling for other explanatory factors such as housing price, housing structural characteristics, social characteristics of residents, and distance to central city. For example, the tax rates in the suburban cities of Iselin and Allschwil are 6.2 and 5.1 percent respectively for an average income family; for a family in the top income

56. Inman (2003).

57. Econsult (2003).

58. Schmidheiny (2006). A canton is a Swiss state, but it is closer in size and economic function to a typical U.S. metropolitan area than to a U.S. state.

bracket, the rates are 24.4 and 21.8 percent respectively. According to the Schmidheiny study, the odds are 1.7 times greater that a family of average income will move to lower-tax Allschwil than not move, while the odds for the wealthy family are 2.2 times greater. Thus, this study offers real-world evidence that households—especially ones with high incomes—consider local income tax rates when deciding where to reside in a metropolitan area. This regression analysis does an adequate job of controlling for factors other than local income taxation that can also drive where a person decides to live.

Of the six regression studies just described, only the ones by Haughwout and others and Econsult account for the simultaneous impacts that a change in the local income tax rate has on both the provision of local public services and the degree of economic activity in a municipality. The other four studies examine the effect of a local income tax change holding other factors constant; thus the results of these four studies should be interpreted to mean that any decrease in the local income tax rate is funded by cutting local services that are not valued by residents or businesses or by eliminating waste and inefficiency. Municipal policymakers generally believe that there are few non-valued local services and few opportunities to eliminate true waste and inefficiency. Hence, such policymakers might be quick to dismiss the findings of all but Haughwout and Econsult. Therefore, it is important to note that the studies by Haughwout and others and Econsult distinguish themselves by explicitly accounting for the reality that a local income tax increase (decrease) must be thought of in the balanced-budget sense that it will lead to an increase (decrease) in the city's ability to provide public services.

Computable General Equilibrium Studies

An alternative to regression analysis for investigating the effect of local income taxation in a metropolitan economy is the use of a computable general equilibrium (CGE) model. CGE employs economic theory, competitive market and equilibrium assumptions, and optimization by economic actors to model the various market (labor, capital, and land) adjustments in a metropolitan area after the imposition of a tax or a change in the tax rate. Calibrated to data from a real-world situation, all of the CGE models discussed below account for the fact that a local income tax change occurs within a balanced local budget. Thus, depending on the modeling strategy, a local income tax decrease would need to result in a decrease in local expenditures on public services and/or an increase in a different local revenue source to offset the tax decrease. That should increase the real-world relevance of the CGE findings; however, policymakers must understand that CGE studies are useful only for assessing long-run policy impacts that occur under the restrictive assumption that all relevant markets are competitive.

A study by Nechyba was one of the first to use CGE to examine the use of local income taxes in a metropolitan area.[59] Of particular interest in that study was why most local governments in the United States prefer to tax property—not income—to finance the provision of municipal services. In the model, local voters set local property tax rates in a community, while a community's professional planners set local income tax rates. Planners must find the best local tax mix given the expected responses of other planners in nearby communities. Planners understand the price, voting, and migration consequences of their choices. Nechyba's study allows for the fact that community planners may pursue various objectives in setting local tax policy. In the study planners may seek to maximize the following: community income; property value; wealth; total resident satisfaction; the size of the public sector; or median voter satisfaction. The model is set to 1987 data from Camden County, New Jersey. Nechyba finds that for all six possible objectives, the best choice for a local planner is to set the local income tax rate to zero. If a community deviates from that, it experiences a reduction in income, property values, wealth, and ultimately the ability to provide local public services within its boundaries. When interpreting that result for the real world, a policymaker must realize that Nechyba's no-local-income-tax result hinges on his assumption of the costless mobility of residents. As the costs of mobility rise, the ability of a community planner to choose a local income tax with less detrimental effects on the community increases.

Haughwout and Inman offer a CGE model of a central city that includes both firms and households.[60] Firms use workers, machinery, and land. The central city's tax revenue rises with local property values, taxable sales, resident income, and commuter income. The city uses the revenue from taxes and outside aid to produce local infrastructure. In addition, poor people live in the central city and survive on transfer payments whose funding is shared by the city and the federal government. The poor are assumed to be unable to move from the city. The CGE model is set up to match closely the city of Philadelphia's economy in 1998. Haughwout and Inman's model is most appropriate for the subject of this chapter because it explicitly ascertains the effects of a central city resident and commuter wage tax.

Haughwout and Inman use the CGE model to explore whether Philadelphia can remain a viable central economic base for its metropolitan area if forced to shoulder a rising burden of welfare payments to the poor through increased local wage taxation. Their study finds that increasing Philadelphia's share of welfare payments from 9.5 to 25 percent will reduce the size of the city's economy by

59. Nechyba (1997).
60. Haughwout and Inman (2001).

about 15 percent. If the city is required to assume any more than 85 percent of the share of welfare paid to its poor, the study forecasts a decimated central city economy. Those findings come in part from the mapping of "revenue hills" for the central city's resident and commuter wage taxes. A revenue hill for a particular city is plotted on a graph in which tax revenue is on the vertical axis and tax rate is on the horizontal axis. The diagram shows the influence of tax rate on tax revenue, holding other factors expected to influence tax revenue constant. It is a hill because as the tax rate rises from zero, tax revenue also rises. However, at some high tax rate, the discouraging effect of taxation will drive economic activity from the city and tax revenue can actually fall with a further increase in tax rate—thus producing a revenue hill when graphed. Such a hill for Philadelphia's resident wage tax was at its peak in 1998. During that period, small changes in rates (up or down) would have neither increased nor decreased total revenue. The city of Philadelphia's nonresident wage tax rate was beyond its peak in 1998, meaning that a decrease in tax rates would have resulted in increased revenues and an increase in rates would have resulted in decreased revenues.

Finally, a later study by Haughwout and Inman offers an even more realistic CGE model that better accounts for movement of people and businesses between a central city and a suburb.[61] (The model assumes for simplicity that there is only one suburban government.) In this model, both local governments provide infrastructure as a local public service. Central city public funding comes from a local property tax, a resident wage tax, a commuter wage tax, and a tax on a firm's gross receipts. The suburban government raises revenue through the property tax and a resident wage tax. This CGE model is set to mimic the Philadelphia metropolitan area, where the central city pays 9.5 percent of the annual cost of assistance to poor residents through local taxes. Under the assumptions of this CGE model, funding a portion of the assistance offered to the poor results in a smaller central city, in economic terms, than if Philadelphia did not make such a transfer. The authors simulate the result of the suburban government's funding all of the central city's assistance to its poor and find that in the long term doing so is likely to offer a net benefit for the suburb. When suburban taxes are held constant, suburban land values will initially decline because of the necessarily reduced provision of suburban public services because public resources from the suburbs go to the central city's poor. However, over time, the suburban subsidy allows the central city to provide additional infrastructure. An increase in infrastructure increases the productivity of central city firms, benefiting the entire metropolitan area.

---

61. Haughwout and Inman (2004).

The Haughwout and Inman study offers a balanced treatment of the trade-offs involved when a central city raises its resident and commuter income tax rates to provide for the increased public services that its disproportionately greater number of low-income residents need.[62] The study also accounts for the likelihood that if these rates are too high, they may drive away the more affluent tax base that necessarily supports the redistributive actions. The authors explicitly choose to simulate the impact of a local income tax cut equivalent to the revenue that Philadelphia spends on local public services that largely benefit the poor. The lost revenue is made up through an income transfer (through either the state or federal government) from suburban residents equivalent to Philadelphia's lost income tax revenue. The simulated result is private sector job growth in the central city that is not balanced on the back of service cuts to the poor. The authors show that through the increased spillovers that suburban residents receive from a stronger central city economy, such a scheme can ultimately benefit the suburban residents initially asked to support the central city's poor. This is a powerful policy idea, supported by a real-world simulation, which policymakers should not ignore.

As discussed, levying a local resident or commuter-based income tax, or a firm-based occupation tax, can induce residents and/or firms to leave the jurisdiction levying the tax. However, exodus is not costless, and the actual extent of it generated by such taxes has been investigated. A review of the investigations suggests that a central city income and/or commuter taxes can generate such flight and its economic consequences. Nevertheless, it is important to note that the vast majority of those studies focus on Philadelphia, which has some of the highest resident and commuter wage tax rates in the country. Thus, the simulated results may not be applicable in places with lower local income tax rates or with a less mobile group of central city residents and firms.

The Politics of Taxing Suburban Commuters and Alternatives

The use of local commuter taxes in the United States is possible only if a state allows it. The politics surrounding a state's decision are complex. In making such a decision, a legislature and governor must weigh the need to assist fiscally troubled jurisdictions against conflicting ideas of what is fair for all state residents and what is best for the state's economy. As summarized by Goodman: "Talk about a politically charged phrase. 'Commuter tax' is such a loaded term that people who support one often try to find some other way of saying it."[63]

62. Haughwout and Inman (2004).
63. Goodman (2007).

As already discussed, some will claim that it is fair to tax commuters only if the value of the locally provided services that they consume while commuting and at work are greater or equal to the commuter taxes that they pay to support those services. Nevertheless, others argue that a state legislature should never allow the option for localities to tax commuters. Give them an instrument to do so, critics say, and central city politicians will be unable to resist the temptation to shift the payment of local taxes to suburbanites—or ask suburban commuters to pay for an unfairly larger portion of the central city's publicly provided services than they actually consume. Furthermore, fairness demands that taxation occur only with political representation, something commuters do not possess in a city in which they only work.

At the same time, conflicting issues regarding what is best for a state's economy arise. One side can claim that commuter taxes ensure that a central jurisdiction has the resources necessary to maintain its place as an economic engine that benefits the entire region. Alternatively, others point to commuter taxes as ultimately inducing a further decline in the jurisdiction that adopts them by spurring additional residential and business outmigration. Once a state allows the local adoption of commuter taxes, local politics usually favors adoption and commuters pay their fair share—and perhaps more—for local services. However, in some states that currently allow local income taxation, no local governments have adopted income taxes (Alaska, Arkansas, Connecticut, Georgia, Kansas, and Vermont). Non-adoption demonstrates that some local politicians and/or citizens consider the possibility that local income taxes do more local economic harm than good.

The fact that most states have more residents living in suburban and rural areas than central cities is very likely the reason that the use of commuter income and wage taxes is limited to only twelve states and commuter occupational taxes to another nine (see table 4-1). Furthermore, Americans have consistently exhibited a bias against the use of state and local income taxes when other alternatives are available.[64] Baldassare and Hoene report that when asked how they would like their city to raise new revenue, 73 percent of Americans responded positively to user fees, 37 percent to the property tax, 30 percent to the sales tax, 30 percent to other taxes, and only 14 percent to the local income tax.[65] In California, only 5 percent favored the local income tax as a way to raise local revenue.[66] In Philadelphia, where commuters to the city face the highest wage tax rates in the country, polls have confirmed that a commuter wage tax raises political ire. A survey of city residents found that 53 percent cited the

64. Brunori (2007, p. 89).
65. Baldassare and Hoene (2004, p. 9).
66. Baldassare and Hoene (2004).

wage tax as the most important reason to leave the city, while 60 percent of Philadelphia's workers questioned cited its wage tax as what they like least about working there.[67]

I have found only three data-based studies that attempted to evaluate the political environment surrounding the decision to adopt local income taxes and/or to set the tax rate. I found no comparable studies on the issue of commuter taxes directly. Ohio's school districts raise revenue through local property taxation alone, or through a combination of local property and income taxation. In examining the factors in local income tax adoption, Spry finds that an additional school district within ten miles of a given district reduces by 10 percent a jurisdiction's likelihood of adopting a local income tax.[68] That supports Nechyba's finding that localities are more likely to avoid adopting local income taxes as the potential for competition (and hence the mobility that it can induce) becomes greater.[69]

Edmark and Agren test the politics behind setting local income tax rates using a set of panel data from 283 Swedish local governments that all used local income taxes between 1993 and 2006.[70] The study finds that a 1 percentage point increase in average local income taxation in neighboring jurisdictions is correlated with about a 0.7 percent decrease in own local income taxation. Finally, Ashworth and Heyndels examine the opinions of Flemish politicians on what determined the public's opinion on whether the local income tax rates were rather high, average, or rather low.[71] They found that the ideological position of their electorate and interest group pressure were the primary determinants of the politicians' opinions on how the public viewed local income taxation.

Alternatives

In view of the strong arguments made both for and against the use of commuter taxes and the limited amount of empirical evidence that supports one side's argument over the other's, the use of this form of taxation remains politically charged. Therefore it is reasonable to ask whether other viable alternatives could achieve the same objectives. First, it is necessary to be clear about which objectives most economists and I believe are met when a city adopts a commuter tax.

The reasons described earlier for the historical adoption of local income and commuter taxes in the United States were fiscal stress, popular revolt against rising property taxes, and central jurisdictions' desire to export their own tax burdens to

---

67. IssuesPA (2003).
68. Spry (2005).
69. Nechyba (1997).
70. Edmark and Agren (2007).
71. Ashworth and Heyndels (1997).

surrounding suburban residents. Fiscal stress, or what a city experiences by not having the fiscal resources necessary to pay for the services that it feels it must provide to its residents and firms, is by far the greatest reason that central jurisdictions have sought to use commuter taxes. Such stress is usually the outcome of forces previously characterized as falling under the categories of natural evolution and flight from blight. Such forces have existed in the United States since the late 1950s and have caused the population, employment, and tax bases of many central jurisdictions to shrink relative to the suburban jurisdictions that surround them. Fiscal stress exists because demand for local public services has not shrunk to the same extent.

Bradbury, Downs, and Small were among the first to offer a book-length examination of the existence and causes of central city decline in the United States.[72] Using a sample of the 153 most populous cities in the United States between 1970 and 1975, they found that 95 cities lost population. Between 1975 and 1980, 85 of those cities continued to lose population. Expanding on the broad causal notions of natural evolution and flight from blight, they offered no less than thirty-seven different theoretical explanations for that decline, which fall into six categories: central city's lack of amenities; central city's taxes; positive attraction to suburbs; economic evolution; biased policies; and demographic trends. In a similar examination, Ladd and Yinger confirmed that central city population decline has resulted in a corresponding decline in central city fiscal health.[73] For a 1982 sample of the seventy-one largest central cities in the United States, they calculated a measure of fiscal health that is calibrated as the difference between a city's revenue-raising capacity and its needed services (based on what local public services the average city with similar characteristics is providing), divided by its capacity to provide those services. The more negative that percentage, the more severe a city's fiscal stress. More than half of the cities in the sample exhibited negative values, with four cities (Atlanta, Los Angeles, Memphis, and New Orleans) exhibiting more than negative 50 percent.

I purposefully use two older studies to document the presence of fiscal stress in American central cities during the 1970s and 1980s. As described earlier, that period corresponds to the last time that central places in the United States widely considered and adopted commuter taxes. Nevertheless, fiscal stress continues to be a major concern for many U.S. central cities,[74] and during the current recession, fiscal stress in many U.S. central cities is only likely to increase. Thus, the primary purpose of any proposed alternative to commuter taxation

72. Bradbury, Downs, and Small (1982).
73. Ladd and Yinger (1991).
74. See Inman (2003, 2006) and Keating (2004). For Canadian cities, see Kitchen (2004) and Kitchen and Slack (2003).

must be to bring additional revenue into central cities from sources that are, at least in part, outside the city, and that has always been an important factor in a city's decision to adopt commuter taxes. Nonetheless, in thinking about alternatives to the commuter tax, I consider it unacceptable to export local taxes only to make others pay for services from which they do not benefit. It is also important to remember that the adoption of local income and commuter taxation has stemmed, and still stems, from a continuing popular desire to reduce property taxes. It is for that reason, good or bad, that I do not consider increasing central city property taxes a viable political alternative to commuter taxes.[75]

Before considering specific alternatives to commuter taxation, it is useful to review some widely held opinions by economists on the provision of local public services and how best to pay for them. Inman posits that economically, the "best" way to finance city services with significant spatial spillovers is to have a higher level of government collect revenue from those who benefit from the spillover and share it with the city producing the spillover.[76] In addition, Inman states that it is best if central cities are not in the business of redistributing income in their own city because doing so will only drive high-income households from the city and possibly attract poor households. Bird also offers a concise summary of seven desirable characteristics by which economists usually evaluate a local tax. It must

—be levied on a relatively immobile base

—produce a stable and predictable yield

—not be easy to export to nonresidents

—be politically perceived as fair

—be levied on a base that helps ensure accountability

—be easy to administer

—produce a yield that is adequate to meet local needs over time.[77]

The commuter tax clearly lacks at least the first five desirable characteristics. It is reasonable therefore to consider some of the alternatives listed below (in alphabetical order, not in order of preference).

ANNEXATION. In a book published more than fifty years ago, Sigafoos noted the fiscal problem created for U.S. central cities when affluent citizens work in a central city but live outside it.[78] He suggested that an alternative to the commuter tax is for the city to absorb its suburban-dwelling workforce into its own

75. See Brunori (2007) for a highly reasoned explanation of why property taxation may be a preferred alternative.

76. Inman (2006).

77. Bird (2000).

78. Sigafoos (1955).

tax base through annexation. Rusk notes a strong positive relationship between healthy municipal credit ratings and "elastic" cities that have grown through annexation.[79] Annexation is far easier to pursue if suburban workers live in unincorporated places, as is more likely to be the case in the South, Southwest, and West. But in other areas of the country, where central cities are surrounded by already incorporated suburban jurisdictions and incorporation laws favor the status quo, annexation is not easily accomplished. Many suburbanites fled a central city to escape its governance and fiscal burdens. They may fight a central city's annexation attempt even more than an attempt to impose commuter taxes.

COMMUTER TAX WITH A CREDIT. Greene, Neenan, and Scott found in their early 1970s study of the Washington, D.C., metropolitan area that commuters fully compensated the district for the nonpecuniary benefits that they received from it but that suburban noncommuters may not have, depending on how the district's redistributive actions on behalf of the poor were valued.[80] The authors concluded that a traditional commuter tax would not be justified but that transferring additional suburban-generated revenue to the district might be. That is possible if a commuter is subject to an income tax imposed by the district and if a credit for the commuter's payment of the tax is allowed on the city or state income tax paid where the commuter resides. Such a credit zeros out the burden of the tax to the commuter and passes it in full to the local or state government where the commuter lives. Facing tax revenue losses from such a credit scheme, local or state governments that surround the district will necessarily compensate by raising their income tax rate and/or cutting their level of services. The result is that D.C. gets the needed revenue from the suburbs. The additional revenue comes from all suburban residents in the D.C. metropolitan area or from all residents in the states of Maryland and Virginia.

DOWNSIZE CENTRAL CITY GOVERNMENT. It would be remiss to ignore a widely mentioned alternative to the commuter tax: downsizing the amount spent on local government services by an amount equal to the anticipated revenue from the tax. That is precisely the solution that Keating offered to the budget crisis that New York City faced after the loss of the commuter portion of its local income tax.[81] He suggested that contracting out some public services to private providers could save tax dollars and even improve service quality. The outright elimination of some public services also is possible. Keating and Inman

79. Rusk (2005).
80. Greene, Neenan, and Scott (1974, pp. 170–172).
81. Keating (2004).

both suggest that an area ripe for cutting in both New York and Philadelphia is the overly generous wage and benefit packages of city employees.[82] However, in considering this alternative, policymakers need to be aware that if downsizing results in lower-quality services and fewer services of the type desired by residents and/or firms, it can offer further reason for flight from a city.

GREATER INTERGOVERNMENTAL ASSISTANCE. A primary goal of commuter taxation is to collect revenue from nonresidents who benefit from the provision of central local government services but do not pay enough for them. It is possible to do so if additional revenue is collected at the state or federal level and redistributed back to the central city. Studies by Bradbury, Downs, and Small as well as Inman conclude that the appropriate way to address the fiscal stress exhibited by many central cities in the United States is to have additional state and/or federally raised dollars flow back to central cities.[83] They conclude that the best way to maintain this flow is through open-ended matching grants that target specific categories of local expenditures that benefit an entire region. The researchers also suggest that the greater the degree of interjurisdictional spillover in the expenditure category, the greater should be the higher-level government's match rate.

INTERJURISDICTIONAL TAXATION. Central cities in two states currently are pursuing perhaps a more politically feasible alternative to commuter taxes than the ones previously mentioned. Goodman describes how central cities in Ohio, frustrated by failed annexation attempts, instead negotiate with surrounding jurisdictions to create joint economic development districts (JEDDs).[84] In exchange for providing municipal utilities and/or other government services to a recently developed suburban location, the central city receives the right to collect local income taxes from the workers who eventually are employed there. Similarly, central cities and their surrounding jurisdictions in Texas have instituted municipal utility districts (MUDs). Through a MUD, a central city extends its sales tax into a suburban area that under state law cannot use such a tax. In exchange for the promise that the central city will not annex the suburban MUD for at least thirty years afterward, the central city and suburban entity split the proceeds of the tax. JEDD- and MUD-type agreements eliminate the major political threat of central city annexation of a suburban district and provide the central city with at least a portion of the resources that it would get through annexation—a solution that many see as a win-win. Unlike with the

---

82. Keating (2004); Inman (2003).
83. Bradbury, Downs, and Small (1982); Inman (2006).
84. Goodman (2007).

commuter tax, there is no punishment for suburban workers commuting to a central location to work.

REGIONALIZATION. An alternative to commuter taxation that achieves the objectives sought is the regionalization of local governments in a metropolitan area. Though long prescribed by urbanists who recognize it as a sure way to internalize all of the costs and benefits of private and public sector activity in a metropolitan area, it is highly resisted by many suburban voters because it necessarily infringes on local control of fiscal and land use choices. Thus, like Inman, I suggest greater regionalization only of public services that clearly spill over local boundaries in a metropolitan area.[85] Things that immediately come to mind are the provision of local roads; public safety services; large parks and recreation facilities; and goods and services that benefit primarily the poor. The first three items have already been widely discussed as being consumed by commuters. The fourth item is a burden unfairly borne by central cities if concern exists among all residents in a metropolitan area for the region's poor.

Inman compares the municipal fiscal situations in Philadelphia and Pittsburgh as examples to consider regarding the regionalization of local government services to the poor.[86] In both cities, about 20 percent of the population is poor. Pittsburgh is a small city in a large county. Philadelphia is a large city in a coterminous county. In Pennsylvania, counties are the primary funders of local government services for the poor. Inman reports that 1.4 percent of all income earned in Philadelphia goes to funding such services, while in Pittsburgh the amount is only 0.23 percent.[87] He calculated that in 2002 the five central counties in the Philadelphia metropolitan area spent about $552 million on public health, human services, corrections, and emergency services that benefitted primarily the poor and that the city of Philadelphia was paying a disproportionate share of the total. The regionalization of total expenditures for the poor in this metropolitan area would require an additional transfer of $191 million ($220 per household) from the four suburban counties to Philadelphia. Inman reports that that additional revenue could reduce Philadelphia's commuter tax rate by 22 percent. Using a CGE simulation, Inman showed that the long-term result of instituting this alternative to Philadelphia's commuter tax would not only raise the central city's average home value by 2.1 percent but also raise the average suburban home value by 1.8 percent. He concludes, "Regional fiscal reform can be a true win-win, enhancing house values in the city and suburbs alike."[88]

85. Inman (2006).
86. Inman (2003).
87. Inman (2003, p. 32).
88. Inman (2003, p. 23).

Commuter Taxes: The Good, the Bad, and a Not-So-Ugly Future Policy Path

While a commuter tax extends the fiscal reach of the enacting jurisdiction, it can by no means be claimed that this is the instrument of first choice for this purpose. The ultimate, of course, is metropolitan financing of governments, but realities indicate that this movement moves—when it does—at a glacial pace. Similarly, increased state financial assistance for programs of heavy "spillover" benefits—education being the prime example—seem clearly preferable to the commuter tax, indeed to the municipal income tax itself. Lacking progress on these fronts, however, local policymakers are confronted with the choice of raising needed additional revenues from an income tax or the property levy. . . . [The local income tax} is more responsive to the growth of the economy and less regressive in impact than the property tax. . . . Judging by these objectives—and their rapid spread—the local income tax appears far more likely to spread than wither away.[89]

I open the last section of this chapter with the quote above from an ACIR report, *The Commuter and the Municipal Income Tax*, that is nearly forty years old. After reviewing what has transpired in this area since 1970, I find the first half of the ACIR statement to be prophetic. Commuter taxes should not be the first choice for local policymakers wanting to raise an appropriate amount of revenue from nonresidents. A regional governance effort to coordinate the provision and funding of locally provided goods whose benefits are not wholly contained in a jurisdiction remains the first choice of most urbanists examining this issue. Nevertheless, institutions and politics in the United States have continued to prevent the implementation of regional governance in all but a few metropolitan areas. However, states and the federal government have made some progress in recognizing the desirability of having higher levels of government provide funding for locally provided goods and services whose benefits spill over across local government boundaries. Unfortunately, it seems that the presence of such spillovers and their external effects have grown faster than the political will of citizens and of the higher levels of the governments that they elect to intervene in their financing.

In retrospect, the ACIR report was wrong in 1970 in thinking that the choice for future funding of urban governments in the United States would be between the property tax and the income tax, and that the income tax was likely to prevail. As forecast by the ACIR, the late 1970s marked the beginning of a nationwide

89. ACIR (1970, p. 20).

revolt against local property taxation that continues unabated. As not forecast by the ACIR, however, the 1970s also marked the height of new adoptions of city income and commuter taxes in the United States. Local income and commuter taxation has not spread in the United States since then. In fact, given the direction of movement on this front in New York and Philadelphia, and the lack of movement in the District of Columbia, both forms of taxation are perhaps closer to withering away. Large cities in the United States have turned instead to local option sales and excise taxes, various user charges and fees, and reliance on greater intergovernmental revenue sharing to backfill the void left by declining property tax revenue.

The relevant policy issue to consider in 2010 is whether the existing use of commuter taxes in the United States should continue, decline in certain situations, and/or expand in other situations. To aid policymakers in assessing this issue and to support the recommendation with which I conclude, I offer below a concise list of the pros and cons of commuter taxes previously covered in this chapter.

First the Good

For better or worse, many large cities in the United States have come to rely on local income taxation, with a commuter component, as a significant source of funding in their portfolio of own-source revenues. To eliminate that source of revenue, or even the commuter portion alone, without replacing it would increase the degree of fiscal stress experienced in these cities. It is very likely that the increased fiscal stress would place additional pressure on local politicians to reduce local services that disproportionately benefit the poor, the result being greater inequality in central cities than already exists.

What about cutting commuter taxes and replacing the lost revenue with an alternative revenue source? The politically viable own-source revenue options (sales taxes, fees, and charges) available to replace the lost revenue from a commuter income tax cut are already used extensively in most cities. In addition, any further expansion of sales taxes, fees, and/or charges as a substitute for commuter taxation would require the poor to a pay a greater proportion of their income to fund city services than they do under commuter taxes. Furthermore, central cities that use local income and commuter taxes are able to provide the local infrastructure and public services that help generate benefits within a central city that lead to greater employment, wage, retail, and intermediate good production opportunities, which in turn benefit suburban residents and firms. A loss in such revenue would surely result in some loss of those benefits and funding that central cities use for assisting the disproportionate portion of their metropolitan area's poor that reside there.

Now the Bad

It is easy to find fault with some characteristics of a commuter tax. The first is that it very likely encourages a central city's policymakers to over-export their local tax burden to commuters who reside in the suburbs but work in the central city. Suburban residents may not be paying fully for the benefits that they receive from the central city in their metropolitan area. Nevertheless, commuters to the central city represent only a small portion of most metropolitan areas' suburban residents, and to ask them to pay for those benefits is very likely to result in the over-exportation of central city taxes to them alone. Even if central city politicians/policymakers care little about the inherent injustice of that effect, they do need to be concerned that the exportation of tax burdens could eventually drive central city employers to the suburbs as their suburban work-force seeks to avoid commuter taxation by seeking employment in a business located in the suburbs.

Second, there remains a general perception among the public that commuter taxes are inherently unjust. "Taxation without representation" is an easy rallying cry to muster among Americans familiar with Boston's Tea Party and those who belong to the current grass-roots group named after it. Moreover, a commuter tax is levied on a potentially mobile base. If the economic base of a city is truly mobile (as is more likely to be the case in places like Detroit and Philadelphia than in New York City), then the tax is likely to reduce that base. If some juris-dictions use the local commuter income tax, while other jurisdictions viewed as alternative locations for a household or firm do not, use of the local commuter income tax by some can spur movement to places that do not use it.

It is hard to tell policymakers with any certainty whether the good outweighs the bad in regard to use of commuter taxation in the United States. The advice that I offer policymakers looking to preserve or even expand the use of commuter taxation is that there is an absolute need to promote its good aspects extensively, and to design commuter tax proposals and revisions that recognize and attempt to mitigate its bad aspects. The lower the rate of commuter taxation overall and the lower the rate relative to the rate of resident income taxation in the central city, the lower the potential for bad effects from a commuter tax. Constructing "revenue hills" as Haughwout and others did for Philadelphia and New York is one way to determine whether local income tax rates have become too high.[90] From their work and other CGE and regression/simulation evidence described earlier, it appears that Philadelphia's current rates of 3.50 percent of nonresident

90. Haughwout and others (2004).

wages and 3.93 percent of resident wages fail on both fronts: the commuter rate is too high overall, and it is too close to the resident rate.

The evidence is clear that such rates have generated residential and business flight from the city. A 2003 study from the Philadelphia Tax Commission, which spent 10,000 hours on a comprehensive review of the influence of the city's tax structure on its development (including commissioning the Econsult study discussed earlier), concluded that its unusual local tax structure definitely contributed to its loss of 250,000 jobs and 430,000 residents since 1970.[91] Furthermore, the commission concluded that about 60 percent of those losses were exclusively attributable to increases in the city's wage tax rates over that period. However, it is also important for policymakers to understand that any local income or commuter tax rate above zero does not induce residents and firms to leave the city levying it. That is the case only when mobility is costless and the alternative location is nearly as attractive to the mobile household or firm as the central city.

As did the ACIR statement quoted above, I wrap up my review of commuter taxation with the belief that a commuter tax is not the best way to finance the provision of central city goods and services that offer benefits to nonresidents of the city. Nevertheless, I also recognize that given the politics and institutions in some states, it may be the only option available. To the central city policymaker looking for an antidote to the fiscal stress generated by suburban residents not paying their fair share for city-provided services, my concluding advice is to consider other avenues before resorting to a traditional commuter tax. That advice also applies to a city looking to replace revenue lost from a self-imposed cut (which has been widely suggested for Philadelphia) or a mandated cut (which previously occurred in New York City) in its commuter tax rates.

Earlier I offered six policy alternatives to a traditional commuter tax, in no order of preference. Below, I rank those alternatives according to which I believe offer the greatest political and logistic legitimacy based on the theory, evidence, and opinions covered in this chapter.

—*First, downsize as much as possible.* The political arguments against a central city seeking revenue from surrounding suburbs are less persuasive if the central city's policymakers demonstrate that they have exhausted all other options for reducing fiscal stress. Efforts should include very public campaigns to reduce the voter's favorite category of public service cuts: cuts in "waste and inefficiency" in the provision of local services. Efforts should also include retention of only what the majority of residents and businesses views as "desirable" city services. In addition, central city policymakers should consider implementing cost-cutting

---

91. Philadelphia Tax Reform Commission (2003, p. 1); Econsult (2003).

efforts that include privatization and renegotiation of city worker salaries that are high by local standards. Nevertheless, as mentioned earlier, extreme care must be exercised to ensure that downsizing does not result in further fiscal blight and even greater flight from it.

—*Second, pursue regional funding/provision of central city services whose benefits spill over to the suburbs.* I am aware that the implementation of such a proposal is likely to move at a glacial pace because statewide approval is required and there are well-established institutions that will work against it. However, urban planners and academics widely favor this approach, and it should be tried if only to eliminate the criticism that it has not been tried. Unfortunately, politics and existing institutions in most places in the United States strongly disfavor this second-preferred option.

—*Third, attempt to annex jurisdictions receiving the greatest spillover benefits from central city services.* Though it is likely to be as difficult as achieving regionalization, this strategy offers another opportunity to convince central city and suburban residents that other options are preferable to a commuter tax. Moreover, in some areas of the country it may actually have a chance of realization.

—*Fourth, enter into an interjurisdictional taxation agreement.* Like the JEDDs and MUDs described earlier, such agreements are more likely to work between central cities and unincorporated suburban areas. Most attractive is the possibility of achieving a win-win for all jurisdictions involved.

—*Fifth, seek open-ended matching grants for central city services whose benefits clearly spill over to the suburbs.* This effort to draw additional fiscal resources into a central city is more likely to succeed if the matching grants come from the state rather than the federal government. It is appropriate to mention the fifth alternative to state policymakers when negotiating for the sixth, as it is the last alternative offered before requesting a form of commuter taxation.

—*Sixth, request a commuter tax with a full (or partial) tax credit.* A commuter tax would need approval by the state legislature and governor (and in some instances an amendment to the state constitution). The credit could be against another local income tax paid by commuters or against the state income tax if no local income tax is in place in the commuter's place of residence. Exploring this alternative will generate less resistance from commuters than a traditional nonresident local income tax with no credit. If implemented, it will also result in a more equitable distribution of the cost of central city services whose benefits spill over to all suburban or state residents instead of just commuters.

Of course, the likelihood of actually implementing any of these six suggestions depends on the institutional, economic, and political constraints under which central city policymakers operate. In 2010, with one of the most severe recessions in United States history still ongoing and budget cuts, layoffs, and employment furloughs a reality in nearly all central cities, most would say that the option of downsizing local government as much as possible is well under-way. In addition, a slow economy, well-established institutions, and a strong political tradition of local control make interjurisdictional revenue sharing or public service provision nearly impossible—or at the very least difficult—in most areas of the United States. Similarly bleak is the likelihood of central city annexation of suburban areas in the Northeast and much of the Midwest. How-ever, the options of annexation or formation of joint tax districts are not so eas-ily dismissed in the South and West, where communities that surround central cities are less likely to be incorporated. Thus, the two options that remain for most of the country involve asking a higher level of government (such as the state) either to raise revenue from a statewide tax and transfer it disproportion-ately back to central cities or to allow the suburban payers of nonresident local income taxes to receive a full state tax credit for payments made. Given the cur-rent constraints, I believe that these are the most politically feasible options, and they are the ones that I encourage city policymakers wishing to cut their local income tax—or to avoid the institution of a new one—to pursue.

Detroit and Philadelphia both plan for slow cuts in their resident and com-muter income tax rates. The evidence presented here has shown that such cuts are desirable. Tax bases in central cities like these are mobile; therefore it is polit-ically important to recognize the disincentives for business and residents to remain. At the same time, such central cities need to pressure their state legisla-tures to develop offsetting revenues to compensate for the decreased service pro-vision that the tax cuts will require in the short run. In that regard, the 2003 Philadelphia Tax Commission recommended acceleration of the city's existing plans for incremental reductions in its local resident and commuter wage taxes so that both rates were no higher than 3.25 percent in 2014 (down from 3.93 percent on residents and 3.5 percent on commuters in 2009).[92] Further-more, the same commission suggested that a more desirable policy path is for resident and commuter tax rates to fall to 3.0 and 2.5 percent respectively, but only if the city receives an equivalent amount of intergovernmental revenue transfers from the Commonwealth of Pennsylvania. This chapter offers com-pelling evidence that this is the appropriate policy path.

References

ACIR (Advisory Commission on Intergovernmental Relations). 1993. *Significant Features of Fiscal Federalism*, vol. 1. Washington (February).
ACIR. 1970. *The Commuter and the Municipal Income Tax*. Washington (April).

92. Philadelphia Tax Reform Commission (2003, p. 1).

Ashworth, John, and Bruno Heyndels. 1997. "Politicians' Preferences on Local Tax Rates: An Empirical Analysis." *European Journal of Political Economy* 13, no. 3: 479–502.

Baldassare, Mark, and Christopher Hoene. 2004. *Local Budgets and Tax Policies in California and U.S. Cities: Surveys of City Officials.* San Francisco: Public Policy Institute of California.

Bird, Richard. 2000. *Intergovernmental Fiscal Relations in Latin America: Policy Design and Outcomes.* Washington: Inter-American Development Bank.

Bradbury, Katharine L., Anthony Downs, and Kenneth A. Small. 1982. *Urban Decline and the Future of American Cities.* Brookings.

Brunori, David. 2007. *Local Tax Policy,* 2nd ed. Washington: Urban Institute.

Chernick, Howard, and Olesya Tkacheva. 2002. "The Commuter Tax and the Fiscal Cost of Commuters in New York City." *State Tax Notes* 25 (August): 451–56.

City of Baltimore. 2007. *Report of the Blue Ribbon Committee on Taxes and Fees* (www.ci. baltimore.md.us/mayor/blueribbon.php).

Deran, Elizabeth. 1968. "An Overview of the Municipal Income Tax." *Proceedings of the Academy of Political Science* 28, no. 4: 19–26.

Econsult. 2003. *Choosing the Best Mix of Taxes for Philadelphia: An Econometric Analysis of the Impacts of Tax Rates on Tax Bases, Tax Revenue, and the Private Economy.* Philadelphia (www. econsult.com/files/final_tax.pdf).

Edmark, Karin, and Hanna Agren. 2007. "Identifying Strategic Interactions in Swedish Local Income Tax Policies." *Journal of Urban Economics* 63, no. 3: 849–57.

Gessing, Paul. 2003. "Commuter Taxes: Milking Outsiders for All They're Worth." *NTUF Papers.* Alexandria, Va.: National Taxpayers Union (www.ntu.org/main/press_papers.php? PressID=148&org_name=NTUF).

Gold, Steven D. 1977. "Scandinavian Local Income Taxation: Lessons for the United States." *Public Finance Quarterly* 5, no. 4: 471–88.

Goodman, Josh. 2007. "Cities Are Finding Ways to Raise Revenue from Suburbanites without Actually Calling the Levy a Commuter Tax." *Governing Magazine* (April) (www. governing.com/archive/archive/2007/apr/taxes.txt).

Greene, Kenneth V., William B. Neenan, and Claudia D. Scott. 1974. *Fiscal Interactions in a Metropolitan Area.* Lexington, Mass.: Heath.

Grieson, Ronald E. 1980. "Theoretical Analysis and Empirical Measurements of the Effects of the Philadelphia Income Tax." *Journal of Urban Economics* 8, no 1: 123–37.

Haughwout, Andrew F., and Robert P. Inman. 2001. "Fiscal Policies in Open Cities with Firms and Households." *Regional Science and Urban Economics* 31: 147–80.

———. 2004. "How Should Suburbs Help Their Central Cities?" Federal Reserve Bank of New York Staff Report 186.

Haughwout, Andrew, and others. 2004. "Local Revenue Hills: Evidence from Four U.S. Cities." *Review of Economics and Statistics* 86, no. 2: 570–85.

Hawkins, Brett W., and Douglas M. Ihrke. 1999. "Research Note: Reexamining the Suburban Exploitation Thesis in American Metropolitan Areas." *Publius* 29, no. 3: 109–21.

Henchman, Joseph. 2008. *County and City Income Taxes Clustered in States with Poor Tax Climates.* Washington: Tax Foundation (www.taxfoundation.org/files/ff133.pdf).

Hettler, Paul L. 2004. "Regional Impact of Commuter Wage Taxes." *Atlantic Economic Journal* 32, no. 3: 191–200.

Inman, Robert P. 2003. "Should Philadelphia's Suburbs Help Their Central City." *Business Review* 25, Q2: 24–36.

————. 2006. "Financing Cities." In *A Companion to Urban Economics*, edited by Richard Arnott and Daniel P. McMillen, pp. 311–31. Malden, Mass.: Blackwell.

IssuesPA. 2003. *The Philadelphia City Wage Tax: A 'Special Case" Income Tax.* Philadelphia: Pennsylvania Economy League (www.issuespa.net/articles/4291).

Keating, Raymond J. 2004. "Budget Reforms to Solve New York City's High-Tax Crisis." *Policy Analysis* 522: 1–18.

Kitchen, Harry. 2004. *Financing City Services: A Prescription for the Future.* Halifax, Nova Scotia, Canada: Atlantic Institute for Market Studies.

Kitchen, Harry, and Enid Slack. 2003. "Special Study: New Finance Options for Municipal Governments." *Canadian Tax Journal* 51, no. 6: 2215–75.

Ladd, Helen, and John Yinger. 1991. *America's Ailing Cities: Fiscal Health and the Design of Urban Policy*, rev. ed. Johns Hopkins University Press.

Mark, Stephen T., Therese J. McGuire, and Leslie E. Papke. 2000. "The Influence of Taxes on Employment and Population Growth: Evidence from the Washington, D.C., Metropolitan Area." *National Tax Journal* 53, no. 1: 105–24.

McMahon, E. J., and Fred Siegel. 2005. "Gotham's Fiscal Crisis; Lessons Unlearned." *Public Interest* 158: 96–110.

Mieszkowski, Peter, and Edwin S. Mills. 1993. "The Causes of Metropolitan Suburbanization." *Journal of Economic Perspectives* 7, no. 3: 135–47.

Nechyba, Thomas J. 1997. "Local Property and State Income Taxes: The Role of Interjurisdictional Competition and Collusion." *Journal of Political Economy* 105, no. 2: 351–84.

O'Cleireacain, Carol, and Alice M. Rivlin. 2002. *A Sound Fiscal Footing for the Nation's Capital: A Federal Responsibility.* Brookings.

Philadelphia Tax Reform Commission. 2003. *Final Report.* Philadelphia (www.philadelphia taxreform.org).

Rusk, David. 2005. *Cities without Suburbs*, 2nd ed. Johns Hopkins University Press.

Sasaki, Komei. 1991. "Interjurisdictional Commuting and Local Public Goods." *Annals of Regional Science* 25, no. 4: 271–85.

Schmidheiny, Kurt. 2006. "Income Segregation and Local Progressive Taxation." *Journal of Public Economics* 90, no. 3: 429–58.

Shields, Martin, and David Shideler. 2003. "Do Commuters Free-Ride? Estimating the Impacts of Jurisdictional Commuting on Local Public Goods Expenditures." *Journal of Regional Analysis and Policy* 33, no. 1: 27–42.

Sigafoos, Robert A. 1955. *The Municipal Income Tax: Its History and Problems.* Chicago: Public Administration Service.

Smith, R. Stafford. 1972. *Local Income Taxes: Economic Effects and Equity.* Institute of Governmental Studies, University of California, Berkeley.

Spry, John Arthur. 2005. "The Effects of Fiscal Competition on Local Property and Income Tax Reliance." *Topics in Economic Analysis and Policy* 5, no. 1: 1–19.

Stull, William J. 1987. "The Effect of Local Taxes on Residential Real Estate Values in the Philadelphia S.M.S.A." In *Local Fiscal Issues in the Philadelphia Metropolitan Area,* edited by Thomas F. Luce and Anita A. Summers, pp. 66–75. University of Pennsylvania Press.

Stull, William J., and Judith C. Stull. 1991. "Capitalization of Local Income Taxes." *Journal of Urban Economics* 29: 182–90.

Tax Policy Center. 2009. *State and Local Data Query System.* Washington: Urban Institute and Brookings.

U.S. Census Bureau. 2002. *Demographic Trends in the 20th Century.* Washington (www.census.gov/prod/2002pubs/censr-4.pdf).

U.S. Census Bureau. 2009. *State and Local Government Finances: 2005–06.* Washington (www.census.gov/govs/www/estimate06.html).

Vincent, Phillip E. 1975. "Book Review of *Fiscal Interactions in a Metropolitan Area.*" *Journal of Economic Literature* 13, no. 2: 552–54.

Von Ins, Tracy. 2001. "Local Income Taxes: A Tale of Four Cities." *Nation's Cities Weekly,* August 13.

Wassmer, Robert W. 2008. "Causes of Urban Sprawl in the United States: Auto Reliance as Compared to Natural Evolution, Flight from Blight, and Local Revenue Choices." *Journal of Policy Analysis and Management* 27, no. 3: 536–55.

Ziegler, Joseph A., and Carl L. Dyer. 1975. "Are Nonresidents Contributing Their Share to Core City Revenues? A Comment." *Land Economics* 51, no: 1: 98–100.

5

Getting into the Game:
Is the Gamble on Sports as a Stimulus
for Urban Economic Development a Good Bet?

ROBERT A. BAADE

Contemporary discussions of commercial sports often focus on financial issues. The extraordinary salaries commanded by the current generation of athletes, those of the free-agency era, have resulted from substantial increases in team and event revenues. The growth of those revenues emanates in large part from the new generation of playing facilities, built largely through taxpayer subsidies. Advocates of such subsidies have defended them on the grounds that they are a winning economic strategy not only for the teams and players but for host cities as well. Enhancing the financial privilege of owners, managers, and players may be tolerable to the host communities if it can be demonstrated that they too benefit economically from the subsidies provided. Communities, like fans, are more likely to accept the excesses of those who provide sports entertainment if their interests also are served. Is there a dovetailing of the economic interests of those who provide sports entertainment and the neighborhoods, metropolitan areas, and regions that host teams?

This chapter evaluates the impact that teams, events, and sports facilities have had on city and metropolitan economic development, with the intent of addressing the counterfactual: how would host city economies appear in the absence of professional sports subsidies?

Following this introduction, the second section of the chapter discusses the history of sports facility construction, including the costs involved for communities to get into the commercial sports game. The pattern of costs incurred to construct stadiums, secure the rights to host sports mega-events, and retain teams in the face of the escalating financial demands that they impose are analyzed, and the benefits derived from accommodating teams or events are then discussed to facilitate a cost-benefit analysis.

The third section discusses the techniques used by advocates of subsidies for commercial sports to justify their use. The economic promises used to rationalize subsidies require projections of their future economic benefits, also known as ex ante analyses, to support those promises. Some discussion is devoted to the problems of forward-looking analysis as it relates to the economic impact of commercial sports subsidies.

The fourth section discusses reasons for careful scrutiny of sports boosters' claims that subsidies represent a win not only for the team but also for the community. There can be little question that subsidies enhance the income and wealth of the producers of professional sports, team owners, and players. That increase in financial privilege for those who are already wealthy is difficult to defend unless it can be demonstrated that the increase is simply part of an increase in output and income that has lifted the entire economy, not just a subset of it.[1]

The fifth section compares the differences among outcomes of the prospective and retrospective analyses discussed in the third and fourth sections. The sixth section discusses how publicly financed sports subsidies should be conceptualized, particularly as they relate to quality of life issues and/or indirect economic benefits. The final section provides conclusions and policy implications.

Sport Subsidies: A Historical Perspective

In testimony before the Senate Judiciary Committee on November 29, 1995, Mayor Bob Lanier of Houston, Texas, made the following observations:

> The real demand is for luxury boxes, not more seats. So the average working person is asked to put a tax on their home or pay sales or some other consumer tax to build luxury boxes in which they cannot afford to sit. Frequently, the new stadium is smaller. The working person is asked to be satisfied with the "sense of pride" they get from this arrangement, which will last until another team bids more for their players, or until another city bids for the team.[2]

Mayor Lanier's lament compels further analysis of the subsidy issue. How extensive is the phenomenon that he describes? Is there more to the story?

---

1. Economists refer to a change that makes at least one person or group better off without making any other person or group worse off as a Pareto improvement.

2. Bob Lanier, *Professional Sports Franchise Relocation: Antitrust Implications: Hearing before the House Committee on the Judiciary*, 104 Cong. 2 sess., February 6, 1996, p. 36.

Namely, do the subsidies that taxpayers finance generate compensating benefits or income that justifies the largesse that the mayor describes? Before evaluating the benefits that may be induced by subsidies for commercial sports, the extent of such subsidies and the explanations for them need to be identified. An assessment of the efficacy of expenditures on infrastructure for commercial sports requires an analysis not only of the benefits but also of the costs that host communities incur. Greater expenditure on sports facilities necessarily implies smaller expenditures on other things that could induce urban economic development, the economist's concept of opportunity cost. The tables, figures, and narrative that follow provide information that indicates that the commercial sports industry, either by accident or by design, has positioned itself to wring substantial and arguably growing financial accommodation from host communities. Cities and metropolitan areas that expect to induce economic development through commercial sports should soberly appraise the costs involved to "get in the game."

The narrative that follows provides information on the number of facilities constructed, the costs incurred, and the extent of the public subsidies for major league sports and sports mega-events as represented by the Summer Olympic Games. Additional information is provided on facility costs for minor league baseball because a significant number of smaller cities have sought to boost their economies by attracting and accommodating minor league baseball. The financial pressures that exist when commercial sports are accommodated also are discussed. Those communities contemplating a sports growth strategy have to be mindful of likely future developments in relation to the costs that they can expect to incur.

Relocation of franchises, new stadium construction, and subsidies for sports mega-events have occurred in response to circumstances beyond the commercial sports sector. Changes in general economic and political conditions have induced the movement of teams and the construction of facilities. Upheavals in the commercial sports sector trace larger tremors in the American economic landscape. Population and economic activity have spread west and south, and technological changes have allowed for the expansion of fan bases and the construction of larger stadiums. Metropolises have sprawled for a variety of reasons and the movement of people to the suburbs has encouraged the development of sports facilities closer to fans. The character of stadiums has mirrored the changing character of spectators. Growing affluence and changes in the distribution of income and wealth have inspired alterations in stadium design and function. The owners of professional sports teams reacted to social and technological change slowly in many instances, but as the commercial promise of sports has become more apparent, the bottom-line implications have dominated decisionmaking more.

Figure 5-1. *Stadiums Built or Proposed*

Number of stadiums

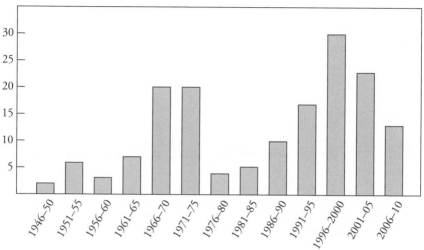

Sources: Data before the 1990s: Baade (1999). Data after the 1990s are author's estimates based on information in "Stadiums of National Football League" (www.stadiumsofnfl.com [March 10, 2009]); "Present National Football League Stadiums," "Present National Basketball Association Arenas," and "Present National Hockey League Arenas" (www.ballparks.com [March 10, 2009]); "Ballparks of Baseball" (www.ballparksofbaseball.com/ [March 10, 2009]); and "Summary of Total Cost and Public Subsidy for NFL Stadiums Constructed or Significantly Renovated since 1990," "Summary of Total Cost and Public Subsidy for MLB Stadiums Constructed or Significantly Renovated since 1990," "Summary of Total Cost and Public Subsidy for NBA Arenas Constructed or Significantly Renovated since 1990," and "Summary of Total Cost and Public Subsidy for NHL Arenas Constructed or Significantly Renovated since 1990" (www.leagueoffans.org/[April 6, 2009]).

During the last century, sports facility construction has followed a clear pattern. Except for Yankee Stadium in New York and Soldier Field in Chicago, virtually no new stadiums were constructed between World War I and 1946, a time dominated by the Great Depression and World War II. As the evidence in figure 5-1 indicates, the pace of stadium construction accelerated modestly in the 1950s until the mid-1960s. Growing prosperity and technological development enabled the construction of steel-and-concrete playing facilities during the ten years from 1965 through 1975. New stadium construction projects retreated to the levels of the 1950s and early 1960s between 1975 and 1985. However, that lull ended in 1986, and facility construction surged beginning in the early 1990s. The accelerated pace continued through 2000, abating only when much of the sports infrastructure had been replaced.

Not only has there been an identifiable pattern regarding the number of facilities constructed, but the evidence indicates some discernible regularities as it

Figure 5-2. *Real Cost of Stadiums*

Millions of 2007 dollars

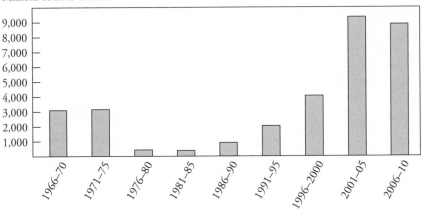

Source: See source note for figure 5-1.

relates to stadium construction costs. Figure 5-2 provides information on stadium construction costs, in 2007 dollars. How have stadiums been financed over time? Figure 5-3 records data on the proportion of the expense shouldered by taxpayers.

Although the evidence appears to indicate a decrease in public subsidies from 1980 to the present, one should not conclude that this indicates that the financial demands imposed on the taxpaying public have abated. The full measure of the burden shouldered by taxpayers requires consideration of not only the amount of money contributed by the private and public sectors for the various projects but also the sharing of revenues from new stadium operations compared with sharing of revenues from the replaced facilities. The increased financial contributions from teams for the construction of facilities have resulted in the receipt of a smaller share of stadium revenues by host cities to an extent that has compelled at least one host government to take legal action. Hamilton County, Ohio, sued the National Football League (NFL), claiming that the league and the Cincinnati Bengals had violated federal antitrust laws in obtaining a heavily subsidized lease arrangement from Hamilton County and its taxpayers.[3] Combining the upfront costs of financing stadium construction with reduced stadium revenues reveals that host communities have incurred a far more signifi-

---

3. *Hamilton County Board of Commissioners* v. *National Football League*, 491 F.3d 310 (6th Cir. 2007).

Figure 5-3. *Percentage of Cost of Stadiums Financed by the Public*

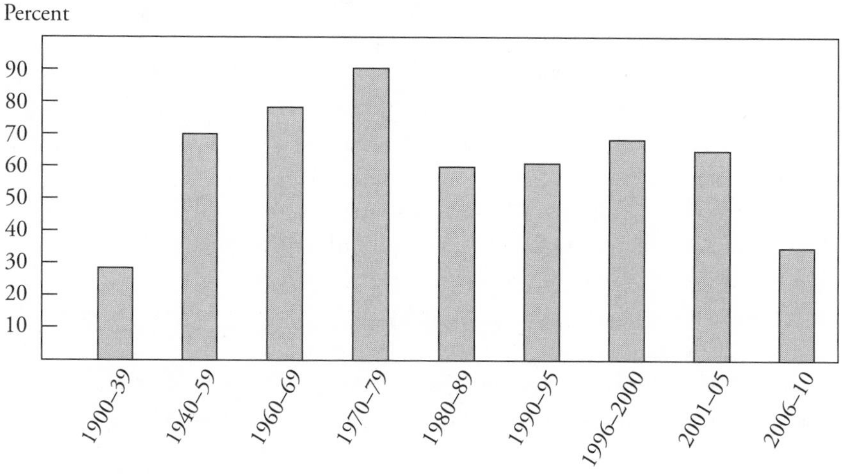

Percent

Source: See source note for figure 5-1.

cant cost in constructing the new generation of stadiums than is suggested by statistics detailing the mix of public and private funds for construction. Furthermore, teams generally earmark funds generated by the new stadium, such as stadium naming rights or a portion of club seat revenues, to fund their portion of stadium construction costs. Therefore, the private risk assumed in the construction of the new facility is not equivalent to that ordinarily associated with entrepreneurial activity.

The evidence provided in figures 5-1 through 5-3 indicates that the pace of stadium construction accelerated in the 1986 through 1990 period and abated only after much of the infrastructure for professional sports had been replaced; that the cost of stadium construction has increased (billion-dollar stadiums were constructed in New York and Dallas in 2009); and that the most of the cost continues to be borne by the public sector through direct subsidization during the construction phase of the project and/or reduced public appropriation of stadium operating revenues.

These patterns can be explained further. In particular, the year 1987 may well represent a stadium construction watershed. After multiple attempts, Joe Robbie, the owner of the NFL Miami Dolphins at the time, had been unable to secure public funding from the city of Miami for the renovation of the Orange Bowl. Robbie decided to build a stadium with private funds by employing a strategy that involved parlaying the upfront money that he received from the sale or lease of luxury seating and personal seat licenses (PSLs) into the financing that he needed to construct the stadium.[4] Professional sports teams are renowned for mimicking successful strategies both on and off the field, and other teams quickly recognized that Robbie had provided a blueprint for increasing revenues. Robbie's financial creativity significantly enhanced revenues generated by stadiums. However, this new financing model ultimately did not provide a substitute for public funding; rather, it intensified competition among cities to retain or attract teams.

Subventions for commercial sports take many forms, and even if teams and leagues are not able to convince host communities to provide funds directly, the public sector can provide financial support in other ways. Constructing infrastructure such as better roads and public transportation to enhance access to the stadium; providing land at below-market value; and offering tax increment financing, which has been used as a justification for eliminating taxes, are but a few of the ways in which municipal, county, and state governments support commercial sports. Even the federal government has been involved in subsidizing sports, through the use of tax-free municipal bonds. Tax-exempt bonds continue to be used to fund the construction of sports facilities despite a number of legislative attempts to eliminate or limit them.[5] It is safe to say that every major league sports facility project has received some public support in some form.

What factors explain the flow of funds from the public to the commercial sports industry? Conditions that influence demand for commercial sports entertainment have permitted the construction of a new generation of stadiums that cater to an elite audience. The distribution of wealth and income became more skewed in the 1980s, and that trend continued into the early 2000s. The top 20 percent of Americans commanded 81.3, 83.5, 83.9, and 84.7 percent of the wealth in 1983, 1989, 1995, and 2004, respectively. The number of households with net worth of more than a million dollars in the United States grew from 2.41 million in 1983 to 6.47 million households in 2004.[6]

Developments and conditions within the commercial sports sector arguably provide perhaps even more compelling reasons for explaining the acceleration in stadium construction. Adding to Robbie's identification and mining of new revenue sources are powerful league and team incentives for pursuing a more aggressive strategy for wringing financial concessions from host governments. Consider first the pressures on leagues that translate into increased financial demands on communities. Leagues have to be concerned with competitive, on-the-field par-

---

4. For a discussion of the origins of Joe Robbie Stadium, also known as Dolphin Stadium, including the financing of the structure, see "Sun Life Stadium" (www.ballparks.com/baseball/national/propla.htm [July 22, 2010]).

5. For an extensive discussion of the use of tax-exempt bonds see Fox (2005).

6. Wolff (2007, p. 14, table 3).

ity. Fan interest across a league and collective league revenues depend vitally on the uncertainty of the outcome of any contest. If a game's outcome is a fait accompli because the wealthier teams can "buy" the best players and thereby win a disproportionate number of games by lopsided scores, fan interest will likely wane, particularly in those cities that have difficulty fielding a competitive team.

The evidence would appear to support that observation. Attendance at games, television and radio interest, and team revenues, in short, depend on team success.[7] Leagues have no responsibility greater than ensuring on-the-field competitiveness. Revenue sharing arguably represents the most important means through which leagues foster competitive play. Revenues from the new generation of stadiums, in turn, constitute an increasingly important source of revenue. The pressure that leagues exert on host communities to either replace or renovate existing facilities provides strikingly clear testimony of the financial realities of commercial sports. Leagues cannot generate support for more comprehensive revenue sharing programs if each team does not do its part to contribute as much as possible to shared or pooled revenues that are distributed among the teams that make up a league.

Free agency has only served to exacerbate the pressures that exist on leagues to ensure playing parity. The clubs that generate the most revenue not subject to league pooling and sharing (*local* or *retained revenues* in the vernacular) dominate the standings. The problem has become so acute in Major League Baseball (MLB) that clubs are identified as large- or small-market (a euphemism for rich and poor teams) rather than as a member of a particular division. The league can enlist the support of the clubs that are financially successful for more comprehensive revenue sharing only if there is a clear financial quid pro quo for the successful teams. Large-market clubs appear to recognize the financial potential for their own bottom lines of new stadium construction for all member teams.

The individual teams exert pressure on their host cities for subventions for the same reasons. When revenues generated within the stadium are pooled and distributed among all clubs, the percent of the revenue going to visiting teams represents a "tax" on the home team.[8] The home team can avoid the tax by diverting revenues from those that are pooled to those that are "tax-exempt." The trend toward a greater emphasis on luxury seating and other luxury amenities reflects the current conventions relating to revenue sharing.[9] A reality of

7. See, for example, Baade and Tiehan (1990).

8. In the case of the NFL, the percent split between the home and the visiting team is 60-40 for revenues that the teams have agreed to share. Much of the revenue generated through the sale of luxury seating, other luxury amenities, and stadium naming rights is not subject to pooling.

9. Jerry Jones, the owner of the Dallas Cowboys, removed seats that were available for sale to the general public and replaced them with luxury boxes in the old Cowboys Stadium.

construction is that it is typically more lucrative and cost effective to include luxury seats in a new stadium or arena than it is to retrofit an old stadium to accommodate them.[10]

Teams understand, as do the leagues, that if they want to put "fannies in the seats," they need to field a competitive team. A new stadium does not ensure that they will draw more fans; only winning can. Three of the seven teams with the lowest attendance in MLB (the Pittsburgh Pirates, Detroit Tigers, and Milwaukee Brewers) played in stadiums that were three years old or less in 2003.[11] All three teams had losing records. A new stadium, despite the novelty, cannot encourage above-average attendance for long, but the revenues generated by the stadium provide funds that can be used to secure the players necessary to allow the team to compete.

The federal government has reacted to the pressure exerted on host cities to construct new facilities by changing the tax laws in a way that it hoped would discourage new stadium construction with public funds. The Tax Reform Act of 1986 and subsequent legislation made it more difficult to use tax-exempt bonds.[12] The higher standards imposed for the use of tax-exempt bonds to fund sports facility construction have had at least two consequences. First, the NFL had to find a way to compensate for the increased debt-service costs on new stadium construction, and it did so through low-interest loans to teams through its G-3 program.[13] The NFL is a tax-exempt entity, and it may well have been that the league used its tax-exempt status to help fund those loans. That financial maneuver may well have preserved tax-exempt financing of stadiums to some degree, but the NFL's G-3 program was depleted when it provided low-cost loans for the funding of renovations for the Kansas City Chiefs' stadium, Arrowhead ($42.5 million), and for the new stadium to be shared by the New York Giants and Jets, the Meadowlands ($300 million).[14] It could be that making it more difficult to use tax-exempt bonds for stadium construction intensified the financial demands teams imposed on host cities. The money for new stadium construction or renovation likely has been provided by local governments in some form, including the aforementioned more generous leases for new facilities.

10. The construction of the United Center, home of the National Basketball Association's Chicago Bulls, for example, came about because it was far more lucrative to build a new arena than to fit luxury seating into Chicago Stadium.

11. "MLB Attendance Report: 2003," ESPN (www.proxy.espn.go.com/mlb/attendance?sort=home_avg&year=2003&seasonType=2).

12. Fox (2005).

13. G-3 refers to the G-3 Resolution, adopted by the NFL in March 1999. The resolution authorized the NFL to advance up to 50 percent of the total private financing for the construction of the stadium, up to $150 million dollars.

14. For a discussion and some analysis of the NFL's G-3 program, see Baade and Matheson (2007).

Similar pressures to construct new facilities exist at the minor league level—an assertion best exemplified by minor league baseball, which, of the four major league sports, has the most extensive and intimate agreement with its major league counterpart. Professional baseball exhibits some fiscal autonomy at its various levels, but baseball's structure has a clear hierarchical character. MLB's financial support of minor league baseball through its player development contract (PDC) has been vital in sustaining baseball's chain of command.[15] MLB sought to moderate its financial support for the minor leagues by requiring a significant upgrade in minor league stadiums through attachment 58 of the 1990 Professional Baseball Agreement.[16] Attachment 58, which refers to the attachment to the *Official Professional Rules Book* entitled "Minor League Facility Standards and Compliance Inspection Procedures," imposed significant burdens on minor league host cities as teams began to request subsidies to comply with major league demands. Eighty-three teams at the AAA, AA, and A levels built new stadiums or renovated old ballparks after 1990; in all probability, many of those projects were undertaken to comply with the demands imposed by attachment 58.[17]

Of course, MLB benefited from attachment 58, or it never would have promulgated it. MLB benefits in two ways. First, increased revenues for minor league clubs potentially imply a reduction in MLB financial succor for minor league teams. Second, higher ticket prices, which generally occur when new stadiums become operational, make minor league baseball a less appealing substitute for major league baseball, all else equal.

The costs involved in hosting sports mega-events follow a similar pattern. They compel public subventions, and the subsidies are rationalized on the grounds that host cities experience substantial economic gains if they are fortunate enough to secure such an event.

The effects of subsidies to finance the construction of infrastructure for commercial sports provide substantial benefit for those who use the facilities. Not only are debt-service costs avoided, but revenues are enhanced, with a predictable

15. Although MLB owners arguably have the final voice on a variety of issues, it is worthwhile to identify and briefly discuss professional baseball's organizational structure. The National Association of Professional Baseball Leagues (NAPBL) governs the minor leagues. The relationship between MLB and NAPBL is defined by the Professional Baseball Agreement. Major league teams supply players to their NAPBL affiliates. The specific financial arrangements between a major league club and its affiliates is established by a player development contract (PDC). These contracts are for short periods of time, usually two years, and at expiration, the affiliates and their parents are free to negotiate a new PDC or change their affiliation (Adelson 1995).

16. Attachment 58 can be found in National Association of Professional Baseball Leagues, "Professional Baseball Agreement" (St. Petersburg, Fla., 1996), pp. 212–30.

17. Author's estimates based on information in www.ballparksofbaseball.com/, which involved counting the stadiums listed in *Single A Ball Parks, Double A Ball Parks, and Triple A Ball Parks.*

Table 5-1. *Proportion of Public and Private Sector Financing of New Facilities and Impact of New Facilities on Revenue and Income, by League*

League	Average total cost ($ millions)[a]	Contribution (percent) Public	Contribution (percent) Private	Incremental revenue ($ millions)[b]	Incremental income ($ millions)[c]
Major League Baseball	269	77	23	19.1	12.7
National Basketball Association (NBA)	169	31	69	17.4	5.4
National Football League	257	74	26	18.8	12
National Hockey League (NHL)	148	42	58	15.7	7.7
Shared NBA and NHL facilities	191	11	89	20.3	11.6

Source: See table entitled "MLB Team Valuations" in Michael K. Ozanian with Cecily J. Fluke, "Inside Pitch," April 28, 2003, Forbes.com (www.forbes.com/forbes/2003/0428/064.html).

a. Figures are for facilities opened since 1990.

b. Per-team annual average generated from new facilities, net of operating expenses. Excludes naming rights and personal seat licenses.

c. Annual incremental revenue less debt service on the facility.

impact on franchise values where applicable. Table 5-1 provides information on the impact that new facilities have had on team revenues and operating income for MLB, the National Basketball Association (NBA), the NFL, and the National Hockey League.

Few would dispute that the suppliers of sports entertainment, owners and players, are financially privileged. Taxpayers often are people of modest means, and some have no interest in commercial sports. Nonetheless, subsidies generally induce a transfer of income from taxpayers to owners and players. The inequity of that transfer is further exacerbated by the fact that subsidies have enabled the construction of a new generation of facilities that cater to the elite spectator. Therefore, subsidies for this type of facility arguably subsidize sports spectating for society's well-heeled members, often at the expense of those who cannot afford to attend games at the new structure.

Public sector subsidies clearly enrich the owners and players of professional sports franchises, and it is worthwhile to take a closer look at how sports facilities have affected their fortunes. The following analysis borrows heavily from an article published in the *Oxford Review of Economic Policy* in 2003.[18] Consider first the implications for owners. The information in table 5-1, although identified for the previous decade, provides a metric for assessing the financial benefit

18. Baade (2003).

that owners have derived from new facilities up to the present. The returns on private investment in new structures were 20.5, 4.6, 18.0, 9.0, and 6.8 percent for MLB, NBA, NFL, NHL, and shared NBA/NHL facilities respectively. It is no surprise then that of the thirty-one teams in the NFL, fourteen changed ownership over the period from 1991 through 2001.[19] (Houston is not included since there has been no change in ownership since the team's relatively recent entry into the league.)

That extraordinary incidence of change in ownership is remarkable in the NFL, a league that is renowned for its stability, and it correlates with the increase in franchise values, which resulted from the construction of new facilities. Data indicate that nineteen of thirty-one teams in the NFL experienced double-digit increases in their franchise valuations in 2002, for example.[20] The stadium-induced increase in teams' financial fortunes, in turn, encourages profit taking. It is reasonable to expect that at some point, a percentage of owners will sell their franchises to realize the gains that have accrued from significant increases in franchise values.

Baseball and football stadiums are the most expensive to build and maintain of all the professional sports facilities. That reality, along with the popularity of football and baseball, accounts for the larger subsidies to teams in these sports in both a relative and absolute sense, as indicated in table 5-1. As noted previously, although the public share of construction costs has decreased during the past decade, that reduction has come at another cost—more generous leases for teams. Until the subsidies are analyzed in tandem with the lease agreements, it cannot be concluded that the taxpayers' burden in supporting commercial sports has been moderated. However, the fact that new stadiums have been built at an unprecedented rate provides prima facie evidence that teams are financially better off with the current financial arrangements, which are characteristic of the new stadiums, than they were with the old stadium partnerships.

Assessing the financial responsibilities assumed by cities seeking a commercial sports presence requires consideration of more than the current financial outlay. It also necessitates an assessment of future costs. Teams have exhibited substantial risk aversion in the construction of new facilities, and that same aversion carries over to the operation and maintenance of the structures, including their revenue-generating potential. It bears noting once again that the model used here assumes that the financial dynamic descriptive of the professional sports industry implies that the most lucrative stadium design and lease become the league standard. Any team that does not have a state-of-the-art facility or a

---

19. Kurt Badenhausen and others, "Inside the Huddle: Which National Football League Teams Have the Money to Compete—and Which Ones Do Not," *Forbes*, September 2002.

20. Michael K. Ozanian and Cecily J. Fluke, "Inside Pitch," *Forbes*, April 28, 2003.

favorable lease will find itself at a financial disadvantage, which in turn will impair its ability to compete on the field.[21]

Those interested in how the new generation of stadiums has influenced the financial fortunes of the NFL can find ample and compelling evidence in the testimony and documents revealed during the 2001 Oakland Raiders lawsuit against the NFL. The legal discovery process provided an unprecedented glimpse into team financial statements, which indicated that average team operating profit increased to $11.6 million in 1999 from $6.9 million in 1994, an increase of 68 percent.[22] The evidence indicated that a majority of the increased profitability was attributable to an increase in local revenues (those not pooled to be redistributed among teams). Local revenues increased by 80 percent between 1994 and 1999.

The new generation of sports facilities has also clearly served the interests of players. Average MLB player salaries increased from $438,729 in 1988, the year after Joe Robbie Stadium (now Land Shark Stadium) was built, to $3,131,041 in 2008, a staggering increase of 714 percent. Salaries for NFL players over the 1998–2008 period increased from $307,000 to $1,886,734, or 615 percent.[23] The effect that the new playing facilities have had on player salaries can be brought into sharper focus by observing team payrolls for MLB teams that built stadiums during the 1991–2001period (see table 5-2). Payrolls have been identified for the two years $(t - 2)$ and one year $(t - 1)$ before the stadium was constructed, for one year $(t + 1)$ and two years $(t + 2)$ after it was constructed, and for the year in which the stadium began operation (t).

Table 5-2 indicates that, with few exceptions, team payrolls increase rather substantially after a new stadium is built. The exceptions—Detroit, Milwaukee, and Pittsburgh (shown in bold)—have been discussed previously. It is important to note that Milwaukee and Detroit recently increased their spending on players substantially, and their improved play resulted in improved attendance. The Milwaukee Brewers, for example, increased their payroll to $80.9 million in 2008 from $67.3 million in 2007, and attendance increased from an average of 2,869,144 in 2007 to 3,068,458 in 2008. Brewer attendance eclipsed the 3 million mark again in 2009, a notable achievement for a small-market club.

Fans have also been affected by new stadiums, but in ways that are both good and bad. The new generation of stadiums comes complete with more plentiful and functional restrooms, concourses, and concession stands. Ticket prices,

21. Baade (2003).

22. Alan Abrahamson and Sam Farmer, "NFL Ledgers," *Los Angles Times*, May 13, 2001, p. 7.

23. *USA Today*, "Salaries Databases." For Major League Baseball, see http://content.usatoday.com/sports/baseball/salaries/default.aspx; for the National Football League, see http://content.usatoday.com/sports/football/nfl/salaries/default.aspx?Loc=Vanity.

Table 5-2. *MLB Payrolls before and after New Stadiums Built, 1991–2001*[a]
Millions of dollars

Team (year new stadium opened = t)	Team payroll for year t	Total payroll t − 2	Total payroll t − 1	Total payroll t + 1	Total payroll t + 2
Arizona (1998)	29.16	n.a.	n.a.	70.37 (241)	77.88 (267)
Atlanta (1997)	50.49	45.2 (90)	47.93 (95)	59.54 (118)	75.07 (149)
Baltimore (1992)	20.99	10.04 (48)	14.63 (70)	26.92 (128)	37.67 (179)
Chicago White Sox (1991)	16.83	7.60 (45)	9.49 (56)	28.41 (169)	34.60 (206)
Cleveland (1994)	28.49	8.24 (29)	15.72 (55)	35.19 (124)	45.32 (159)
Colorado (1995)	31.15	8.83 (28)	22.98 (74)	34.92 (112)	42.87 (138)
Detroit (2000)	61.74	22.63 (37)	34.96 (57)	**49.36 (80)**	**55.05 (89)**
Houston (2000)	52.36	40.63 (78)	55.29 (106)	60.39 (115)	63.45 (121)
Milwaukee (2001)	45.10	42.93 (95)	35.78 (79)	50.29 (112)	**40.63 (90)**
Pittsburgh (2001)	57.76	24.22 (42)	29.56 (51)	**42.32 (73)**	**54.81 (95)**
San Francisco (2000)	53.54	40.32 (75)	46.06 (86)	63.28 (118)	78.30 (146)
Seattle (1999)	44.37	39.67 (89)	52.03 (117)	59.22 (133)	74.72 (168)
Texas (1994)	32.42	29.74 (92)	35.64 (110)	**32.37 (100)**	35.86 (111)
Average		**(57)**	**(73)**	**(125)**	**(147)**

Source: "USA Today Salaries Database" (www.usatoday.com/sports/baseball/salaries/default.aspx).

a. In parenthesis, percent of payroll for year *t*, the time at which stadium construction was completed, of the payrolls for other years. Boldface figures are less than 100 percent, meaning that team payrolls actually fell in certain instances after the new stadium became functional.

however, have not decreased, as some boosters for new stadium subsidies suggested that they might. Increases in ticket prices, parking fees, and concessions as well as PSLs made a day at the ballpark a more expensive proposition in a real sense from 1991 through 2001, a period that has been studied because it exhibits the greatest increase in new stadium construction. Information on the fan cost index (FCI) indicates that the cost of spectating rose sharply from 1991 through 2001. MLB is generally considered the most moderately priced of the four major professional sports leagues operating in the United States, and on average, the FCI for MLB rose from $77.79 to $144.98 between 1991 and 2001, an increase of 86 percent.[24] By contrast, the consumer price index (CPI) for the same period rose only 30 percent, or approximately one-third as much as the MLB FCI for what is considered the best bargain in professional sports in the United States.

The correlation between the FCI and stadium construction can be brought into sharper focus by compiling information on the FCI and stadiums built during the 1991–2001 period (see table 5–3). The same conventions were used in table 5-3 and table 5-2 to relate construction and ticket prices—that is to say, ticket prices have been assembled for one and two years before and after a stadium was constructed.

Table 5-3 suggests that new stadiums have moderated the ticket price increases overall. It should be noted, however, that Detroit, Milwaukee, Pittsburgh, and Texas all had attendance problems despite playing in new ballparks. A portion of the moderated ticket price increase, therefore, may be attributable to teams that attempted to entice fans to the ballpark by reducing the price of their product.[25]

The evidence gathered to this point indicates the extent to which the explicit costs of getting and staying in the game pose significant financial challenges for host cities, particularly those whose economies are small relative to those of the cities with which they compete. A community assessing the wisdom of an investment in sports as an economic development tool must also assess risk. The current global recession and the financial meltdown in the United States demonstrate the economic vulnerability of the sports industry. Systemic excesses in professional sports trace the fault line of excesses that have riddled and devastated economies across the world currently. Once owners saw how new stadiums and arenas could lead to an increase in operating incomes and a spike in franchise values, teams argued that they could not compete either financially or on the playing field without a new facility. Leagues understood that parity required equal dispersion of playing talent and that that could be accomplished in the free-agent era only through financial parity. New York and Green Bay, Wisconsin, are inherently unequal economically, and two such disparate economies can compete in the same football league only if New York agrees to share some of its inherent financial advantage with Green Bay.

While new stadiums have provided greater revenues for all cities, they also have exposed new financial inequities and have required the wealthier cities

---

24. Team Marketing Report, "Team Marketing Report," 1992 and 2002 (www.teammarketing.com).
25. Baade (2003, p. 592).

Table 5-3. *Ticket Prices before and after New Stadiums Built, 1991–2001*[a]
Dollars

Team (year new stadium opened = t)	Ticket prices for year t	Ticket prices t − 2	Ticket prices t − 1	Ticket prices t + 1	Ticket prices t + 2
Atlanta (1997)	15.54	12.00 (77)	13.06 (84)	17.78 (114)	19.21 (124)
Baltimore (1992)	9.65	n.a.	**10.30 (107)**	11.12 (115)	11.12 (115)
Chicago White Sox (1991)	10.28	n.a.	n.a.	11.70 (114)	11.70 (114)
Cleveland (1994)	12.06	7.70 (64)	8.70 (72)	12.06 (100)	14.52 (120)
Colorado (1995)	10.61	7.91 (75)	7.90 (74)	10.61 (100)	11.38 (107)
Detroit (2000)	24.83	10.40 (42)	12.23 (49)	**23.90 (96)**	**20.44 (82)**
Houston (2000)	20.01	11.88 (59)	13.30 (66)	20.03 (100)	**18.87 (94)**
Milwaukee (2001)	18.12	11.02 (60)	11.72 (65)	**17.63 (97)**	n.a.
Pittsburgh (2001)	21.48	10.71 (50)	11.80 (55)	**19.51 (91)**	n.a.
San Francisco (2000)	21.24	11.47 (54)	12.12 (57)	23.38 (110)	**20.84 (98)**
Seattle (1999)	23.42	14.94 (64)	19.01 (81)	**23.38 (100)**	24.60 (105)
Texas (1994)	12.07	8.93 (74)	8.93 (74)	12.07 (100)	**11.96 (99)**
Average	16.71	(60)	(66)	(102)	(104)

Source: Baade (2003).

a. In parenthesis, percent of the price for year *t*, the time at which stadium construction was completed, of the prices for other years. Boldface figures indicate ticket prices prior to stadium construction that exceeded the price in the year that the stadium was built, or ticket prices following stadium construction that were equal to or less than the price that prevailed at the time the stadium opened.

(that is, large-market clubs) to agree to share the revenue streams that the new stadiums were intended to exploit. The large-market clubs have been reluctant to share their local revenues. Retained revenues include 60 percent of home gate receipts, stadium naming rights, luxury suite revenues, concessions, and local broadcast revenues.[26] Following the spate of new stadium construction in the

26. Terrell and others (2004).

NFL, retained and shared revenues constituted 41 and 59 percent respectively of NFL total revenues.[27] Given the importance of retained revenues, those teams that generated the most local revenues had a significant financial advantage over the other teams. The NFL recognized the potential threat to parity on the playing field and sought to remedy that potential problem by increasing shared revenues and imposing a salary cap based on "defined gross revenues."[28]

The NFL has proved to be the most forward-looking league when it comes to implementing and managing a salary cap and revenue sharing, but problems due to inequities still exist even in that league. The teams that produce lower revenues have argued that if all the clubs face the same salary cap, salaries would constitute a larger fraction of their revenues than is true for more lucrative teams. That, of course, has implications for the profitability of small-market clubs and their ability to compete with large-market clubs in ways that may affect playing parity— for example, greater expenditures on marketing, training facilities, and coaching.

Despite the problems in the NFL, the other professional sports leagues have not done nearly as well at managing the escalating player costs and maintaining on-the-field competitiveness in the free-agent era as has the NFL. The most egregious example occurred during the 2004–05 NHL season, when the NHL teams locked out their players for the entire season. The current recession threatens the NBA in ways that offer disturbing parallels to the 2004–05 NHL experience. On February 26, 2009, the NBA opened up a $200 million line of credit to its financially stressed clubs. As of February 2009, twelve teams had expressed interest in tapping that fund.[29]

The financial implications for host cities are profound. Communities have partnered with teams in a financial sense and, because teams are not accountable for the public largesse, host cities have been exposed to substantial risks. Teams have signed players to long-term contracts at high salaries without any assurance that demand will exist for their product over the life of the contracts. That, of course, is a risk that all businesses assume, but in the case of professional sports the substantial infrastructure expense has been borne disproportionately by the

---

27. Terrell and others (2004) reports that total income for teams averaged between $123 and $127 million dollars in 2002. Between $51 and $55 million was categorized as retained. The 41 percent figure identified assumes a retained revenue of $51 million and total revenue of $123 million per team in 2002. It should be noted that shared revenues are represented by national broadcast rights fees, 40 percent of the gate for visiting teams, and licensing.

28. The salary cap in the NFL is based on the formula $C = (1/n) \times S \times DGR$, where C represents the salary cap, S is players' share of gross revenues, and DGR is defined gross revenue. For a discussion of the NFL salary cap, see "Salary Cap FAQ" (www.askthecommish.com/salarycap/faq.asp).

29 Bill Simmons, "Welcome to the No Benjamins Association." ESPN, February 27, 2009 (http://sports.espn.go.com/espn/page2/story?page=simmons/090227).

taxpaying public. Prior to the most recent economic downturn, few industries could be identified in which public sector support was as pronounced.

To consider professional sports an effective local economic development tool requires a comparison of the costs incurred and the risks assumed to get in the game, which are considerable. Professional sports leagues function as unregulated monopolies. Monopolies serve to restrict supply, which results in excess demand for franchises. Cities compete vigorously with one another for the available clubs, a reality that has been exacerbated by macroeconomic developments such as reduced revenue sharing at the federal and state levels in the late 1980s. Cities became more entrepreneurial during that time as they sought to replace lost revenues, and urban areas began reinventing themselves as tourist destinations. Sports have played a vital role in that development strategy.

The disparities in income and wealth inherent among metropolitan areas necessarily mean that some will be more successful in supporting commercial sports than others. The expansion of professional sports leagues necessarily has resulted in smaller, less affluent cities pursuing a sports development strategy, and teams have often abandoned markets that were ill-equipped to support them. Aggressive financial innovation among team owners as they sought a competitive edge on the playing field served to increase team demands for new, more lucrative facilities, jeopardizing the ability of some communities to retain their franchises. Then too, the stadiums constructed for some sports were smaller (MLB being the most notable example), and these new facilities, built at taxpayer expense, cater to an elite audience. If cities sought to retain their franchise, they often had to accept the inequities involved.

Despite the significant costs and risks identified and analyzed here, it may well be that the public benefits associated with hosting a professional sports team more than compensate for the public costs. If so, then a decision to host commercial sports is justifiable on economic grounds. The next section considers how those who support the use of public subsidies for commercial sports justify their position.

The Economic Justification for Sports Subsidies: Boosters' Promises

One mantra supporting stadium construction borrowed a line from the movie *Field of Dreams*: "If you build it, they will come." The line had sentimental appeal, but to pragmatic people, the idea of a pilgrimage to a sports cathedral had undeniable commercial appeal. During this time of acute economic stress, the quote below from Lester Bagley suggests a new mantra: "If you build it, the economy will heal."

Minnesota lawmakers heard last month that a $954 million Vikings stadium would employ 8,000 construction workers, another 5,400 people supported by construction-related spending, and 3,400 in the new facility. Team vice president Lester Bagley called it a "significant jobs and economic stimulus package."[30]

But is it just hyperbole—another egregious example of corporate welfare? The purpose of this section is to identify and analyze the claims by those who advance economic arguments to defend the use of public funds to subsidize construction of sports infrastructure for professional sports teams and to accommodate sports mega-events.

As noted, the decades-old stadium construction boom has been financed to a substantial extent by taxpayers. Economics justify the expense, according to those who support public subsidies. Apologists would argue that stadium construction costs should not be construed as an expenditure, but rather as an investment. Sports facility projects do not force painful civic trade-offs, the booster's logic goes, but rather provide funds that will enable school construction, highway expansions, police protection, and sewer repair. Stadiums will, in short, contribute to the public coffers, not deplete them.

The theoretical blueprint is not hard to follow. Stadium events attract nonresident spendthrifts who not only buy tickets to games but stay in local hotels and eat at local restaurants. The stream of spending is embellished by the expanding incomes of those who work in the hotels and restaurants, who spend their increased income locally, multiplying the spending directly attributable to the sports activities several fold. Increased incomes also yield greater tax revenues, and the public expenditures enabled by those revenues serve to benefit the very taxpayers who enabled all of it in the first place, through their investment in the sports facilities.

The windfall promised for the Twin Cities economy through investment in a new stadium for the NFL Vikings is a claim that has been repeated hundreds of times before—and to great effect, as attested to by the number of stadiums constructed in the relatively recent past. The public sector, much of the time, requires some prodding, as the owners of teams and event promoters represent the wealthier strata of society that stand to benefit substantially from stadium largesse.[31] The prods employed have been made effective by conditions that exist

---

30. Martiga Lohn, "Some Owners' Rx for the Economy: Build Us a Stadium," Associated Press, March 5, 2009 (http://abcnews.go.com/Business/wireStory?id=7016220).

31. One of the most widely publicized examples of a controversial stadium subsidy for a wealthy owner was seen in Seattle in 1997, when taxpayers were asked to approve a $350 million expenditure to raze the Kingdome and replace it with an open-air stadium for the Seattle Seahawks. Paul Allen, the

in the professional sports industry—for example, maintenance of excess demand for teams, as noted previously. Team owners, leagues, and promoters argue that investment in sports enables other public investments instead of precluding them and that the enhancement of income and wealth of the financially privileged can be viewed as a cost of doing business.

Economic impact studies are difficult to critically assess for several reasons. First, studies usually refer to several categories of expenditure, which can confuse or obscure the true impact of a team, facility, or event. The terms *direct, indirect,* and *induced* (or *multiplier-related*) *spending* are commonly used. Direct spending, as most economists use the term, refers to spending relating to an event, which could include spending on infrastructure to accommodate the event and spending undertaken by spectators as a direct consequence of the event—for example, on tickets, parking, and concessions. Most economists identify indirect spending as spending that occurs as a consequence of direct spending. For example, spectators spend money at restaurants, hotels, and gas stations in the stadium environs, and the income thereby created for workers in those establishments will be respent on goods and services in the host community. The particulars relating to the location of respending identify what economists refer to as the "multiplier effect." The size of the multiplier will depend on the extent to which newly created income is respent in the local economy.

Second, the use of technically sophisticated models, an input-output structure for example, lends an air of authenticity and authority to economic impact studies. State-of-the-art methodology does not guarantee accurate assessments, however. All input-output models are based on the fundamental proposition that all goods are both inputs and outputs, and coefficients can be identified describing the amount of one good minimally necessary to produce a unit of another. An input-output table identifies the entire set of relationships that exist among all goods. It is possible through the use of input-output relationships, therefore, to describe how it is that a change in one sector of the economy—the sports sector, for example—will affect all other sectors, including employment.

It should be added, however, that the changes projected to occur in direct and indirect spending are at least as vital to a precise calculation of the economic impact of sports spending on an economy as a correct rendering of the interrelationships (coefficients) among goods. If changes in direct and indirect spending are improperly valued, the changes induced by sports spending on other segments

---

cofounder of Microsoft and a billionaire, made it clear that he would not exercise an option to buy the Seahawks and keep them in Seattle if the public did not subsidize the majority of the construction costs for the project. Eventually, that project and another for a nearby stadium for the MLB Seattle Mariners were approved (Griffin 1997).

of the economy will be improperly valued. Some might refer to this somewhat indelicately as the "garbage-in, garbage-out" principle. If errors, furthermore, are made in estimating the direct and indirect changes in spending, then the induced or multiplier effects will be incorrectly estimated as well.

Another way of stating this is to note that errors made at the first stage of an impact analysis are compounded when the induced effects are estimated. Critical to estimating the economic impact of sports accurately is an arithmetically accurate measure of direct and indirect spending changes attributable to the team, facility, or event. Much of the difference in economic impact estimates can be explained by significant disparities in direct and indirect spending estimates. This issue will be discussed in greater detail later in this chapter.

A justification for subsidies necessarily involves prospective analysis. The quote attributed to Lester Bagley earlier in this section contained numbers that were produced through an economic analysis of some sort. A very crude economic analysis might go no further than to multiply the number of fans who attend a game or event by the amount of money that they are projected to spend. That product, in turn, could be multiplied by an "entertainment multiplier" that is published in a public or private sector document.

Suppose, for example, that a sports promoter argues that a city should spend $100 million to host the Pan American Games. Suppose further that in defending that use of public funds, the promoter asserts that the games will attract 100,000 spectators who will spend $100 per day each day for the fourteen days of events. The total amount of spending, according to the primitive analysis noted above, would be $140,000,000 (100,000 × $100 × 14). That would suggest a 40 percent return on the initial public investment, and if a multiplier of two is used, the return on the investment is an astounding 180 percent.

The difficulty, of course, rests with accurately estimating the benefits and costs as well as using the appropriate multiplier. All aspects of the analysis can be debated by reasonable people, but certain economic fundamentals and realities have to be observed in generating credible numbers. That is especially important if taxpayers are going to be asked to shoulder an additional financial responsibility. One important way in which estimates are embellished is that gross spending induced by an event, not net spending, is commonly used to estimate benefits. However, only the spending of nonresident spectators (net new spending) should be included because the spending of resident spectators ordinarily substitutes for spending that would otherwise occur. Transparency and accuracy are critical not only in estimating the impact of an event but also in identifying who enjoys the benefits and who assumes the costs. As noted earlier, the direct benefits of public subsidies for sports facilities are appropriated primarily by owners and players.

Another cause for concern in economic impact studies relates to what might be called "advocacy research." If a person or firm is hired to do an economic impact analysis, it is not too cynical to argue that the results of the study will conform in many cases to the outcome preferred by the hiring entity. That does not imply fraudulence; it may involve nothing more sinister than making assumptions that favor the desired outcome. If, for example, the spending per day for a fan identified previously ranges from $50 to $100, the analyst may assume that it is $100 rather than $50 or $75 and still remain within the range identified. The actual number used may favor the interests of the client, but it is not necessarily a dishonest estimate. If $50, however, is the correct figure for daily fan spending and if all the other numbers in the analysis are right, assuming a multiplier of zero means that in our example the games would be a losing proposition for the hypothetical city rather than a winning investment.[32] If deception is intended to help achieve a particular outcome, economic impact analysis provides ample opportunity to shape a desired "research" outcome.

Ex ante or prospective analysis is difficult. Precise estimates require extensive knowledge of the way that different sectors of the economy interact. The most sophisticated and current input-output tables do not completely capture the manner in which sectors of the economy relate. That could be, in part, because the nature of the interaction depends on the condition of the economy. It could be, for example, that the economic impact induced through the construction of a new stadium would be far different if the economy is at full employment instead of in the severe downturn characterizing the current U.S. economy. The input-output coefficients that describe the interrelationships cannot account for that difference. The coefficients would be the same in either case, and if the projected changes in direct and indirect spending were assumed to be the same, then the predicted outcome would be the same. Despite the best efforts of economists, a model that explains urban economic growth within acceptable margins of error eludes the profession. That reality makes all ex ante analysis somewhat suspect.

Recognizing the problems with ex ante analysis, some economists have taken a different track. If they cannot assume that they understand the relationships necessary to describe urban economic development well enough, then perhaps they can use ex post or retrospective analysis to at least filter the promises made by those who use ex ante analysis to justify public subsidies for professional sports. The next section of this chapter discusses the reasons for and the methodology underlying retrospective analysis.

---

32. McConnell (2000) gives a good example of how important assumptions are in doing economic impact analysis.

Evaluating the Economic Justification for Subsidies: Economists' Concerns

Economists, philosophers, and politicians have debated the question of whether there is a trade-off between equity and efficiency in some form or another for hundreds of years. The following quote from Henry Simons is one of many that could have been chosen to represent the conventional wisdom that such a trade-off does exist:

> It is reasonable to expect that every gain, through taxation, in better distribution will be accompanied by some loss in production.[33]

Underlying that statement is the notion that the more that the government takes of what people earn—that is, the more that it increases taxes—the less people will work and earn. The increase in taxation induces a decrease in efficiency. Hence, it is thought that taxing the wealthy to promote a more equitable distribution of income and wealth would diminish output.

Subsidies could be construed as negative taxes, and if the argument has symmetry, one might think that subsidies to the wealthy, in this case the producers of commercial sports, would result in an increase in economic efficiency and output. However, the fact is that there is no economic justification for subsidies for commercial sports unless it can be demonstrated that they induce an expansion of the economy. There is no doubt that wealthy owners and players gain. The question is whether that gain translates into an expanded economy that has the potential for benefiting all rather than a few. Boosters claim that that is the case.

There is some reason to be skeptical. After all, apologists for subsidies for commercial sports are likely among those who benefit from the largesse, and it is imperative to verify independently the studies that they cite to corroborate their claims. This portion of the chapter asks two questions. First, do boosters' claims concerning the ability of subsidies to expand the local economy conform to simple economic fundamentals? Second, if suspicions are aroused because bedrock theory is neglected or ignored, how should the real economic impact of commercial sports be assessed?

Nothing is more central to economic theory than trade-offs. Resources are finite and wants are virtually insatiable, and so allocation has to occur. Given that they have limited time and money, consumers confront scarcity each day. Time and money spent attending a commercial sports event necessarily precludes spending that time and money on something else. Critical to understand-

---

33. Simons (1938, p. 19).

ing the impact that more spending on commercial sports has on the local economy is determining what activities and goods are forgone as a consequence.

The prospective analysis of the typical sports economic impact study ignores
the fundamental economic reality of trade-offs, or, at the very least, the early ex
ante subsidy studies did. When independent economists weighed in on the subsidy issue and noted that shortcoming, more sophisticated supportive studies
that ostensibly compensated for it appeared. There is still reason for skepticism.
Accounting fully for the trade-offs requires a thorough understanding of the
character of the sectors that lose and gain from the spending on commercial
sports that subsidies promote. Input-output models, as discussed previously,
account for sector gains and losses to a point, but there is no way of knowing
whether the fixed coefficients that relate all inputs to outputs fully or even adequately capture the changes in spending. Vital to the analysis is an accurate rendering of the changes in spending that do occur. As noted, the net changes in
spending have to be determined, rather than the gross changes in spending.
That is true for all kinds of reasons that economists are trained to identify. I now
consider a few of them.

Suppose that firm A is owned by a local resident and hires people who also are
residents of the community. Suppose that firm B produces a substitute good in
the same locale but is owned by a nonresident. Assume further that the workers
hired by firm B are nonresidents as well. If the local government adopted policies
that promoted the activities of either firm A or B, clearly there would be consequences for the local economy. The technical relationships that exist among all
the different inputs and outputs would not be fundamentally different, but the
flow of funds within the local economy might differ dramatically. If subsidies are
extended to firm B, a significant outflow of funds would occur as the nonresident
owner and workers repatriate their earnings, spending where they live rather than
in the community in which they are employed. The input-output models that
often are cutting-edge in terms of describing technical relationships have no way
of accounting for specific financial leakages. The only way that such leakages can
be captured would be to adjust changes in local spending consistent with the
hypothetical subsidy that encourages the activity of firm A or B.

Subsidies for professional sports encourage their expansion, all else equal, and
increase the income of those working in the professional sports sector. The labor
market for professional sports is decidedly national, not local, in character. If the
subsidy encourages the sports industry or serves to increase the incomes of those
employed by the industry and discourages other locally owned and staffed
industries, it serves to expand an outflow of funds, all else equal. If the athletes
who produce sports locally become nonresidents when the season ends, then the
subsidized facility becomes a conduit through which resident spending flows

from places such as Green Bay, Wisconsin, to southern California when the NFL season ends. That would not be the case if subsidies did not lead to displacement of locally produced entertainment in favor of nationally produced entertainment. If the implications of subsidies are to be truly assessed, an enormous number of details about the functioning of the economy need to be identified and incorporated into the analysis.

Fairness to those doing prospective analysis requires recognition of the herculean nature of the task that they confront. Economists are trained to identify the quintessential elements that allow reasonable conceptualizations of the complex world of commerce. The resulting models inform policy, and their absence or inadequacy can result in significant misallocations of resources. Subsidies for professional sports, as noted, are valued in the billions of dollars. It is important to develop a metric for assessing how accurate prospective impact studies are in providing the information needed to determine whether commercial sports subsidies generate not only a return (accounting return), but one that exceeds that of all of the alternative purposes for which the money could have been used (economic return).

Skepticism of the ability of subsidies to do what their advocates promise relates once again to a substitution effect. If spending on commercial sports by residents of the community providing the subsidy is dollar-for-dollar replacement of spending that they would otherwise have done, then the commercial sports subvention can stimulate the economy only by inducing exports of the sport service or by substituting for the professional sports activity that another community is providing (import substitution). The evidence in general indicates that spectators for commercial sporting events come from a radius of not more than twenty-five miles, although there may be some exceptions. When the weather does not permit watching a game in comfort in an outdoor stadium, fans in cold climates, for example, may attend a baseball game in a domed stadium (as in Milwaukee or Minneapolis) that may be located more than twenty-five miles from their home. Fans in the Southwest or in the Plains states also may be willing to travel distances greater than twenty-five miles because of the relative scarcity of teams in the less densely populated western United States. People living in the West are accustomed to traveling substantial distances to spend discretionary income, so teams in the western part of the country are more likely to sell their sports entertainment to fans living beyond twenty-five miles than are teams in the more densely populated eastern part. East of the Mississippi, professional sports teams exist in sufficient numbers to allow development of geographic loyalties, and fans support teams within a relatively short distance from their homes.

A substitution effect may occur not only at one point in time but also over time in ways that moderate the impact that commercial sports may have on a community. The Olympic Games provide one such example. The games do attract fans from across the world, and a first-blush reaction is that such a hallmark event must bolster the host city economy by a substantial amount. That may be true at the time the event is actually held, but the evidence indicates that before and after the event, the local economy may operate at below-normal levels. The "dead time" before and after the Olympic Games likely occurs because people who might otherwise visit an Olympic host city anticipate that prices for hotels and restaurants might be higher than normal around the time of the event, and so they find alternatives to the Olympic site for things such as business conventions. A recent publication noted not only that is there a period of slack economic activity before and after the games but also that economic activity falls below normal levels as one moves away from the environs in which the events are held. A study by the European Tour Operators Association (ETOA) concluded:

> During the Olympics, a destination effectively closes for normal business. The repercussions are felt before and after: both tourists and the tour operators that supply them are scared off immediately before and during the events. This "absence" then creates its own effect, as the normal conveyor belt of contented customers begetting new arrivals has been broken.[34]

The ETOA study is important not only for recognizing the temporal offset to the spike in tourism related to the event itself but also for disputing the notion that Barcelona experienced a sustained uptick in tourism as a consequence of hosting the 1992 games. Barcelona is often singled out as an example of what a properly prepared and well-run Olympic Games can do for an economy. The ETOA opined that if Barcelona's experience is compared with that of a non-host city such as Dublin or one in any other growing economy, the notion of an Olympic legacy for Barcelona is less compelling.

The chance for a legacy is enhanced in theory if the host city "surprises" visitors in some sense. A surprise occurs when the host city exceeds the expectations of those attending the games to an extent that they plan to return to that community rather than visit another site when planning future vacations or business trips.

Host cities could also sustain an Olympic boost if the community coalesces around financing infrastructure developments or improvements that otherwise

34. European Tour Operators Association (2006, p. 10).

would not occur due to political resistance. Jordi Hereu, the current mayor of Barcelona, provided the following assessment of what the Olympics did for his city and why during the sixteenth anniversary of the 1992 games.

> When we look back we can remember that the Olympic Games gave us an opportunity to think big and plan afresh; they provided the reason to do things on a large scale. The Games were also a great rallying initiative for the city, bringing the people, the business, and other institutions and the city government together in a consensus about the long-term development of the city which has lasted for 16 years with great vitality. The Games created the unstoppable momentum for us.[35]

Mayor Hereu's observations suggest that the ability of the Olympic Games to serve as a catalyst for economic development may well rest with their ability to bring diverse segments of a community together to fashion a plan for growth and development. Not only was a blueprint for development created, but the infrastructure necessary for its execution was also identified and funded. Mayor Hereu noted as much in his speech.

> Barcelona used the Olympics as the organizing idea for a new kind of strategic planning, one that looked deep into the future, and long back at our past, and enabled us to believe that we could be a leading city once again. The Games also left a very tangible legacy of improved architecture, infrastructure, and new development potential, as well [as] many new amenities and facilities which we managed in ways that enabled ordinary citizens to enjoy and use [them] fully.[36]

Often the facilities that are built to accommodate commercial sports are replacement facilities. Teams and their allies often claim that an old stadium or arena has physically deteriorated to the point that there is no viable alternative but to replace it. It would appear, however, that for more than two decades the reason for replacement has been economic rather than physical obsolescence. Consider events in Florida as they relate to construction of arenas there. The arena in Miami where the professional basketball and hockey teams played was eight years old when the facility was judged to be economically obsolete. The arena in which the NBA Heat played had only sixteen luxury suites and 14,053 seats, a low number among NBA facilities. Broward County, just a short distance up the coast from Dade County, where Miami is located, sought to attract the Heat and the NHL Florida Panthers as tenants for a new arena that it proposed to build. From the

---

35. As quoted in Clark (2008, p. 11).
36. As quoted in Clark (2008, p. 11).

perspective of the team owners, a "Solomonic compromise" was struck between the two counties in the ensuing financial tug of war: Broward County constructed a facility for the Panthers and Dade County built a new arena for the Heat. There is now a thirty-mile stretch on I-95 that serves as home for three arenas.[37]

Miami's experience is not atypical. The evidence indicates that teams agitate for new stadiums, with strong league support, whenever their revenues fall below league standards. Financial innovation puts not only teams at risk but also the communities that host them.

Substantial sports infrastructure also is required to accommodate sports mega-events. Beijing reportedly spent $40 billion to host the 2008 Summer Olympic Games, and South Korea spent $5.6 billion to co-host the World Cup in 2002. The justification for South Korea to spend that amount was the claim that it would boost the nation's gross domestic product (GDP) by 2.2 percent.[38]

Theoretically speaking, there are at least two reasons to suspect that the return on infrastructure is small. First, stadiums accommodate seasonal activities and the use of outdoor stadiums, particularly in colder climates, is limited. Second, there is a lack of synergy between commercial sports and other businesses. Parking garages represent one natural business partner because they are needed to accommodate spectators driving to a game or an event. Both the stadium and parking facilities leave a large urban footprint, however, and they may not optimize the use of large tracts of urban real estate. Although parking lots or structures may be used to accommodate other activities, land in a central business district is relatively expensive and the expense pushes stadiums to the periphery of the urban core or to the suburbs. Land outside the central business district is not only cheaper but also plentiful, and less densely occupied land eases traffic flow to and from a stadium.

Perhaps nothing attests to the power and influence of sports as much as how the construction of new stadiums has defined the space around them. Fenway Park in Boston and Wrigley Field in Chicago, the two oldest professional baseball stadiums in the United States still in use, were fitted into the urban grid, and businesses in the stadium environs share commercial relationships with the facility. By contrast, the stadium in which the Chicago White Sox play, built in 1992, exhibits no such commercial synergy. Aerial photographs of Chicago's two stadiums show many small businesses near Chicago's Wrigley Field, but virtually no businesses around the "Cell" home of the White Sox.[39]

---

37. John Heylar, "For Team Owners, More Is Never Enough," *Wall Street Journal,* May 3, 1996, p. B7.

38. Finer (2002).

39. Baade, Nikolova, and Matheson (2007).

Despite the extensive use of public subsidies, teams, which are primary tenants, have considerable say in how and when a facility is used. Teams often directly and indirectly limit the ancillary or spillover economic activity in the surrounding community. Teams have managed to convince their host governments in some cases to legislate limits on the amount of competitive private economic activity taking place in the stadium environs.

Indirectly, the new generation of stadiums has limited ancillary development in neighborhoods because new stadiums, by providing a range of commercial activities, substitute for commercial activity provided by neighborhood establishments. The new stadiums are "soup-to-nuts," self-contained commercial centers that arguably detract from neighborhood economic activity rather than encourage it. The modern sports facility offers a range of food and drink options, merchandise sales, and even child care. The more the team offers and appropriates revenues from such goods and services, the less community businesses benefit.

Even the economic impact of the construction phase of a stadium project has to be more carefully assessed, and not only because of the other uses to which the money could be put. Construction projects of considerable size can be disruptive. When I interviewed shop owners and other business people in the Plaka, the old commercial center of Athens, four years prior to the Athens Summer Olympic Games, virtually all of them expressed enthusiasm for the games. These entrepreneurs had visions of hordes of nonresident, wealthy consumers descending on their shops. One year prior to the games, their sentiment had shifted dramatically. The extensive construction that had been undertaken had prevented potential customers from reaching their stores and business had fallen substantially, by as much as 90 percent according to some of those interviewed.

All of these complications taken together cast doubt on the claims regarding the efficacy of stadium subsidies as catalysts for urban economic development. A clear need exists to evaluate the question of efficacy, and the remainder of this section identifies a method for doing so.

If teams, facilities, and events do induce substantive changes in economic activity, then it is reasonable to expect that the economic landscape would change by some measure as a result. Conceptually speaking, the test is straightforward: do measures of economic activity respond positively to the addition of a team, the construction of a stadium, or the hosting of a sports mega-event for a particular area studied, be it a neighborhood, city, metropolitan area, state, or country? Specifically, the test involves observing the level of employment, real income, or growth rates for a metropolis and statistically testing how those macroeconomic measures respond to a substantive addition to or deletion from the commercial sports sector. The hypothesis tested is that there will be a measurable change in macroeconomic activity if the impact of commercial sports is as large as advocates of subsidies propose. A related test would determine whether government revenues increase as a consequence of subsidies to commercial sports. The next section of this chapter identifies and discusses the statistical findings for both the retrospective and prospective analyses.

Measured Economic Impacts

Daniel Joseph Boorstin notes that "the greatest obstacle to discovery is not ignorance; it is the illusion of knowledge."[40] The purpose of this section is to identify and discuss the observed economic impacts of professional sports teams and events in order to dispel any illusions about those impacts. The section is divided into three parts. The first provides selected information on estimates of the impacts of teams, stadiums, and events by those who generally support subventions to attract teams and events. The second part provides a summary of ex ante and ex post analyses relating to economic impact for mega-events to highlight the extent to which impact estimates differ. The third part identifies and analyzes the reasons for the divergence between the promises of subsidy boosters and the economic impact estimates of subsidies provided by independent scholars.

Table 5-4 provides information on a selection of boosters' economic impact studies for teams, stadiums, and events.[41]

Several things relating to the numbers in table 5-4 warrant analysis. First, the estimates generally represent results from studies that projected the economic impact of a team, a facility, or an event. Those ex ante results provided a justification for the use of public funds to support a team or event financially. A sports facility, for example, often is constructed with a league's promise that construction will ensure that the community involved will be selected to host a league "all-star" event, such as the NBA All-Star game, or a championship game, such as the NFL's Super Bowl. A substantial economic impact number creates the impression that the facility will go a long way toward paying for itself by hosting a hallmark event. Leagues have a clear motivation for projecting a large impact number, especially in cases in which host communities exhibit parsimony with respect to commercial sports subsidies.

Second, the very size of some of the numbers compels skepticism and, therefore, invites scrutiny. Is it possible that the World Cup, for example, induced a

40. Quoted in Carol Krucoff, "The 6 O'Clock Scholar; Librarian of Congress Daniel Boorstin and His Love Affair with Books," *Washington Post,* January 29, 1984, p. K2.

41. Baade (2003, p. 12).

Table 5-4. *Economic Impact Estimates Provided by Boosters for Selected Teams, Facilities, and Events*

Year of study	Team, facility, or event	Area measured	Impact ($ millions)
1992	NBA All-Star Game	Metro Orlando	35[b]
1995	Summer Olympic Games	Metro Atlanta	5,142[c]
1996	Cincinnati Reds (MLB), old stadium[a]	Metro Cincinnati	158[d]
1996	Cincinnati Reds, new stadium[a]	Metro Cincinnati	192[d]
1998	Arizona Diamondbacks	Metro Phoenix	319[d]
1999	Super Bowl	South Florida (Miami, Dade, and Broward Counties)	396[e]
1999	Boston Red Sox (MLB), current stadium[a]	Metro Boston	120[d]
1999	Boston Red Sox, new stadium[a]	Metro Boston	186[d]
1999	San Antonio Spurs (NBA)	Metro San Antonio	71[d]
1999	Summer Olympics Dallas	Metro Dallas	4,000[f]
2000	Houston Rockets (NBA)	Metro Houston	187[d]
2001	World Cup Soccer	Countries of Japan and South Korea	24,800 (Japan) 8,900 (South Korea)[g]

a. Economic impact estimates based on spending by out-of-area fans only.

b. Robert A. Baade, "Los Angeles City Controller's Report on Economic Impact: Staples Center" (http://controller.lacity.org/stellent/groups/ElectedOfficials/@CTR_Contributor/documents/Contributor_Web_Content/LACITYP_008662.pdf).

c. Jeffrey M. Humphreys and Michael K. Plummer, "The Economic Impact on the State of Georgia of Hosting the 1996 Summer Olympic Games," *Georgia Business and Economic Conditions*, May–June 1994, pp. 18–21.

d. Jordan Rappaport and Chad Wilkerson, "What Are the Benefits of Hosting a Major League Sports Franchise?" *Federal Reserve Bank of Kansas City Economic Review* 86, no. 1 (2001): 55–86.

e. National Football League, "Super Bowl XXXII Generates $396 Million for South Florida," *NFL Times*, vol. 58 (1999), p. 7.

f. Rusty Cawley, "The Olympic Race: The Metroplex Bid for the 2012 Games Has a Parallel in Atlanta, Where the '96 Games Generated Less Gold than Expected," *Dallas Business Journal* (April 5, 1999).

g. John Finer, "The Grand Illusion," *Far Eastern Economic Review*, March 7, 2002, pp. 32–36.

0.6 and 2.2 percent increase in Japan's and South Korea's GDPs, respectively? Can a single event such as the Super Bowl do more for the economy of a region or a metropolis than a baseball team that plays eighty-one home games?

Third, because of the substitution effect described earlier, more recent economic impact studies focus spending by nonresidents and exclude the spending of residents. Resident spending on professional sports substitutes for spending within the community that would occur on other goods and services in the absence of spending on commercial sports. Teams, leagues, and politicians understand that the public has become more educated and that there has to be a legitimate basis for the impact numbers provided. Some number is not necessarily better than no number if the methodology used to generate it violates fundamental principles of economic behavior.

Fourth, the estimates vary widely. Do the NBA Rockets really induce an economic impact in Houston that is more than two and one-half times that induced by the NBA Spurs in San Antonio? Such divergent results require a closer look at the assumptions used to generate them.

Subsidy critics are in a position to contend that estimates generated by those who potentially benefit from a project should be viewed with skepticism. Funding approval depends at least to some degree on "proof" that a team or event is worth it. Can the groups that stand to benefit be trusted to provide a fair appraisal of the potential economic contribution of a sports facility or event? It is prudent for those charged with making decisions on commercial sports subsidies to review economic impact estimates in light of boosters' motivations.

Table 5-5 represents a sample of the findings of independent scholars relating to the economic impact of mega-events contrasted with those provided by boosters for subsidies for such events.

Independent scholarship auditing the economic impact of hallmark events generally fails to confirm the substantial positive impact asserted by subsidy advocates. Table 5-5 indicates that on occasion boosters forecast a positive impact of an event that audits indicate had an actual negative impact. Events can be disruptive to the normal course of commercial life to an extent that net spending stays the same or actually declines rather than increases in conjunction with the event.

Similarly, some scholars have found that teams and facilities have negligible or negative impacts on metropolitan economies. Baade found no correlation between the real growth differential in real per capita personal income for a city experiencing some change in its professional sports industry and cities experiencing no such change or having no professional sports presence.[42] That analysis included all cities hosting a team in one of the four major professional sports (baseball, basketball, football, and hockey) and covered more than three decades beginning in 1958. Coates and Humphreys similarly examined all thirty-seven cities that had at least one big-league football, baseball, or basketball franchise at any point between 1969 and 1996. They found that per capita income actually fell by $10 and $73 as a consequence of building a new baseball stadium or basketball arena, respectively.[43]

42. Baade (1996).
43. Coates and Humphreys (1999).

Table 5-5. *Economic Impact Estimates Provided by Boosters and Independent Economists for Selected Events*

			Impact and authors			
			Boosters (ex ante)		Independent economists (ex post)	
Event	Year	Sport	Impact	Author	Impact	Author
Super Bowl (Atlanta)	1994	Football	$166 million/ 2,736 jobs	Jeffrey Humphreys, Georgia State University	$91.9 million/537 jobs[a]	Robert Baade and Victor Matheson
Super Bowl (Miami)	1999	Football	$393 million	Kathleen Davis, Sports Management Research Institute	$91.9 million/537 jobs[a]	Robert Baade and Victor Matheson
Super Bowl (San Diego)	2003	Football	$367 million	Marketing Information Masters, Inc.	$91.9 million/537 jobs[a]	Robert Baade and Victor Matheson
MLB All-Star Game	1999	Baseball	$75 million	Bud Selig, MLB	Employment down 0.38 percent[b]	Robert Baade and Victor Matheson
MLB World Series	2000	Baseball	$250 million	Comptroller of New York City	Personal income: $6.8 million[c]	Robert Baade and Victor Matheson
NCAA Men's Final Four (St. Louis)	2001	Basketball	$110 million	St. Louis Convention and Visitor's Bureau	Personal income down $6.4 to $44.2 million[d]	Robert Baade and Victor Matheson

Multiple events	1969–97	Multiple	Personal income/per capita: no effect	Dennis Coates and Brad Humphreys
Daytona 500	1997–99	Car racing	Taxable sales: $32–$49 million	Robert Baade and Victor Matheson
Super Bowl	1985–95	Football	Taxable sales: no effect	Phil Porter
Multiple events (Florida)	1980–2005	Multiple	Taxable sales: down $34.4 million (average)	Robert Baade, Rob Bauamann, and Victor Matheson
Multiple events (Texas)	1991–2005	Multiple	Gross sales: varied, positive and negative	Dennis Coates
Multiple events (Texas)	1990–2006	Multiple	Sales tax revenue: varied, positive and negative	Dennis Coates and Craig Depken, II
NHL regular season games	1990–99	Hockey	Hotel occupancy: slight increase	Marc Lavoie and Gabriel Rodriguez

Source: Matheson (2006).

a. All Super Bowls (average), 1970 through 2001.
b. All MLB All-Star Games (average), 1973 through 1997.
c. All MLB Playoffs and World Series (average), 1972 through 2000.
d. All NCAA Men's Basketball Final Fours (average), 1970 through 1999.

Coates and Humphreys's negative results require additional explanation. The authors cited three reasons for a negative relationship between the presence of commercial sports and real incomes for workers. First, workers may accept lower real wages in exchange for the presence of commercial sports in a city. Second, public subsidies for sports may reduce spending on public infrastructure in other sectors of the economy, which reduces incomes. Third, the presence of sports may reduce worker productivity as a consequence of their preoccupation with teams.

Other independent economists who have studied the economic impact of teams, facilities, and events by and large have reached conclusions that echo the findings in table 5-5. In fact, in reviewing the collected research on the subject, Siegfried and Zimbalist (2000) concluded:

> Few fields of empirical economic research offer virtual unanimity of findings. Yet, independent work on the economic impact of stadiums and arenas has uniformly found that there is no statistically significant positive correlation between sports facility construction and economic development.[44]

What accounts for the substantial disparity in the prospective economic impact estimates of boosters and the retrospective estimates of economists highlighted in tables 5-4 and 5-5? Answering that question requires repeating the fundamental problems associated with prospective analysis discussed previously. Painting in the broadest possible strokes, exaggerations of the net economic impact (benefits less costs) from constructing a sports facility generally occur because costs are underestimated, benefits are overestimated, and opportunity cost is ignored. The relevant issue, as it relates to opportunity cost, should not be whether a new stadium or arena has any net impact on area development but whether its impact is larger than that of alternative development projects. The following discussion focuses on the explanatory power of theoretical issues discussed previously in describing the schism between the economic-impact estimates of subsidy advocates and independent scholars.

The exaggeration of benefits occurs because the reality of consumer budget constraints often is ignored. Entertainment spending, including that which occurs at a sports event, involves trade-offs. It is axiomatic that the more time and money that consumers spend at a sports event, the less time and money that they have for other activities that involve spending time and money. Tickets sold to a sports event may mean that fewer tickets are sold at local theaters. Similarly, consuming food and drink at the stadium implies that less food and drink is

---

44. Siegfried and Zimbalist (2000, p. 98).

consumed elsewhere. Clearly, to the extent that those who attend activities at the sports venue are residents of the community, the sports facility or event may simply reallocate entertainment spending in the local economy while leaving total spending unaltered.

The difference between gross and net expenditures is not trivial. Consider the economic impact that the MLB's Mariners generated for the city of Seattle, King County, and the state of Washington as estimated by the firm Dick Conway and Associates for King County in 1994.[45] Net direct spending as a percentage of gross direct spending was 35.4 percent for the city and county ($40.4 million/$114.0 million for both the city and the county) and 25.5 percent ($29.1 million/$114.0 million) for the state. The difference between gross and net total economic impact is more pronounced since multipliers compound differences in gross and net measures of direct economic impact. Total net economic impact as a percentage of total gross economic impact as calculated by Conway and Associates was 23.9 percent ($42.9 million/$179.7 million), 38.5 percent ($53.3 million/$138.3 million), and 40.1 percent ($47.7 million/$119.1 million) for the state, county, and city respectively.

One other observation with regard to the difference between estimates of gross and net spending merits mention. The Conway and Associates report suggests that in relative terms, gross economic impact is likely to be most pronounced in the neighborhood in which the stadium is located. It can be argued then that the magnitude of the impact that professional sports has on an economy, in relative terms at least, varies inversely with the size of a circle drawn around the point where the event actually occurs. Stated somewhat differently, the economic effect achieves greatest relative strength at "ground zero," the exact location of the event. As the circumference of the circle expands, net impact diminishes as dollars spent on the sporting event are more completely offset by reduced spending elsewhere.

Following that logic as it relates to leisure spending, the global impact of even the largest sporting events, such as the Summer Olympics, approximates zero if an increase in global net spending is not induced by the event itself. That is true even if people travel great distances and spend time and money at the Olympics host city: absent the games, those attending would have spent their money elsewhere. The local impact, therefore, depends on the extent to which spending and respending occurs by those residing outside the environs where the event is held or by local residents who spend money on the local sports event rather than outside their neighborhood. Theoretically, a local government might decide to

45. Dick Conway and Associates (1994).

subsidize sports if the audience is distinctly nonlocal. Even within a neighbor-hood, however, there are outflows associated with team and stadium activities; therefore, even at the local level, commercial sports might fail to provide much of an economic boost.

Eliminating the spending by residents of the community would at first blush appear to eliminate a potentially significant source of bias in estimating direct expenditures. Conducting a survey on expenditures by those attending a sports event, complete with a question on place of residence, would appear to be a straightforward way of estimating direct expenditures in a statistically acceptable manner. Although surveys may well provide insight on spending behavior of those patronizing an event, they offer no data on changes in spending by resi-dents not attending the event. It is conceivable that some residents may shift their spending out of the stadium's environs on game day simply because they want to avoid the accompanying chaos and congestion. A fundamental short-coming of economic impact studies is not the information on spending by those who are included in a direct expenditure survey but the lack of information on spending by those who are not.

Second, if errors are made in assessing direct spending, those errors are com-pounded in calculating induced indirect spending through standard multiplier analysis. Tips given to a server at a restaurant operating within a stadium, for example, could generate additional spending in the community when the server spends his or her tips at some other business in the host community. The addi-tional spending in the stadium arguably multiplies as it is spent again and again within the economy of the host community.

The multiplier process, however, has the potential to overstate economic impact if it is not recognized that the tips for the serving staff at a stadium restaurant simply substituted dollar for dollar for the tips another waiter or wait-ress would have received in the host city had the stadium restaurant not existed. Suppose, furthermore, that the server who received tips at a stadium restaurant resides outside the metropolis in which the stadium is located. If the server spends her tip money in another city, it creates a leakage from the flow of spend-ing in the host city. Unsophisticated multiplier analysis that does not account for details related to spending and respending likely exaggerates the impact that stadium activities have on the economy of the host city. Precise multiplier analy-sis includes all leakages from the circular flow of payments and uses multipliers that are specific to the entertainment industry and adequately describe the econ-omy of the host city.

Depending on the state of the economy, leakages may be significant. If the economy of the host city is at or very near full employment, it may be that the labor required to accommodate events at the stadium will require workers who reside in other communities where there is a labor surplus or unemployment.[46] To the extent that that is true, the indirect spending that constitutes the multiplier effect must be adjusted to reflect the leakage of income and subsequent spending that is thought to exist.

Labor is not the only factor of production that may repatriate income. What fraction of increased earnings remain in the host community if the hotels that experience higher than normal occupancy rates during sports events are owned by national chains?[47] An accurate assessment of the impact of the sports facility or event, in short, requires consideration of not only the dollar inflows broadly induced by the facility but also the dollar outflows that occur as a consequence of operating the venue. Input-output models used in the most sophisticated prospective analyses require accurate information on net spending changes as well as updated representations of the fixed relationships between inputs and outputs to generate accurate estimates of the economic impact induced by some economic development. Such models do not automatically account for the subtleties of spending substitutes, full employment, and capital ownership noted here.[48] As a consequence, it is not clear whether economic impact estimates based on them are overstated or understated.

Evidence indicates that the rate of growth induced by a sports development strategy lags behind the rate of growth associated with generating development in other ways. After examining economic growth for numerous cities that built or renovated professional sports facilities, Baade and Dye concluded:

> The impact of stadium construction or renovation on the metropolitan area's share of regional income is negative and significant. This result is

---

46. The stadium construction accident at Miller Park in Milwaukee on July 14, 1999, illustrates this point. A crane collapsed, killing three ironworkers and seriously injuring the crane operator. Of the four people, only two resided in the Milwaukee metropolitan statistical area. The third steelworker was from Kimberly, Wisconsin, and the crane operator was from Houston, Texas.

47. It is not altogether clear whether occupancy rates increase during sports events. If a host city is a popular convention destination, it may be that overnight stays in conjunction with sporting events displace some hotel reservations that would occur as a consequence of other activities that would have occurred in their absence.

48. The potential shortcomings in calculating the multiplier values described above apply also to the uncustomized versions of the most recent version of the U.S. Department of Commerce's Regional Input-Output Systems (RIMS II), a popular tool used by forecasters. Even when the models used to forecast are customized, the possibility remains that essential pieces of information will be ignored, and the forecast may miss the mark as a consequence. The models constructed by Regional Economic Models, Inc. (REMI), to their credit, specify an endogenous labor sector, which gives more accurate readings on the employment and wage implications of an "economic event," but the accuracy of the REMI projections depends on the quality of the model that predicts the future of the regional economy in the absence of an event (control forecast) and the economy's future (alternative forecast). The event's economic impact is estimated as the difference between the control and the alternative forecast.

consistent with the kind of economic activity that stadiums and professional sports spawn. Professional sports and stadiums divert economic development toward labor-intensive, relatively unskilled labor (low-wage) activities. To the extent that this developmental path diverges from less labor-intensive, more highly skilled labor (high-wage) activities characteristic of other economies within the region, it would be expected that the sports-minded area would experience a falling share of regional income.[49]

The reasons should now be clear. Sports with resource markets that are largely national in character may displace locally owned and operated industries. Value added locally may well be replaced by value added nationally or internationally. Local governments must endeavor to limit the leakage of economic activity to maximize the local benefits of any economic development project. The importance of this fact should not be ignored in generating credible economic impact estimates.[50]

To date, an adequate description of the value-added process for immense urban economies has eluded the grasp of scholars. It is not cynical to say that estimates of the value added by sports facilities, teams, and events have not been developed with sufficient care in the prospective analyses used to evaluate the efficacy of sports subsidies. That deficiency explains why ex ante economic impact estimates financed or conducted by those who stand to benefit from public subsidies have been greeted with such skepticism by scholars. If prospective estimates are to be used in assessing the merits of subsidies for sports facilities, then they should, at the very least, be filtered through retrospective analyses of cities of a similar economic character to lend some context or supportive evidence.

It should also be noted that at least in some cases, the seemingly divergent results for ex ante and ex post studies can be reconciled by elaborating on the meaning of statistical insignificance and confidence intervals. When a statistician concludes that the impact of a team, facility, or mega-event is not meaningfully different from zero, that does not equate to saying that the impact is zero. The impact could be a positive or negative number that, in the context of a large metropolitan economy, is not sufficient to reject the hypothesis that its value is meaningfully different from zero. If the Super Bowl generates an economic impact of $50 million for a host city, for example, it would not qualify as a statistically significant economic event in the large metropolises that host the game. If, however, the host city knew that the impact of the game was $50 mil-

---

49. Baade and Dye (1990, p. 12).

50. For a description of the mathematics involved in calculating what a team, event, or stadium/arena contributes to a local economy, see Noll and Zimbalist (1997, p. 75), and Baade and Matheson (2000).

lion, then the benefit side of the cost-benefit ledger would properly include the $50 million in economic impact. It is difficult, of course, to identify what amounts to a needle in an economic haystack in the case of a small economic impact. The challenge for the scholar who is auditing the impact of commercial sports is to create a model capable of teasing out of a constantly changing economic landscape that portion of change attributable to sport.

Finally, economic impact results will differ according to the size of the area analyzed.

As previously noted, a reduction in spending associated with residents leaving a community during an event to avoid crowds and congestion would decrease spending and income in the metropolis, all else equal. The effect on economic activity in the metropolitan area beyond the neighborhood in which the event is held, would depend, of course, on particulars related to the location of changed resident spending. The impact on the metropolitan economy could be zero or less than zero, while the impact on the neighborhood economy could be positive.

Policymakers must distinguish among local, metropolitan, and national economic impacts, including fiscal impacts. As observed above, the substitution effect will be larger as the area of analysis expands outward from the location of the event (economic ground zero). Spectators who reside outside the neighborhood in which the event is held will contribute positively to economic activity within the event's neighborhood since nonresident spending boosts net spending within the neighborhood. As the area of analysis expands, the likelihood increases that spending in conjunction with the event will simply substitute for spending that would otherwise occur. The Olympic Games attract a global audience and are more likely to contribute to an increase in spending locally, regionally, and nationally than would a smaller event, all else equal.

A policymaker must be cognizant of those realities as they relate to spending substitutions since they have significant implications for tax revenues from the event. For example, in subsidizing the construction of a stadium, a state government needs to consider the relocation of spending from areas outside a host city to the host city as a consequence of the subsidy. The state would need to find a justification for reallocating spending from one locale in its jurisdiction to another. The federal government, following the same logic, would have to identify a rationale for subsidizing a mega-sports event such as the Olympic Games, since the games divert income from some communities and regions to others within the nation.

In summary, the consensus of scholars is that subsidies for sports franchises and mega-events do not induce economic development on a scale that justifies them. Dennis Coates and Brad R. Humphreys surveyed scholarly work on the subsidy question and drew a conclusion echoing that drawn by Siegfried and Zimbalist.[51] To wit:

> Although the intuitive argument and survey evidence do not deny the possibility of certain local economic benefits from sports subsidies, the empirical findings also strongly reject sports subsidies on the grounds of a lack of economic benefits. The large and growing peer-reviewed economics literature on the economic impact of stadiums, arenas, sports franchises, and sports mega-events has consistently found no substantial evidence of increased jobs, incomes, or tax revenues for a community associated with any of these things. Focusing our attention on research done by economists, as opposed to that of scholars from public policy or urban development and planning departments, we find near unanimity in the conclusion that stadiums, arenas and sports franchises have no consistent, positive impact on jobs, income, and tax revenues.[52]

Although a large majority of independent scholars who study the economic impact question hold that view, as Coates and Humphreys noted, it is not unanimous. There are researchers who argue that the urban context in which a stadium or arena is constructed does matter and that if careful thought is given to that context, then sports facilities have the capacity to induce a statistically and economically significant economic impact.[53] A public policy planner should not necessarily conclude that a downtown ballpark is a panacea for a deteriorating central business district (CBD). There is more to the "context," according to Ziona Austrian and Mark S. Rosentraub, who recognize the potential benefit of a downtown facility.[54] Quoting Austrian and Rosentraub as it relates to the experience in Cleveland and Indianapolis:

> The experiences of Cleveland and Indianapolis indicate that a downtown sports strategy can help to sustain the centrality of an urban center's core area, but not as a result of tangible outcomes related to the sports investment itself. In other words, the presence of the teams and their facilities did not spawn the creation of a large number of new jobs.[55]

Commercial sports as part of a larger development strategy may induce economic development, but the ability of sports to do so alone is doubtful. The key

---

51. Coates and Humphreys (2008); Siegfried and Zimbalist (2000).
52. Coates and Humphreys (2008, p. 310).
53. See, for example, Santo (2005).
54. Austrian and Rosentraub (2002).
55. Austrian and Rosentraub (2002, p. 561).

to development through sports may well be connected to the fact that a community coalesces around sport and agrees on a broader development strategy that serves as a catalyst for growth. The work of Rosentraub and Austrian recognizes that possibility.

Indianapolis in particular has attempted to integrate sports and its infrastructure more fully into its economy. In trying to induce development, it has emphasized amateur sports in addition to professional sports and has been successful in integrating amateur activities with the relocation of the administrative entities that govern many amateur sports. Indianapolis currently hosts approximately twenty-five sports-related organizations, including the National Collegiate Athletic Association (NCAA). It is erroneous to attribute Indianapolis's sports-induced growth to the presence of professional sports alone; it is the city's integrated sports development strategy, including both amateur and professional sports, that has boosted the city economy. The permanent presence of the amateur sports bodies and their resident staffs accounts for the majority of the boost that sports have provided.

Holger Preuss, a highly regarded German economist, expressed a similar sentiment in speaking to members of London Legacy 2020. Summarizing Preuss's remarks, the London Legacy reporter observed:

> These infrastructure and location factors drive up costs of Olympic projects, and yet they are the investments that long term drive legacy benefit. The Games are a catalyst and an excuse that can justify this additional spend[ing].
>
> The implication of this seemed to be that strategically planned infrastructure spend[ing], whilst increasing the headline budget, is key to capturing benefits to a host city.[56]

The scholarship that argues that sports can stimulate economic development if the context is "right" does not distinguish between development attributable to the team and facilities and that attributable to the broader development plan. Can an economic justification be identified for subsidizing a team, facility, or mega-event in the absence of additional infrastructure development? The following discussion identifies and analyzes other possible benefits from sports subsidies, including the quality of life in a community and economic benefits that are tangential to the team, facility, or event.

---

56. London Legacy 2020, "The Economics of Securing an Olympics Legacy" (London: East London Business Alliance, 2009) (www.sport.uni-mainz.de/Preuss/Download/%20public/081220_Holger_Preuss_on_economic_impact_of_2012.pdf).

Quality of Life and Indirect Economic Benefits from Subsidies

Oscar Wilde once observed, "Nowadays people know the price of everything and the value of nothing"—a remark that has been modified on occasion to reflect a popular perception of economists.[57] Do economists know the price of everything and the value of nothing with respect to commercial sports teams, facilities, and mega-events? Is there value associated with commercial sports other than that associated with the economic impact of the team, facility, or event? If so, what is it and how might it be measured? It is conceivable, for example, that the hedonic value and/or benefits tangential to those commonly associated with commercial sports are substantial enough to justify the public expenditure? Moon Landrieu, the mayor of New Orleans at the time that the Superdome was built, believed that they were: "The superdome is an exercise of optimism. A statement of faith. It is the very building of it that is important, not how much it is used or its economics."[58]

John L. Crompton described the benefits associated with teams, facilities, and events that need to be considered in assessing the efficacy of sport subventions:

> The need for an affirmative vote at the polls before a project can be con-
> structed means that extensive emotional public debate invariably sur-
> rounds these decisions. The author's analysis of these debates suggests that
> advocates use five lines of argument to support their case: (1) economic
> impact from the spending of visitors to the community; (2) increased
> community visibility; (3) enhanced community image; (4) stimulation of
> other development; and (5) psychic income.[59]

Argument 1 has been discussed in detail in the previous sections of this chapter. Arguments 2, 3, and 4 might be collectively identified as economic "signaling"—a message that a city, region, or country communicates to the rest of the world making it known that it is physically and dispositionally open to expanding its trade with the outside world. Is there a measurable economic benefit in signaling? One advantage of a retrospective analysis is that if there is a signaling effect, it should translate into increased levels of economic activity due to a collection of initiatives, for which the sports event serves as a proxy, that expand trade. If the signaling claim is valid, a change in output, income, or employment in the area analyzed should follow the openness-to-trade signal symbolized by a

---

57. Oscar Wilde, *The Picture of Dorian Gray and Three Stories* (New York: New American Library, 1995), p. 63.

58. Quoted in J. D. Reed, "Louisiana Purchase: Superdome in New Orleans," *Sports Illustrated,* July 22, 1974, pp. 66–72.

59. Crompton (2001, p. 16).

change in the commercial sports sector. As previously noted, retrospective analysis, for the most part, fails to provide economic support for a signaling phenomenon. Holger Preuss reportedly noted the following as it relates to the importance of signaling in addressing the possibility of an economic legacy following the 2012 Summer Olympic Games in London:

> Holger then looked in more detail at the drivers of genuine legacy from the Games. He noted that the injection of money from tourism and visitors to the Games leaves no noticeable impact two years post Games. In Germany it was estimated the World Cup boosted the German gross domestic product by just 0.13 percent. . . . The real benefit comes from: (1) change of location factors; and (2) signaling effect.[60]

Preuss's "location factors" refers to changes in infrastructure in addition to those required to accommodate the actual events that contribute to economic activity following the event. Change in location factors as it relates to teams and stadiums refers to the facility "context" discussed previously—that is, the movement of a stadium from the suburbs to the central business district. The physical context, to reiterate, involves development beyond the team and stadium, and an analyst needs to be careful not to ascribe any observed meaningful change in the economic landscape to the team, facility, or event alone.

Preuss reportedly focused on the impressions that a community creates in describing the signaling phenomenon as it related to the Summer Olympic Games hosted by Beijing in 2008. Preuss made reference to the significance of the Bird's Nest, the spectacular stadium built for the opening ceremonies and for track and field events. Specifically,

> Games and the way they are staged has signaling effects. That is to say they carry subliminal signals about the host city. The Chinese could have built a budget stadium. By building the Bird's Nest, they sent messages to their own population and to the world at all sorts of levels. Whatever London does will also send messages, and we would do well to orchestrate those.[61]

Do these psychological signals take economic form? The evidence is mixed. Andrew K. Rose and Mark Spiegel have concluded that signals relating to the

60. London Legacy 2020, "The Economics of Securing an Olympics Legacy" (London: East London Business Alliance, 2009) (www.sport.uni-mainz.de/Preuss/Download %20public/081220_Holger_Preuss_on_economic_impact_of_2012.pdf).

61. London Legacy 2020, "The Economics of Securing an Olympics Legacy" (London: East London Business Alliance, 2009) (www.sport.uni-mainz.de/Preuss/Download %20public/081220_Holger_Preuss_on_economic_impact_of_2012.pdf).

Olympic Games do translate to statistically significant changes in economic activity as it relates to exports:

> Our results suggest that the Olympic effect on trade in the data is not associated with hosting the games but rather from bidding for them; bidding to host the games seems to send a signal that has a sizeable trade-expanding effect. . . . Our model is of the "burning money" type. In keeping with our empirical results, we assume that countries that intend to pursue liberal trade policies in the future can signal this intent by engaging in the costly activity of bidding to host the Olympic Games. The payoff for sending this signal is that countries which expect to liberalize receive increased investment in the export sector (the sector whose prices are raised by liberalization).[62]

The authors conclude then that bidding for the Olympics serves as a proxy for declaring a more liberal trade policy. It is not the bidding itself that causes the approximately 30 percent increase in exports for the bidding country, but the fact that the country is now behaving in a way that encourages trade. However, the assertion that bidding for the Olympics correlates with a liberal trade policy is not equivalent to saying that bidding for the Olympics causes an increase in exports and induces an increase in national income, output, and employment.

Crompton noted that the question of whether subsidies stimulate other forms of economic development needs to be considered. All else equal, it can be expected that a city that hosts professional sports offers an additional amenity that makes it a more attractive place to live and work. It is reasonable to expect, therefore, that cities that have a commercial sports presence experience rates of economic growth that exceed those of communities that are sports deprived. The evidence indicates that sports does not rate as a major location factor, at least as measured by changes in manufacturing activity: a study by Baade and Dye concludes that the evidence does not suggest a correlation between major league sports and the location of manufacturing firms.[63]

The Baade and Dye study is, in fairness, somewhat dated, but the evidence gathered would support what is theoretically appealing. It is doubtful that a professional sports presence would rank high on the list of considerations when businesses relocate. The existence of a skilled labor force, favorable tax rates, and adequate infrastructure would arguably trump the existence of a particular leisure activity. Context and signaling may be important, however, and the presence of

---

62. Rose and Spiegel (2009, p. 19).
63. Baade and Dye (1988).

professional sports may be a proxy for other aspects of a city's economy or culture that may be important in determining where businesses locate.

Sports impart benefits to the community that are hedonic in character. The word "hedonics" is of Greek origin, and it translates as "pleasure doctrine."[64] A psychologist studying hedonics would note that it includes both pleasant and unpleasant sensations and states of mind. Sports provide benefits and impose costs that may be difficult to measure but that require consideration if prudent decisions regarding subsidies are to be made.

The contingent valuation method (CVM), also known as the "stated preference" method, can be used to provide valuable information on the elusive concept of psychic income as it relates to commercial sports and could potentially justify subsidies for sport. CVM was first applied to the study of ecosystem and environmental services.[65] It can be used to study both "use" and "non-use" values, but the term, particularly as it relates to environmental issues, has almost become synonymous with the estimation of non-use or passive values.[66] The CVM has been extended to the study of the non-use values of a range of amenities, including the arts, cultural pursuits, and sports entertainment.[67]

The CVM generally involves directly surveying people about their willingness to pay "contingent on a specific hypothetical scenario."[68] Criticisms of the CVM are numerous, but most have to do with the inability of surveys to gauge consumer preferences accurately. Surveys, no matter how clever the design, cannot easily replicate the information that the market provides on the willingness of people to pay and the benefit derived from their purchases.

The substantive problem with the CVM is the absence of information gleaned from market transactions relating to "use values" on which to base non-use valuations. Kibitzing around a water cooler on Monday morning following an NFL game on Sunday may generate utility for those participating in such

64. Antony Mueller, "The Illusions of Hedonics," *Mises Daily,* July 29, 2005, www.mises.org/story/1873.

65. Dennis M. King, Marisa J. Mazzotta, and Kenneth J. Markowitz Jr., "Ecosystem Valuation: Contingent Valuation Method," U.S. Department of Agriculture and National Oceanic and Atmospheric Administration (www.ecosystemvaluation.org/contingent_valuation.htm).

66. Non-use value, as the term suggests, means value derived not from the use of the good but from its very existence. Non-use value, therefore, is often identified as existence or passive value. Non-use value emanates primarily from three sources: the desire to preserve something, holding something because of uncertainty about the future demand for or supply of it, and the altruistic pleasure derived from the use of a good by others.

67. See, for example, the September 2004 *Journal of Arts Management, Law, and Society* for several articles focusing on using CVM for valuing arts and culture.

68. Dennis M. King, Marisa J. Mazzotta, and Kenneth J. Markowitz Jr., "Ecosystem Valuation: Contingent Valuation Method," U.S. Department of Agriculture and National Oceanic and Atmospheric Administration (www.ecosystemvaluation.org/contingent_valuation.htm).

discussions, but there is no information that can be extracted from market trans-actions to help inform the valuation of the benefits to those who participate. Contrast that to oil spills, where losses to the commercial fishing and tourist industries can be gauged through measurable market activity. Non-use value does not provide any readily apparent behavioral clues that can be employed to measure that value.

The issue is complicated by the fact that teams, facilities, and mega-events may qualify, at least in part, as public goods. (If they are a source of civic pride then everyone in a metropolitan area may benefit from their presence even with-out attending a game.) The optimal provision of a public good is theoretically defined as the point at which the sum of the individual benefits for the last unit of the good provided (sum of the individual marginal benefits) equals the social cost of providing that unit. The CVM requires reasonably accurate information about preferences for all of those affected.

The fact that sports are culturally important and yield value is not at issue, but the question of how much value they yield is vital to public practice as it relates to the allocation of resources in support of commercial sports. Then too, teams, stadiums, and events may mean more to citizens in one community than another or provide benefits over a larger area in some locales than in others. It can be argued that the Green Bay Packers are a Wisconsin team and, by compar-ing the list of cultural options in Green Bay with those in Los Angeles, that the Packers are more important to residents of Wisconsin than the Raiders or Rams were to residents of Los Angeles. The fact that the Packers are publicly owned provides testimony to the historical importance of the team to Green Bay and Wisconsin and to the extent to which the city's and state's identity has been linked to the team. That fact argues for separate CVM studies of specific teams, facilities, and events. No two communities are identical in the benefit that teams, facilities, and events impart to them.

Bruce K. Johnson, Michael Mondello, and John C. Whitehead used CVM to estimate the value of public goods that the NFL's Jaguars produced for their host city, Jacksonville, Florida:

> The present value of public goods created by the Jaguars is $36.5 million or less, far below subsidies provided to attract the Jaguars. For a basketball team the figure is less than $22.8 million. The results add to the growing body of CVM literature indicating that sports public goods probably can-not justify the large public expenditures on stadiums and arenas.[69]

---

69. Johnson, Mondello, and Whitehead (2005, p. 2).

Johnson, Mondello, and Whitehead noted a systematic bias that has been ascribed to CVM studies:

> If some critics of CVM are correct, even the low figures found in CVM sports studies are overstated. They claim CVM overstates willingness to pay for public goods and that willingness to pay estimates should be calibrated to correct for hypothetical bias. The National Oceanic and Atmospheric Administration in 1994 proposed a default calibration of dividing reported willingness to pay by two to correct for bias in environmental CVM analyses. To the extent the critics are correct, the estimates reported in this paper for the value of public goods generated by the Jaguars, low as they are, may nevertheless be biased upward.[70]

Gerald Carlino and N. Edward Coulson proposed another method, referred to as "compensating differentials," for estimating the value of professional sports teams that makes use of information gleaned directly from markets other than the market for professional sports. That method involves recognizing that a difference in price for the same good in different markets may reflect the value of something other than that good. For example, a person may be willing to accept a lower wage or pay higher rent for living and working in a warm, sunny city than for living and working in a cold, rainy one. The wage or rent differential provides a measure of the value placed on the more pleasant climate and thus compensates for the wage differential. Carlino and Coulson proposed measuring the amenity value of the NFL using compensating differentials.

> [I]f people like having professional sports teams in their community, they are presumably willing to pay for it—if not directly through the purchase of season tickets, then indirectly through an increased willingness to pay for housing in the area and an increased willingness to accept marginally lower wages. . . . We found that the presence of an NFL team raises annual rents, on average, 8 percent. We also found that wages were about 2 percent lower in cities that host an NFL team, but the differential was not statistically significant. . . . The annual quality-of-life benefit of $139 million found in our study is substantially larger than the annual subsidy suggesting that these subsidies were good investments for the typical city. Our study showed that the quality-of-life benefit to households easily exceeds the subsidies granted in all cities that hosted an NFL team during the 1990s.[71]

70. Johnson, Mondello, and Whitehead (2005, p. 18).
71. Carlino and Coulson (2004, p. 11).

The compensating differentials argument is hampered by the fact that cities that can afford professional sports teams also can afford other cultural amenities. The difficulty is to tease out the portion of the compensating differential that is attributable to sport. Coates, Humphreys, and Zimbalist used several alternative "reasonable specifications" to retest the Carlino and Coulson compensating differentials argument to justify subsidies for NFL teams. They found that the results did not withstand further testing. The authors concluded that the presence of an NFL franchise did not increase rents for apartments in the center city.[72]

Other studies that used the compensating differentials technique failed to support Carlino and Coulson's finding that the presence of professional sport correlated with higher property values. Carolyn A. Dehring, Craig A. Depkin II, and Michael Ward concluded that residential property values declined by 1.5 percent in Arlington, Texas, when it was announced that the Dallas Cowboys would be building a new stadium there. The authors of the Arlington study noted that the decline in property values approximated the increase in sales taxes for the average household to subsidize the stadium. They concluded that the amenity effect of hosting the Cowboys was not meaningfully different from zero.[73]

There is little doubt that commercial sports do provide amenity value, but the evidence regarding the amount is ambiguous. CVM studies generally conclude that citizens of a community do not derive sufficient value from teams to justify the large subsidies for them. However, one study using the compensating differentials methodology concludes that the improvement in the quality of life imparted by NFL football does justify subsidies for NFL teams. The question remains whether the compensating differentials truly reflect a quality-of-life enhancement attributable to professional sports alone or whether they reflect the sum of cultural amenities in communities affluent enough to accommodate commercial sports. The most recent empirical work suggests that even for a sport as popular as NFL football, the amenity effect is negligible.

Conclusions and Policy Implications

Public subventions for sport have been substantial over the past two decades, and the producers of sport entertainment have clearly benefited. The windfall for players and owners has been criticized, but the additional social value that sports create may justify the largesse. Has the money been well spent from the public's point of view? Has the return on the expenditures on sports not only

---

72. Coates, Humphreys, and Zimbalist (2006).
73. Dehring, Depken, and Ward (2007).

been positive but also greater than what would have been realized from the best alternative use of the funds?

A preponderance of evidence suggests that sports subsidies alone do not produce social value in excess of their social costs. As part of a larger redevelopment plan, expenditures on teams, facilities, and sports mega-events may induce an increase in economic activity in an urban core, but that increase may come at the expense of other parts of the metropolitan or regional economies. Logic suggests that stadium environs/neighborhoods are more likely to experience a positive economic impact if one occurs because the substitution effect is weakest closest to the stadium locale or event. Spending on the team or event activities is likely to be mitigated by reduced spending on other things further from economic ground zero. While the stadium neighborhood has the greatest potential for experiencing an increase in net spending as a consequence of the influx of non-residents, the further from the locus of play or the event, the less the increase.

Because the modern sports facility provides a greater range of culinary and retail options, it is not certain that even the neighborhood experiences a significant increase in net spending in conjunction with commercial sport events. That is due to the fact that the spillover of economic activity into the neighborhood is negated—either indirectly, by the provision of a range of spending options within the stadium walls or directly, by the reduction in commercial activity related to sports outside the facility. Independent vendors in some host cities are not allowed to market their wares within a certain distance of the stadium, and only league-sanctioned paraphernalia or memorabilia can be manufactured and sold.[74]

Some cities have implemented more comprehensive economic development plans that include sports facilities but do not rely on them. Indianapolis and Cleveland are two cities that have planned mixed-use developments in which sports facilities play an important role but represent only a part of a plan. Such developments are designed to capitalize on the synergies that exist between residential and commercial activities, including sports. It is erroneous to attribute an increase in economic activity to the construction of sports facilities alone if they represent only a portion of a development project or plan.

The intensity with which a facility is used is critical to the return to the public sector from its investment in a subsidized facility. The Staples Center in Los Angeles received a $71 million dollar subsidy from the city of Los Angeles, and it has been estimated that the city receives a tax increment of $710,000 annually on its

---

74. The U.S. Supreme Court heard arguments in *American Needle, Inc.* v. *National Football League, cert. granted* 129 S. Ct. 2859 (2009) on January 13, 2010, on the question of whether a league can function as a single entity in contracting for production rights with a single firm for paraphernalia. The Supreme Court ruled against the NFL in a unanimous decision on May 24, 2010.

investment.[75] Although the fiscal return on the Staples Center is positive due to its intensive use (more than 200 use dates annually), it is very likely not economically profitable, since alternative uses of the subsidy, in all probability, would have yielded a return in excess of 1 percent.

The transfer of income and wealth from taxpayers to owners and players and from federal, state, and county coffers to those of local governments has numerous and substantial policy implications. Painting with the broadest strokes, the benefits associated with "efficiency" as it relates to public subsidies for sports do not appear to compensate for the negative equity implications of the subventions. There is some dovetailing of the interests of a portion of the taxpaying public, some fans, and the producers of sports, but the shared interests do not appear to be large or comprehensive enough to justify sports subsidies.

The fact that the subsidies are provided with such frequency is not testament to the political leadership's understanding of their economic efficacy, as some have suggested.[76] It more likely points to predictable outcomes related to the functioning of the unregulated monopoly that is the sports industry and to the operation of political coalitions, particularly related to political decision-making when a community is threatened with the loss of a team if a subsidy is not provided. Arguably the most significant policy challenge involves devising a strategy that would allow government to become an equal partner in negotiations with teams and leagues. That cannot happen as long as the leagues, which represent owners, make the decisions with regard to franchise relocation and league expansion. When leagues can sustain excess demand for teams, the choice for parsimonious communities threatened with the loss of a franchise is crystal clear: provide subsidies consistent with the current standard or lose your franchise.

Finally, since the preponderance of evidence does not support the notion that sports subsidies alone can serve as a catalyst for economic development, subsidy debates should focus on the public benefits as they relate to any enhanced quality of life imparted to a community by teams, facilities, and sports mega-events. Future research should focus on techniques for estimating the hedonic component of sports subsidies, and both the contingent valuation and compensating differentials methods show promise in that regard. Moon Landrieu may have been right in saying that "it is the very building of it that is important, not how much it is used or its economics."[77]

75. Baade (2003).
76. Carlino and Coulson (2004).
77. Quoted in J. D. Reed, "Louisiana Purchase: Superdome in New Orleans," *Sports Illustrated,* July 22, 1974, pp. 66–72.

References

Adelson, Bruce. 1995. *The Minor League Baseball Book.* New York: Simon and Schuster.

Austrian, Ziona, and Mark S. Rosentraub. 2002. "Cities, Sports, and Economic Change: A Retrospective Assessment." *Journal of Urban Affairs* 24, no. 5: 549–63.

Baade, Robert A. 2003. "Evaluating Subsidies for Professional Sports in the United States and Europe: A Public-Sector Primer." *Oxford Review of Economic Policy* 19, no. 4: 585–97.

———. 1999. "An Analysis of Why and How the United States' Judiciary Has Interpreted the Question of Professional Sports and Economic Development." In *The Economic Impact of Sports Events,* edited by Claude Jeanrenaud (Neuchatel, Switzerland: Centre International d'Etude du Sport), pp. 43–45.

———. 1996. "Professional Sports as a Catalyst for Metropolitan Economic Development." *Journal of Urban Affairs* 18, no. 1: 1–17.

———. 2003. *Los Angeles City Controller's Report on Economic Impact: Staples Center.* City of Los Angeles.

Baade, Robert A., and Richard F. Dye. 1988 . "An Analysis of the Economic Rationale for Public Subsidization of Sports Stadiums." *Annals of Regional Science* 22, no. 2: 45–46.

———. 1990. "The Impact of Stadiums and Professional Sports on Metropolitan Area Development." *Growth and Change* 21, no. 2: 1–14.

Baade, Robert A., and Victor Matheson. 2000. "High Octane? Grading the Economic Impact of the Daytona 500." *Marquette Sports Law Journal* 10, no. 2: 413–15.

———. 2007. "NFL Governance and the Fate of the New Orleans Saints: Some Observations." In *Governance and Competition in Professional Sports Leagues,* edited by Plácido Rodríguez, Stefan Kesenne, and Jaume García, pp. 141–68. Gijon, Spain: Universidad de Oviedo.

Baade, Robert A., Mimi Nikolova, and Victor Matheson. 2007. "A Tale of Two Stadiums: Comparing the Economic Impact of Chicago's Wrigley Field and U.S. Cellular Field." *Geographische Rundschau International Edition* 3, no. 1: 53–58.

Baade, Robert A., and Laura J. Tiehan. 1990. "An Analysis of Major League Baseball Attendance, 1969–987." *Journal of Sport and Social Issues* 14, no. 1: 14–32.

Carlino, Gerald A., and N. Edward Coulson. 2004. "Should Cities Be Ready for Some Football? Assessing the Social Benefits of Hosting an NFL Team." *Business Review* (Federal Reserve Bank of Philadelphia), 2nd quarter, pp. 7–17.

Clark, Greg. 2008. "Local Development Benefits from Staging Global Events." Paris: Organisation for Economic Co-operation and Development.

Coates, Dennis, and Brad Humphreys. 2008. "Do Economists Reach a Conclusion on Subsidies for Sports Franchises, Stadiums, and Mega-Events?" *Econ Journal Watch* 5, no. 3: 294–315.

———. 1999. "The Growth Effects of Sports Franchises, Stadia, and Arenas." *Journal of Policy Analysis and Management* 18, no. 4: 601–24.

Coates, Dennis, Brad R. Humphreys, and Andrew Zimbalist. 2006. "Compensating Differentials and the Social Benefits of the NFL: A Comment." *Journal of Urban Economics* 60, no. 1: 124–31.

Crompton, John L. 2001. "Public Subsidies to Professional Team Sports Facilities in the USA." In *Sport in the City: The Role of Sport in Economic and Social Regeneration,* edited by Chris Gratton and Ian P. Henry, pp. 15–34. London: Routledge.

Dehring, Carolyn A., Craig A. Depken II, and Michael R. Ward. 2007. "The Impact of Stadium Announcements on Residential Property Values: Evidence from a Natural Experiment in Dallas–Fort Worth." *Contemporary Economic Policy* 25, no. 4: 627–38.

Dick Conway and Associates. 1994. *Seattle Mariners Baseball Club Economic Impact.* Report prepared for King County, Washington.

European Tour Operators Association. 2006. *Olympic Report.* London (www.etoa.org/Pdf/ETOA%20Report%20Olympic.pdf).

Finer, John. 2002. "The Grand Illusion." *Far Eastern Economic Review* 165, no. 9: 32–36.

Fox, Gregory W. 2005. "Public Finance and the West Side Stadium: The Future of Stadium Subsidies in New York." *Brooklyn Law Review* 71, no. 1: 477–518.

Griffin, Tom. 1997. "Pro Sport's Impact on the Economy Is Closer to a Bunt than a Home Run, but There May Be Other Reasons to Keep Teams Swinging at Home." *Columns* (University of Washington Alumni Association), June 1997 (www.washington.edu/alumni/columns/june97/game1.html).

Johnson, Bruce K., Michael J. Mondello, and John C. Whitehead. 2005. "The Value of Public Goods Generated by a National Football League Team." Economics Department Working Paper 0415. Appalachian State University.

Matheson, Victor A. 2006. "Mega-Events: The Effect of the World's Biggest Sporting Events on Local, Regional, and National Economies." College of the Holy Cross Working Paper Series (October 1–25).

McConnell, Beth. 2000. "An Economic Analysis of the Impact of Proposed Taxpayer-Subsidized Sports Stadiums on Philadelphia." Philadelphia: PennPIRG.

Noll, Roger G., and Andrew Zimbalist. 1997. *Sports, Jobs, and Taxes.* Brookings.

Rose, Andrew K., and Mark M. Spiegel. 2009. "The Olympic Effect." NBER Working Paper 14854. Cambridge, Mass.: National Bureau of Economic Research.

Santo, Charles. 2005. "The Economic Impact of Sports Stadiums: Recasting the Analysis in Context." *Journal of Urban Affairs* 27, no. 2: 177–91.

Siegfried, John, and Andrew Zimbalist. 2000. "The Economics of Sports Facilities and Their Communities." *Journal of Economic Perspectives* 14, no. 3: 95–114.

Simons, Henry C. 1938. *Personal Income Taxation.* University of Chicago Press.

Terrell, Ellen, and others. 2004. "The Sports Industry: The Business of Professional Football." *Business and Economics Research Advisor,* Issue 3–4 (www.loc.gov/rr/business/BERA/issue3/football.html).

Wolff, Edward N. 2007. "Recent Trends in Household Wealth in the United States: Rising Debt and Middle-Class Squeeze." Working Paper 502. Levy Economics Institute, Bard College.

6

Public Transit as a Metropolitan Growth and Development Strategy

GENEVIEVE GIULIANO AND AJAY AGARWAL

For more than half a century, urban policy has focused on a remarkably consistent set of problems: the economic decline of central cities, rapid suburbanization, and growing disparities between the urban core and its periphery. Over the decades, the decentralization of population and jobs—urban sprawl— has been associated with a variety of external costs, such as congestion, air pollution, energy consumption, loss of open space, and more recently obesity and global climate change.[1] Urban sprawl is also associated with problems such as loss of social capital and spatial segmentation by race and class. Those who see urban sprawl as the problem see compact cities as the solution. In the tradition of Jane Jacobs, economically and socially healthy metropolitan areas should have density and diversity.[2]

More than half a century of urban policy has been aimed at reversing decentralization trends by promoting a variety of local economic development strategies, from 1950s urban renewal to the "new generation" urban rail investments of the 1970s, convention centers and sports stadiums of the 1980s and 1990s, and most recently, efforts to attract Richard Florida's "creative class."[3] In some states and metropolitan areas, growth management, growth boundaries, concurrency requirements, and other planning strategies have also been employed. Public transit, particularly rail transit, has been viewed as an essential component of reversing decentralization trends and supporting the revitalization and growth of cities. Public transit is also seen as an important means for restructuring the suburbs and guiding the growth of newer cities to transform them according to what

1. External costs are costs borne by people other than those who generate them.
2. Jacobs (1961).
3. Florida (2002).

205

are now accepted among urban planners as "smart growth" principles: cities with moderate to high population and employment densities, intermixed housing and jobs, heterogeneous neighborhoods, a high degree of walkability and access to public transit, and limited use of the private automobile.

The commitment to rail transit as an urban policy tool is reflected in its funding and its expansion to metropolitan areas throughout the United States. By 2006, fifty metropolitan areas had at least one form of rail transit in operation. Annual transit capital expenses increased from $5.1 billion in 1991 to $8.9 billion in 2007 in constant 1991 dollars.[4] In addition, the nationwide fare recovery for operating expenses is 31 percent. All capital expenses and more than two-thirds of operating expenses (totaling about $32 billion in 2006) are subsidized by federal, state, or local governments. Public funding of that magnitude suggests broad political support for public transit, and that support is in part built on expectations that the investments will solve traffic congestion and environmental, energy, and quality-of-life problems.

This chapter addresses one of those expectations: transforming the spatial form of metropolitan areas. More than three decades of research on the influence of public transit on urban form—particularly rail transit—has generated a rich literature on the topic. Although in theory investment in public transit could lead to a more compact urban form, the evidence is quite mixed. This chapter presents a critical review of the influence of rail transit on travel behavior, land use, and urban form in order to answer the following questions: What are the theoretical expectations from transit investments? Under what conditions might transit investment lead to a more compact urban form? What has been learned from the research? Finally, in view of the mixed evidence, why is transit investment still perceived as a critical policy tool for shaping cities?

The remainder of the chapter has four parts. The next section presents a theoretical discussion of the transportation/urban form connection in general and the transit/urban form connection in particular. The section that follows discusses the evidence on the impact on urban form of investment in public transit The section after that presents three brief case studies. The final section summarizes findings and discusses policy implications

Theory

Provision of transport infrastructure, both highway and transit, lowers transport costs by improving accessibility—the ease of moving from one location to

---

4. Federal Transportation Administration, "National Transit Database," 2007 (www.ntdprogram.gov/ntdprogram/data.htm).

another. As movement becomes less costly, the propensity for interaction between any two places increases. Transportation systems are networks. Locations near entry points (transit station or highway ramp) or points of intersection (highway interchanges) are valued for their accessibility. Improved accessibility is capitalized in land values, which in turn leads to higher-density development at those locations. Reduced transport costs also lead to economic productivity gains, as lower transport costs can be substituted for cheaper but more distant inputs. The underlying premise is that the new transport infrastructure significantly improves network accessibility.

Applying the concept to a rail transit system, accessibility within the rail line corridors would increase relative to accessibility within corridors not served by the rail system. All other things being equal, then, economic activity should gravitate toward the rail corridors, implying that rail transit redistributes or redirects future development. That shift should be reflected in land values—that is, property values around transit stations should be higher, thereby stimulating higher densities around rail stations. Differences between the effects of highway and transit investments are a function of the accessibility patterns that they generate. Highways are served by a ubiquitous local road system, yielding a pattern of accessibility that declines gradually from access points. In contrast, because transit systems are mainly accessed by foot, accessibility is concentrated around station areas and declines steeply with distance. It is the concentration of transit access that is the basis for using transit investments to promote higher densities and more concentrated development patterns.

If transportation costs were the key factor in determining urban form and transit investment reduced transport costs significantly, transit impacts on urban form would be straightforward. Location decisions of households and firms would result in concentrations along rail corridors. While the access patterns of transit imply concentration within the corridor, it is important to note that like any other transportation investment, transit improvements promote decentralization, because lower transport costs allow longer trips. One example is the nineteenth-century streetcar suburbs in Boston and Philadelphia.[5] During the late nineteenth century, rail transit allowed cities to expand along corridors, while the downtown prospered as a result of its location at the center of the transport network.

Muller ascribes the urban form of any given metropolitan region to the transport technology dominant during its formative stages.[6] For example, the structure of cities that developed during the late nineteenth-century streetcar era is

5. Jackson (1985); Warner (1978).
6. Muller (2004).

quite different from that of cities that developed during the freeway era, such as Atlanta or Dallas. Even today, the downtowns of older U.S. cities retain a larger share of regional employment than those of newer U.S. cities. But the freeway era suburbs of Boston or Chicago are not very different from those of Atlanta or Dallas. The explanation is the durability of capital stock and the dependence of outcomes on the historical processes that produced them. The earlier spatial forms are preserved even as transport costs and technologies change.

Muller's ideas are based on the dominant transportation technology. Today, public transit carries only a small proportion of all trips, even in the largest U.S. metropolitan areas. From this perspective, then, public transit would not be expected to influence the structure of today's metropolitan areas. In an article on future trends in metropolitan structure, Chinitz ascribed changes in urban form to "locators"—those who make location decisions.[7] The two main groups of locators are households and firms. If public transit investments are to have any impact on urban form, the investments must affect the decisions of locators.

Transport Costs and Residential Location Decisions

The rather straightforward mechanism by which development is concentrated along rail corridors, described above, is grounded in standard economic theory. The earliest urban models of location explained residential and employment location decisions as a trade-off between transport costs and all other costs. Households choose the locations that they most prefer, taking into account land rent, commuting cost, and the costs of all other goods and services.[8] The simplest version of the standard urban model is based on many simplifying (and unrealistic) assumptions, but it is useful for illustrating the basic principles of location choice and its implications for urban form.

Starting with a city or metropolitan area where all employment is located at the center and where only work travel is considered, standard economic theory predicts an urban form in which the highest land value and population density are at the city center because households are willing to pay more per unit of housing as transport costs decline. If housing price per unit is plotted as a function of distance from the center of the city, a downward-sloping curve is observed, with the slope getting flatter with distance from the center. Since households pay more per unit closer to the center, they consume fewer units of housing, yielding higher population density near the center and a corresponding population density curve that declines with distance from the center.

---

7. Chinitz (1991).
8. Alonso (1964); Muth (1969); Mills (1972).

The four basic factors that determine a metropolitan area's physical size in the standard urban model are population, income, transport costs, and agricultural land value. Some stylized comparisons are provided as illustrations. A population increase will increase metropolitan area size but not affect the slope of the density curve. If households desire more housing as their incomes rise, then an increase in income will generate more housing demand per household and thus increase metropolitan area size and decrease density throughout the metropolitan area. If transport costs decline, then more housing is consumed, the metropolitan area expands, and the slope of the density curve becomes flatter. If the price of agricultural land increases, metropolitan area size is reduced and the slope of the density curve becomes steeper.

Figure 6-1 and table 6-1 provide some stylized illustrations of these ideas, for peak density (population density at the center) and metropolitan area size.[9] Case 1 is the base case. Case 2 shows the effect of either reducing transport costs or increasing household income (represented by reducing the gradient, or the rate at which the slope changes, by 25 percent) while holding total population constant. Transport cost and income effects are equivalent, because both have the same effect—they increase housing demand. Metropolitan area size increases by one-third, and peak density decreases by 43 percent; density decreases throughout the metropolitan area as households consume more housing. Case 3 shows the effect of increasing population by 25 percent, holding all else constant. In this case, peak density increases by 25 percent and metropolitan area size increases by just 10.9 percent. The additional population is accommodated by raising density throughout the metropolitan area. Case 4 shows the combination of cases 2 and 3. This case yields a 30 percent reduction in peak density and 50 percent increase in city size. It can be observed that metropolitan population growth accompanied by increased household income and decreased transport costs can lead to large increases in metropolitan area size—which is just what has been seen in recent decades.

Evidence tends to support the standard theory, albeit in a very general way. Over the past several decades, per capita income has increased and real transport costs have declined. Population density declines with distance from the city center, and the population density curve has flattened over time.[10] The spatial extent of metropolitan areas has increased, as documented by several studies of urban sprawl.[11] Lower-income households tend to live near the city center and

---

9. Figure 1 and table 1 are derived analytically using an exponential density function, which is conventional in the urban economics literature. The spatial units in the figure and table have no inherent meaning but can be thought of as miles or square miles, as appropriate.

10. Anas, Arnott, and Small (1998); Giuliano, Agarwal, and Redfearn (2009).

11. Galster and others (2001); Ewing, Pendall, and Chen (2002); Glaeser and Kahn (2003).

Figure 6-1. *Population Density Gradients for Four City Forms*

Population density (population per acre)

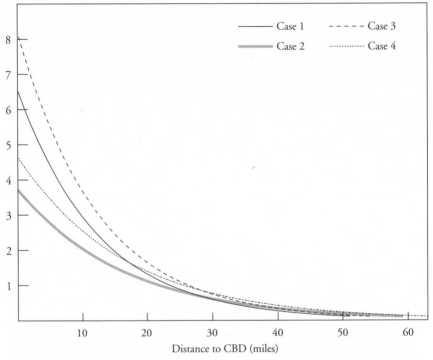

Distance to CBD (miles)

Source: Authors' illustration.

have shorter commutes, while higher-income households are more likely to live in the suburbs.[12]

The reality of metropolitan areas is, of course, far more complex than it is assumed to be in standard economic theory. In reality, even after controlling for socioeconomic and demographic characteristics, households may have different preferences, not the identical preferences assumed in the standard theory. Individual preferences often are strong predictors of residential location choice. Although the assumption has been that all employment is located at the city center, most metropolitan employment is now located outside the center—some of it concentrated in multiple "employment centers" and some dispersed with the population.[13] It follows that all commute trips are no longer made to the city

12. Mieszkowski and Mills (1993).

13. Giuliano and Small (1991); Cervero and Wu (1997); McMillen and McDonald (1998); Giuliano and others (2007); Redfearn (2007).

Table 6-1. *Four Metropolitan Forms*

Case	Population (millions)	Peak density (population per square mile), in hundreds	Gradient	Metropolitan area boundary (miles from center)	Size of metropol-itan area (square miles)	Percent change in metropol-itan area size from base case
1 Base case	4	6.5	0.08	51.8	8,413	. . .
2 Increased household income or decreased transport costs	4	3.7	0.06	59.8	11,216	33.3
3 Population up 25 percent	5	8.1	0.08	54.5	9,331	10.9
4 Population up 25 percent, plus in-creased household income or decreased transport costs	5	4.6	0.06	63.5	12,668	50.6

Source: Adapted from Giuliano, Agarwal, and Redfearn (2009).

center. Indeed there is significant cross-commuting—that is, traveling to work from a suburban residential location to a suburban work location.

Contrary to the single-worker-per-household assumption, a substantial proportion of households now have two earners. That implies that such households somehow must locate to accommodate multiple job locations. Workers now are more mobile (that is, they tend to have shorter tenure in any given job, and there is higher job turnover), which may lead households to choose their location based not only on present job location but also on ability to maximize access to future jobs as well. Furthermore, moving costs, both monetary and psychological, are high, and households often may choose a longer commute rather than move to a location closer to their workplace.[14]

In a broad sense, "housing" represents a bundle of housing-related services, including site amenities and public services such as schools, parks, public safety, local shopping, and so forth. The quality of public services and amenities varies across jurisdictions, and studies of residential property values show that local services have a significant effect on prices. In addition, durability of housing stock has given rise to a variety of housing types and neighborhoods differentiated by age, size, general condition, and local surroundings.

14. Crane (1996).

Finally, although standard theory considers only the journey to work, such trips constituted just 16.6 percent of daily travel for households earning more than $25,000 a year in 2001 (work-related trips made up another 3.3 percent).[15] Most trips are taken for other purposes (daily household maintenance, school, social activities, and so forth). Thus, access to work is just one of many types of access likely to be considered in choosing household location. And transport costs for the journey to work are a small portion of total household transport costs.

These observations imply that residential location choice is much more nuanced than the simple trade-off between housing cost and commute cost that the standard theory posits. If transport costs are one of many factors considered and households have highly varied preferences, the impact of changes in the transport system on household location choice is likely to be far more modest than stylized examples suggest.

Transport Costs and Employment Location Decisions

In theory, a firm's location choice depends on total transport costs: the cost of transporting labor and other inputs to the production location and the costs of transporting goods to market. If input costs dominate, firms will locate closer to input sources (including labor); if output costs dominate, firms will locate closer to market nodes. The decline in manufacturing and increase in services and information processing observed over the past several decades implies that output costs (costs of shipping products to market) are becoming relatively less important in making location decisions, and the decentralization of employment suggests that access to labor is becoming relatively more important.

The countervailing force to decentralized employment is agglomeration economies: the external benefits accruing to firms from spatial proximity—for example, labor force access, knowledge spillover, and input sharing. There is an active debate among scholars regarding the nature and extent of agglomeration economies.[16] One argument is that transport and information costs are so low that agglomeration economies exist only at the regional or metropolitan level.[17] Another argument is that the fast-moving, knowledge-intensive, global economy relies heavily on face-to-face communication and expert management control.[18] The first argument implies a decentralized employment distribution; the second implies a clustered employment distribution. Changes in the distribution of employment, including the extensive evidence of multiple employment

15. Hu and Reuscher (2004, p. 54).
16. For a more detailed discussion on the subject, see Giuliano, Agarwal, and Redfearn (2009).
17. Gordon and Richardson (1996).
18. Graham and Marvin (1996); Castells and Hall (1994).

centers in metropolitan areas, supports the second argument. The existence of localized agglomeration economies is important in considering the potential impacts of rail transit. Without such economies, firms would be unwilling to pay the higher prices of density—land values and congestion costs.

Finally, as with household location choice, firm location choice is subject to path dependence associated with long-lived capital stock and variations in preferences with regard to amenities and services. Studies of firm location show that many factors besides transport costs influence location choice, including local services and taxes, school quality, access to amenities, and so forth.[19]

Ubiquity of Transport Infrastructure Access

With respect to accessibility, it is important to consider the context in which transportation investments take place. Accessibility is a function of both spatial structure and the transportation system. Today's metropolitan areas are characterized by a decentralized population and employment distribution, punctuated by higher-density clusters, and by an extensive transport network. For example, we recently conducted research on various types of accessibility in the Los Angeles area, seeking to distinguish accessibility provided by the transport network from accessibility provided by the distribution of jobs and population. Figure 6-2 illustrates how accessibility varies within the area based only on the highway transport network. (The transit network offers a much lower level of accessibility and therefore is swamped by highway accessibility.) It can be readily seen that accessibility is highest in the urban core, but that area includes many square miles. Even if transport access is a significant factor in location choice, there are many possible locations with comparable levels of access.

The potential effect of a new transportation investment may be defined by the extent to which it changes the level and spatial pattern of access. Given the ubiquity of transport network accessibility in metropolitan areas, however, addition of any new transport facility may not have any discernible regional impact on either urban form or travel patterns. New facilities, even if large scale, may have little relative impact when viewed from a regional perspective.[20] Public transit has an even greater challenge. In order to affect metropolitan form, any new transit investment must significantly change accessibility, but metropolitan access is dominated by the road system. The impacts of transit investments, however, are aimed more at the local level: specific investments or policies are used to direct population and economic growth to transit-accessible locations. We turn now to other public policies that may influence location choice at the local level.

19. Gottlieb (1995).
20. Giuliano (2004).

Figure 6-2. *Network Accessibility, Los Angeles Region*

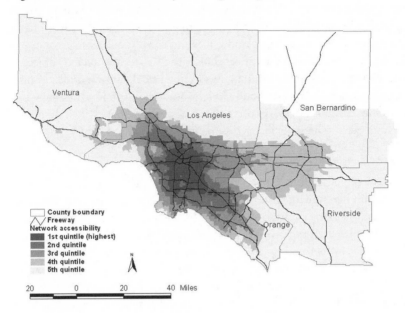

Source: Authors' illustration based on highway network in 2000.

Other Policy Considerations

With few exceptions, local governments have land use control in the United States, and they use their regulatory authority to achieve economic growth and other goals. One of the most important issues on a city's agenda involves maintaining or improving the city's fiscal base.[21] Cities have increasingly enacted "fiscal" zoning regulations that promote development of activities that generate high tax revenues but have low service needs—for example, high-end housing and commercial or retail development.[22] Cities may use incentives such as subsidies, tax breaks, and density bonuses to attract their preferred types of development. They also may use disincentives such as parking requirements, minimum lot size, or density limits to deter nonpreferred types of development. In states where property tax limits have resulted in shifts to other forms of taxation, such as the local sales tax, the distorting effect of local fiscal policy is more pronounced.[23]

Exclusionary zoning includes regulations that implicitly exclude the poor by restricting the capacity to provide low-cost housing—for example, by mandating

21. Peterson (1981).
22. Hanushek and Quigley (1990).
23. Brunori (2004); Pagano (2003).

large minimum lot sizes. A key justification for such regulations is preservation of residential property values by excluding conflicting land uses that may undermine property values. While the basis of zoning lies in mitigating external costs associated with conflicting land uses, exclusionary zoning extends the concept to apartments and multifamily units.[24] It has been argued that land use policies have facilitated the suburbanization and segmentation of metropolitan areas by class and race.[25]

The land use authority of local governments suggests that cities and counties have some influence on the location choices of households and firms. Local governments have other policy tools for attracting or resisting economic activity. They may invest in infrastructure, set business-related taxes, impose fees and delays on development projects, provide subsidies, and so forth. Thus we would expect that local government policies would affect the impact of any transport investment. Interestingly, the evidence on local government influence is quite mixed. Studies of economic development projects, enterprise zones, and employment centers show no consistent effects of local government policies.[26]

Conclusions from Theory

Transit investments can influence urban form. The form and magnitude of impact, however, is subject to two major factors. The first is the quality of transit service in terms of benefits of accessibility, which include comparative cost savings offered by the service and the extent to which the service enhances mobility. In today's metropolitan areas, achieving such benefits requires a significant improvement in accessibility in an already highly accessible network. A light-rail line that replaces an existing bus line, for example, does not constitute increased accessibility; the performance characteristics of the modes would not be measurably different. A subway line that reduces headways and travel times relative to those of bus service would likely constitute a significant increase in accessibility. Thus we would expect significant impacts to be most likely in cases where road congestion is high and the transit investment offers significant benefits in terms of travel time and network connectivity.

The second is local conditions. In a growing metropolitan area, new households and firms must locate themselves. All else being equal, land use impacts are more likely to occur in a growing area. Transit investments in stable or declining metro areas must be sufficiently attractive to influence a redistribution of economic activity. Whether or not land use impacts occur also depends on local government policy. Land use policies that make development cheaper (density

24. Fischel (2001, 2004).
25. Ihlandfeldt (2004).
26. Wassmer (1994); Boarnet and Bogart (1996); Agarwal (2009).

bonuses, tax reductions) will attract new development or redevelopment. Land use policies that make development more costly will have the opposite effect. It is important to note that land use policy alone could affect development patterns. If a city offers special benefits for locating near a transit station and if favorable market conditions exist, development may occur near the transit station, whether or not the transit investment itself contributes to improved accessibility. In this case the motivating factor is the difference in development costs, not the transit investment itself.

Finally, the relative influence of transit will depend on numerous other factors that influence travel demand more generally, including the location of existing activities, future population and employment growth, individual and household incomes, and so forth.

Studies of Land Value Impacts

If transit investment is to have an impact on metropolitan growth and development, it must generate accessibility benefits sufficient to be capitalized into land values. In other words, if provision of transit service improves accessibility substantially, then it will result in significant land value increases near transit stations. Increased land value will be reflected in higher-density development, as expensive land is more intensively used. Population and employment density are therefore proxies for the underlying changes in land values. We focus on evidence related to land value impacts, in part to make the review manageable and in part to restrict ourselves to the most methodologically sound work—an extensive literature that spans several decades. Given our theoretical discussion, it is perhaps not surprising that it provides mixed evidence. The problem is to isolate impacts of transit that are likely to be of small magnitude while controlling for all the other factors that affect land values.

We begin by discussing methodological issues in measuring the impacts of transit investments. We then review, in some detail, studies of three transit systems. We chose these cases for the richness of literature available (in terms of capturing multiple time periods and having a robust research design) and the age of the transit system involved (assuming that older systems may have more measurable impacts than newer systems). We end the section by summarizing the key findings and identifying the questions that research has not yet answered.

Measuring Impacts of Transit Investments

The first issue to consider is how to measure the impacts of transit investments. Since impacts must come from changes in accessibility, the first question is how to measure that.

MEASURES AND VARIABLES. Transit benefits locations near transit stations by making them more accessible.[27] The best measure is land values. If the benefits are significant, they should be capitalized in property values. According to Cervero, for residential properties, the benefits are defined entirely in terms of accessibility.[28] Residents may assign a "disbenefit" to higher street traffic, noise, and air pollution near transit stations, and most U.S. households prefer lower-density living environments. Hence, any observed "premium" in residential property markets near transit stations comes from gains in accessibility, and that premium is a suitable proxy for accessibility impacts. The case for using land values as a proxy is less clear for commercial markets, because both accessibility and agglomeration benefits may be reflected in any observed rent premiums, and it is extremely difficult, if not impossible, to disentangle one from the other.

Land value is not a perfect measure. Numerous factors affect land values, including, for example, distance from natural amenities such as an oceanfront, public amenities such as parks and playgrounds, the quality of schools, highway access, regulation, regional economic health, property market cycle (upswing or recession), and so forth. Some of those factors are spatially correlated with transit access, as discussed further below. Of particular concern are land use policy impacts. If, for example, density bonuses are offered for development around transit stations, both higher property values and more intense development may be observed near stations, even in the absence of any transportation effect of the transit line. Any study of transit impacts has to control for such factors. Policy interventions outside the study area could also be confounding. For example, development constraints introduced in other parts of the city may drive up land values near stations.

A second-best measure of impacts is land use changes. If accessibility increases land values, higher-density development should follow. Thus, changes in commercial square footage—or in employment or population density—could be interpreted as proxies for the underlying land value changes. Of course, residential and commercial development depend on many factors, including local government policies, as discussed above.

One issue to consider in measuring the impacts of transit investment is the appropriate spatial catchment area for a rail line. Most studies limit their study area (the presumed extent of impacts) to a quarter-mile radius, which is roughly the distance that can be covered on foot in five minutes. In reality, however, both benefits and costs of transit stations are more likely to taper off

27. This chapter focuses on rail transit only, because rail transit investment is more likely than bus transit to affect accessibility positively (the exception being bus transitways); most of the empirical literature focuses on rail; and most of the transit policy discussion is about rail systems.

28. Cervero (1997).

(decline with distance) than terminate abruptly. In the simplest form, transit access can be measured as straight-line distance to the transit station or by distance categories (within 1,000 feet of station, between 1,000 to 2,000 feet of station, and so on). Other variations express distance in some nonlinear form—implying that being too close to a station also means being too close to nuisances such as noise and pollution, while being too far reduces the benefit of access to amenities.

The extent to which location near a transit station is valued depends on the improvement in ability to access the network generated by the investment in a station (or line). A transit line that connects major activity centers may significantly improve transit access. A transit line that traverses an area in economic decline or that does not provide a significant travel time advantage will not improve transit access. It is therefore important not only to consider the appropriate catchment area but also to consider the overall impact of the change in transit services. Simply comparing development patterns before and after a transit investment, for example, says nothing about transit impacts.

A second measurement issue is the time frame chosen for examining impacts. Land use changes take place over long periods, owing to the fixed costs and long life of capital stock. How long is long enough? Some may argue that many decades are required. Measuring impacts immediately after the opening of a new rail line or in its early years of operation would underestimate impacts. However, the longer the time period, the more other factors also affect outcomes, including the rate of regional population and employment growth, other transport investments, changes in local government policy, and so forth. Others may argue that changes in land value could occur before construction, reflecting market expectations of the investment. Generally speaking, the older a system, the more likely it is for its benefits to be capitalized in property values.

A third issue is whether property values or development patterns are examined in a single corridor or station area. In a growing metropolitan area, property values can be expected to increase overall. Therefore, demonstrating land price increases within the rail catchment area is not sufficient. Similarly, declining land values do not necessarily imply a negative impact; rather, land values near transit may have declined less than values in other locations. Some studies take the approach of comparing similar corridors, but again, that does not solve the problem. Investment in one corridor could redistribute economic development, exaggerating the effect of the investment.

MODELING APPROACHES.   Researchers have used three major approaches to study the effects of transit on land values: hedonic price models; matched pair comparison; and repeat sales ratios. Hedonic price models use regression analysis to assign monetary value to different attributes of a given property, including building characteristics, neighborhood attributes, and location factors in addition to proximity or distance to a transit station. Hedonic models are based on the assumption that the total value of a given property can be decomposed to the value of each of its attributes. Although there is growing criticism of the hedonic method, it remains a widely used technique for imputing values to property characteristics.[29]

  Hedonic models have some serious shortcomings for investigation of transit impacts. First, because property values are influenced by numerous factors, it is not possible to develop a fully specified model. Omitted variables are likely to be correlated with variables included in the model, leading to various types of estimation problems. When omitted variables are spatially correlated with transit access, the estimated effect of transit access will be biased. For example, if retail shopping opportunities improve (or decline) with distance from transit, the estimated impact of transit is some combination of the value of both transit and retail shopping. Second, hedonic models implicitly assume a homogeneous market. The models assume that attributes such as number of bedrooms or access to parks have the same price effect throughout the market. However, recent research suggests that because housing markets are segmented, that assumption is false.[30] Third, hedonic estimates have been shown to be unstable: small changes in specification or in sample composition can lead to big changes in the access coefficient estimates.[31] Finally, hedonic models typically are estimated on samples of sales data. Sales data do not likely represent the universe of properties from which they are drawn, as the likelihood of a sale is correlated with the attributes of the property itself.

  Matched pair analysis compares prices of properties near transit stations with those of other properties located elsewhere but with attributes similar to those of the properties near transit stations. The biggest challenge in matched pair analysis is finding property pairs that are similar in every way except that one is located near a transit station while the other is not. Finding suitable matches for comparison can be very difficult. In reality, comparison properties are rarely ever exactly the same.

  In repeat sales ratio analysis, changes in sales price between two or more sales transactions for the same property are recorded. The change in property prices near transit stations is then compared with the change in property prices at other

  29. Redfearn (2009).

  30. Therefore, attempting to control for submarket differences through fixed effects models (for example, adding location dummies) is not sufficient because preferences with respect to attributes may vary across submarkets. See Redfearn (2009).

  31. Redfearn (2009).

locations not in close proximity to a transit station. The ratio of the change in property prices at two locations measures the premium that residents are willing to pay for transit access, after other factors have been controlled for. Repeat sales ratio analysis assumes that neighborhood features and parcel attributes remain unchanged across time periods. In reality, that may not be true, especially for long time periods. In addition, repeat sales data for relatively small areas may not be representative of general market conditions.

Two additional measurement challenges are worth mentioning. The first is correlation among various access variables. Many transit lines are located near major highways. In those cases it is difficult to separate out the effects of transit from those of highways. The second is what is technically known as an "endogeneity" problem. If transit planners are investing in response to demand, then transit lines will be located in already dense (and hence high-land-value) locations. Thus, higher land values would reflect the site amenities (agglomeration economies) of the land uses and not necessarily the value of access provided by the transit line. This brief discussion suggests that there are extensive methodological and data challenges to testing the impacts of rail transit investments. Those challenges are one source of differences across the literature.

OVERVIEW OF THE LITERATURE. More than three decades of research has generated an extensive literature that is remarkably varied in terms of method (hedonic model, repeat sales, or matched pair); location (urban, new suburb, mature suburb, greenfield, and so forth); type of transit service, such as heavy-rail transit or light-rail transit (LRT); extent of the study area (within one-fourth to one mile of a transit station); and so forth. The findings from these studies are equally mixed. Given the size of the literature, we have included a sample of studies that are more rather than less methodologically sound; that illustrate the variety in research approaches; and that represent the mixed evidence regarding transit impacts on property values. Table 6-2 provides a summary.

Three studies in table 6-2 allude to property price increases in anticipation of benefits of a proposed rail service.[32] Damm and others examined the influence of proximity to proposed Washington, D.C., Metro transit stations on three property types: single-family residential, multifamily residential, and retail. In all three, locations closer to a proposed rail station drew a premium. The study controls for a variety of building quality and socioeconomic characteristics of the neighborhood. But the study is limited to the District of Columbia; it does not include suburban locations, where results might have been different. Other changes associ-

---

32. Damm and others (1980); Gatzlaff and Smith (1993); Knaap, Ding, and Hopkins (2001).

ated with station locations, such as improved security or new parking facilities, may also be reflected in the premium.

Knaap, Ding, and Hopkins found that the proposed Portland, Oregon, rail transit service resulted in property price increases at locations in close proximity to the proposed stations.[33] The Westside-Hillsboro light-rail service was formally approved in 1993. The authors examined sales prices of vacant residential lots in the proposed rail corridor between 1992 and 1996. Much of the proposed alignment passed through undeveloped greenfield sites. The proposed rail service was likely anticipated to offer development incentives (for example, more flexible development requirements). Thus, the observed premiums may reflect land use policy rather than access provided by the new line.

Unlike the two studies discussed above, Gatzlaff and Smith found that Miami rail station locations were associated with weak effects on single-family home prices.[34] They used two methods: hedonic price models for before and after the station location announcement; and a comparison of repeat sales indices for single family homes located within one square mile of Metrorail stations with identical indices for all other metropolitan properties. The repeat sales indices are estimated for eighteen one-year periods beginning in 1980. The authors assumed that their eight selected stations constituted a representative sample of the entire county. They partitioned observations into two groups to control for neighborhood quality, one representing high-income neighborhoods and the other low-income, economically struggling neighborhoods. They then estimated hedonic price models. The impact of access to rail stations was slightly greater in low-income neighborhoods. The authors found their results to be consistent with lack of ridership on the Metrorail (implying no impact on accessibility) and with planners' efforts to use Metrorail as an economic development tool, locating the system outside Miami's economic growth corridors.

Landis and others examined property values near Sacramento LRT and San Diego trolley (LRT) less than three years after commencement of the rail service.[35] The authors estimated hedonic price models for single-family residential property values in 1990. They used extensive controls for building characteristics and neighborhood quality. In addition to the measure for proximity to an LRT station, the authors also controlled for freeway proximity (a disamenity because of noise and air pollution) and freeway access. The authors reported mixed results. While San Diego stations had a significant and positive influence on single-family home values, Sacramento LRT stations did not have a significant

33. Knaap, Ding, and Hopkins (2001).
34. Gatzlaff and Smith (1993).
35. Landis and others (1995).

Table 6-2. *Selected Studies of Rail Transit Impacts on Property Values*[a]

Author/system	Analysis method	Dependent variable	Time context	Transit accessibility measure
Damm and others (1980)/Washington Metrorail	HP	Property sales price 1969–76 (adjusted for inflation to 1969)	Pre-completion	Linear feet to station
Gatzlaff and Smith (1993)/Miami Metrorail	RSR index for locations near stations compared to an identical index for the MSA; HP	Single-family home sales price	Analysis covers period before and after station locations were announced	Linear distance to the nearest station measured in tenths of a mile
Landis and others (1995)/Sacramento LRT	HP	1990 single-family home sales price	Postconstruction 1–2 years	Roadway distance to the nearest LRT station; dummy for whether the unit is within 300 meters of a rapid transit line
Landis and others (1995)/San Diego trolley	HP	1990 single-family home sales price	Postconstruction >3 years	Roadway distance to the nearest LRT station; dummy for whether the unit is within 300 meters of a rapid transit line

Premium effect	Spatial extent	Weaknesses	Controls/comments
Price elasticity with respect to distance Single-family home (−0.06 – −0.13) Multifamily (−0.09) Retail property (−0.68)	2,500 feet (.5 miles) from LRT station Analysis restricted to Washington, D.C.	No control for highway access because authors claim no substantial variation in travel speeds within Washington, D.C.	Neighborhood quality (income, percent of substandard housing units, percent nonwhites, and so forth); parcel and building attributes (size, condition of the structure, and so forth); densities; zoning; transit station above or below ground
Not significant	One square mile of a rail station; eight stations along the entire line	No control for highway access; no disaggregated controls for neighborhood characteristics and amenities	Building attributes; index for residential property price appreciation in Miami MSA Data partitioned for station locations north of the CBD (representing declining neighborhoods) and south of the CBD (representing economically healthy neighborhoods)
No significant effect on home prices	Not applicable	Accessibility expressed as linear roadway distance to the nearest LRT station	Various building attributes; lot size; neighborhood quality indicators; distance to nearest freeway interchange, dummy for whether the unit is within 300 meters of a freeway; dummy for whether the unit is within 300 meters of an above-ground transit line
Positive premium: $1.66 for every foot closer to station (in 1990)	City of San Diego	Accessibility expressed as linear roadway distance to the nearest LRT station	Various housing, size, age, and amenity attributes; tract income; distance to nearest freeway interchange, dummy for whether the unit is within 300 meters of a freeway; dummy for whether the unit is within 300 meters of an aboveground transit line

(continued)

Table 6-2. *Selected Studies of Rail Transit Impacts on Property Values*[a] *(Continued)*

Author/system	Analysis method	Dependent variable	Time context	Transit accessibility measure
Landis and others (1995)/San Francisco BART and CalTrain	HP	1990 single-family home sales price	Postconstruction >10 years	Roadway distance to the nearest BART/Caltrain station; dummy for whether the unit is within 300 meters of a rapid transit line
Knaap, Ding, and Hopkins (2001)/ Hillsboro light-rail extension (Portland, Oregon)	HP	Sales price per acre of land; residential parcels only	Pre-service; analysis covers period before and after the station locations were announced.	Within one-half mile of a planned station; within one mile of a planned station
Bowes and Ihlanfeldt (2001)/ MARTA (Atlanta)	HP	Single-family home sales price 1991–94	Postconstruction >10 years	One-quarter mile; one-quarter to one-half mile; one-half to one mile; one to two miles; two to three miles

Premium effect	*Spatial extent*	*Weaknesses*	*Controls/comments*
Positive premium in Alameda and Contra Costa counties ($1.96–$2.29 for each foot closer to station) No significant effect in San Mateo County	County	Accessibility expressed as linear roadway distance to the nearest rail station	Various housing, size, age, and amenity attributes; tract income; distance to nearest freeway interchange, dummy for whether the unit is within 300 meters of a freeway; dummy for whether the unit is within 300 meters of an above-ground transit line County dummies
Positive premium: within one-half mile of stations (+31 percent); one-half to one mile (10 percent after station locations were announced)	One mile	Less than 2 percent of the observations in the sample were within one-half mile; less than 10 percent were within one mile.	Extensive neighborhood and site characteristic controls; dummies for whether the parcel lies within 150 feet of a major road and within 150 feet of a minor road Greenfield sites
Negative effect within one-quarter mile radius; positive effect between one-quarter mile and three miles Direct effects stronger than indirect effects	Entire city of Atlanta and DeKalb County		Neighborhood quality; parcel and building characteristics; highway access; city dummies Three separate models for direct effect of rail access and indirect effects of crime rate and retail activity

(continued)

Table 6-2. *Selected Studies of Rail Transit Impacts on Property Values*[a] *(Continued)*

Author/system	Analysis method	Dependent variable	Time context	Transit accessibility measure
Cervero and Duncan (2002)/LRT and CalTrain in Santa Clara County, California	HP	Estimated land values for commercial, light-industrial, and office parcel sales in 1998 and 1999 (in 1999 dollars)	Postconstruction >8 years	Dummies for whether the parcel lies within one-quarter mile of a rail transit station
McMillen and McDonald (2004)/ Midway rapid transit line (Chicago)	HP, RSR, and Fourier RSR	Residential sales prices between 1983 and 1999	Postconstruction >5 years	Distance to the nearest transit station
Hess and Almeida (2007)/ Buffalo LRT	HP	Assessed value of residential properies in 2002	Postconstruction >15 years	Two models: one with linear distance and the other with network distance to the nearest rail station
Redfearn (2009)/ Metro Red Line and Metro Gold Line (Los Angeles)	HP and LWR	1997 and 2002 single-family home sales price for the Red Line 2002 and 2004 single-family home sales price for the Gold Line	Before and after service started	Distance to the nearest rail transit station

Source: Authors' compilation.
a. HP (hedonic price model); RSR (repeat sales ratio); LWR (locally weighted regression).

Premium effect	Spatial extent	Weaknesses	Controls/comments
Positive premium of $25 per square foot within one-quarter mile of a commuter rail station and $4 per square foot within one-quarter mile of an LRT station; negative premium for properties within one-half mile of a freeway interchange	Entire Santa Clara County	Dummy for whether a parcel is within one-half mile of a freeway interchange	Freeway access; labor force access; density; neighborhood quality
Positive premium of 4.02 percent within 1.5 miles of transit line	1.5 miles of the transit line; east of Midway Airport only	No control for highway access; weak control for neighborhood quality	Parcel and building attributes; census tract ethnic mix; community/neighborhood dummies Transit line built on an existing rail right-of-way passing through industrial areas—a potential disamenity effect for property values before transit service
Positive premium of $2.31 for every foot closer to a light-rail station (using linear distance) and $0.99 (using network distance)	One-half mile	No control for highway access	Property characteristics; neighborhood attributes; location amenities
HP: results inconclusive LWR: no capitalization of rail access	Sample drawn from Los Angeles County; exact extent not specified		Controls for distance to the nearest highway ramp Three sets of equations using linear, log, and quadratic specification for the distance variables (both to the nearest rail transit station and the nearest highway ramp)

effect. Furthermore, the San Diego trolley's effects were significant only within the San Diego city limits and not at station locations outside the city proper. The authors attribute their findings to very high ridership on San Diego trolley and to low ridership on Sacramento's LRT. Low ridership is explained by the limited effect of Sacramento's LRT on accessibility. Sacramento has less congestion than San Diego; rail transit therefore offers no travel time advantage.

More recent studies use more sophisticated research methods. For example, one study controlled for local idiosyncratic effects in examining capitalization of rail access in property values along two rail transit lines in Los Angeles.[36] The findings from recent studies, however, are still as mixed as those done earlier. For example, Hess and Almeida found positive price premiums in Buffalo, New York, while Redfearn found no evidence of premiums in Los Angeles and Pasadena.[37]

In a review of the literature on the economic impact of transportation improvements, Ryan noted that the results of the different studies vary according to the ways in which "access" is measured.[38] Ryan observed that to the extent that access improvement is measured to reflect travel time savings accurately, results may be consistent with theoretical expectations. However, since most research does not capture changes in travel time—due to methodological issues or data limitations or both—the results obtained are not consistent with theory.

Conclusions from the Literature

The most robust conclusion to be drawn from our review is that results are quite mixed. The literature does not establish unambiguously whether or not rail transit investments get capitalized in property values. It is much less clear whether rail transit has any impact on investment beyond the narrow geographic scope of most of the studies reviewed—within a quarter-mile to one-mile distance from rail stations or along rail corridors. Mixed results may be attributed to the many methodological and measurement issues discussed previously. Differences may also be the result of unique local circumstances, because transit investments take place in all sorts of locations and conditions. A study of the Midway Rapid Transit line in Chicago is illustrative.[39] The line was built on an existing rail right-of-way that passed through industrial areas; that could have made housing near the transit line less attractive to residents. Although the research findings indicate that the transit service was capitalized in property values, it is not clear whether the effect was completely or in part a result of changes such as the replacement of

36. Redfearn (2009). This study used the locally weighted regression technique.
37. Hess and Almeida (2007); Redfearn (2009).
38. Ryan (1999).
39. McMillen and McDonald (2004).

older, dilapidated buildings that were unattractive to residents with new buildings. Mixed results also suggest that broader, more qualitative studies may provide additional insight on the impacts of investments in transit.

Selected Case Studies

In discussing the three case studies that follow, we broaden the scope of analysis to include multiple indicators of transit impacts, including land values, land use, and transit ridership. We examine changes over long time frames to allow for a sufficient gestation period and in the context of local circumstances. Although not perfect, these case studies address some of the limitations of the land-value studies discussed previously.

The Exemplary Case: Portland, Oregon

Portland, Oregon, is famous throughout the United States for its success in implementing a variety of policies and regulations to foster compact development, promote transit use, and reduce automobile dependence. Most notable among them are the urban growth boundary (UGB); the forty-four-mile-long MAX light-rail system; and an ambitious downtown revitalization program. Since 1979, Portland has also elected a regional government called the Metropolitan Service District (Metro), which has independent budget and land use authority. Portland has employed transit policy, land use policy, and a change in governance structure to reshape its urban form.

THE URBAN GROWTH BOUNDARY. In 1973, Oregon's legislature passed Senate Bill 100, mandating that all city and county governments prepare and adopt comprehensive plans and land use regulations that conformed to the nineteen statewide planning goals.[40] The UGB was a key component of the comprehensive plan. Each region had to define an UGB that contained enough land to meet the region's need for the next twenty years. All plans and land use regulations had to be "acknowledged" (approved) by the State Land Conservation and Development Commission (LCDC), whose members are appointed by the governor. All subsequent local land use decisions had to be in conformity with the acknowledged comprehensive plan. The 1973 mandate established an intergovernmental system of land use regulation and growth control.[41] While local governments enforced land use regulations inside and outside the UGB, state and local governments jointly enforced the UGB.

40. See Oregon Department of Land Conservation and Development, "Statewide Planning Goals" (www.lcd.state.or.us/LCD/goals.shtml#The_Goals).
41. Knaap and Nelson (1992).

On its establishment in 1979, Metro adopted the UGB that had been delineated by the Columbia Regional Association of Governments (CRAG). LCDC was not very satisfied with the proposed boundary because substantial farmland was included within it. However, LCDC did not want to reject a proposal from a recently elected body and hence acknowledged the UGB adopted by Metro. As a compromise, Metro promised to place a temporary moratorium on developing all prime farmland within the UGB for the next ten years. That in effect created an inner growth boundary (IGB) within the UGB. All land inside the IGB could be developed at any time, land between the IGB and UGB could be developed after ten years at the local government's discretion, and land outside the UGB could not be developed until 2000. The UGB, jointly enforced by the state and local governments, was rigidly implemented. The IGB, however, was flexible and could be expanded at the discretion of local government.

PUBLIC TRANSIT IN PORTLAND. The Tri-County Metropolitan Transportation District of Oregon, called TriMet, provides public transit services in most of the urbanized portion of the Portland metropolitan area. The first eighteen-mile segment of the Metropolitan Area Express (MAX) LRT opened in 1986 between Gresham and downtown Portland (see figure 6-3), and an eighteen-mile extension to Hillsboro opened in 1998. The line between downtown and the airport opened in 2000, and the Interstate MAX Yellow Line opened in 2004. Presently, TriMet operates a 44-mile light-rail transit system, 14.7 miles of commuter rail, and more than 700 buses on 93 bus routes.[42] For fiscal year 2008, TriMet reported 63.9 million bus boardings and 35.2 million MAX boardings.

TRANSPORTATION AND LAND USE POLICIES. Portland has pursued inner-core revitalization since 1972 through its Downtown Plan, which involves coordinated land use and transportation policies, several strong landscape and urban design elements, supportive investments in local infrastructure, and extensive housing rehabilitation to recycle older neighborhoods. In 1977, Portland introduced an eleven-block (now thirty-six-block) Transit Mall as a key component of the Downtown Plan. The idea was to concentrate a high-density office core along a transit spine. As a part of the same strategy, Fareless Square, which now covers most of downtown, was introduced in 1975; all transit trips that start and end within the square are free to riders.

Portland has also regulated parking supply in the city in general and within downtown in particular. Portland's zoning code placed an upper limit but no

---

42. TriMet (2009).

minimum requirement on the number of parking spaces permitted for any new development in downtown.[43] Presently, a maximum of 0.7 to 1.5 parking spaces per 1,000 square feet is permitted, depending on the type of development and its proximity to transit. For existing buildings, additional parking space is allowed only if the building is undergoing substantial renovation that establishes a need for additional parking space. In addition, all parking spaces that are open to the general public, whether privately or publicly owned, must be fee parking and all street parking within downtown must be metered.

The city of Portland planned a variety of land use policies and incentives to encourage density in transit corridors in order to support increased transit use and transit-oriented development. Those policies include permitting higher floor area ratios (FARs) along the transit corridors (9:1) and Transit Mall (15:1), as well as incentives to developers to promote higher-density development, including density bonuses and transfers of development rights. Those measures are accompanied by density controls in the several historic districts in the central city (FAR of 4:1). Height and density bonuses are offered for residential use in the downtown commercial zone and for amenities such as child day care centers, rooftop gardens, and so forth.[44]

IMPACTS ON TRAVEL BEHAVIOR. If any changes in spatial patterns in Portland are to be attributed to transit investments, some increase in transit market share must be demonstrated. TriMet, the regional transit agency, reports that between 1998 and 2008, average weekday boardings increased by about 36 percent, from 231,000 to 315,000.[45] Transit trips per capita were 68 in 2006, higher than in other metro areas of comparable size. Jun used census data from 1990 and 2000 to describe travel patterns within the Portland primary metropolitan statistical area (PMSA) and the UGB.[46] Between 1990 and 2000, the commute trip mode share for public transit increased from 4.7 percent to 5.7 percent while that for automobiles decreased from 86.5 percent to 85.2 percent in the PMSA. Within the UGB, however, public transit's mode share increased from 7.2 percent to 9.0 percent and that of automobiles decreased from 87.9 to 85.5 percent during the same period.[47] Note that transit use for commuting was highly concentrated: in 2000, downtown commuters accounted for nearly 44.7 percent of all transit commuters, while the downtown accounts for just 12.1 percent of all

43. City of Portland (2006).
44. City of Portland (1988).
45. TriMet (2009).
46. Jun (2008). The Portland PMSA contains four counties: Clackamas, Multnomah, and Washington counties in Oregon and Clark County in Washington. Only the three Oregon counties have a UGB.
47. Jun (2008).

Figure 6-3. *MAX Transit System*

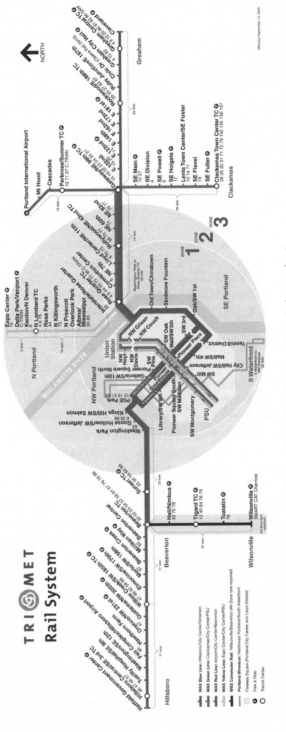

Source: Tri-County Metropolitan Transportation District of Oregon (http://trimet.org/maps/rail system.htm).

employment.[48] That is consistent with the LRT investment's focus on downtown (see figure 6-3). In the case of Portland, there is ample evidence that transit use has increased as a result of the LRT investment.

IMPACTS ON LAND VALUES AND LAND USE. Dueker and Bianco studied the impacts of the eastside LRT on auto ownership, mode share, property values, and development density.[49] They compared data from households that lived along the eastside rail corridor and a parallel bus corridor. The rail line began service in 1986. Two aspects of the eastside LRT are worth noting: first, the rail line eliminated one radial and two express bus lines. Hence, much of the patronage simply shifted from bus to rail. Second, except for rezoning of station areas for higher-density development, no other active transit-oriented development policies were implemented in conjunction with development of the rail line.

Dueker and Bianco used a before-and-after type of qualitative comparison using 1980 and 1990 census data that bracket the opening of the transit line in 1986. The authors noted that land along the rail corridor is "over-zoned" for multifamily units. There was a greater number of multifamily housing units in the rail corridor, but the increase in net residential density (number of residential units divided by the land area zoned for residential use) between 1980 and 1990 was higher in the bus corridor than in the rail corridor. Between 1980 and 1990, the median value for single-family homes in the rail corridor increased at a rate higher than that of comparable homes in the bus corridor. During the same period, the percentage of households owning two automobiles increased by similar rates in both corridors. Given the mixed results, the authors concluded that LRT alone was not sufficient to change development patterns, auto ownership, and travel patterns significantly. However, their findings are based on data from 1990, only four years after the opening of eastside LRT, which may not have been long enough for the benefits of the system to be fully realized.

There have been several studies of the impacts of the UGB on land values in Portland. Knaap used a hedonic pricing model to estimate the effect of the UGB on land values, examining all 455 vacant parcels zoned for single-family homes from Washington and Clackamas counties that were sold in 1980 (four years after the UGB was initially proposed).[50] The sites were located within the IGB, between the IGB and UGB, and outside the UGB. Knaap's findings show that

48. Wendell Cox Consultancy, "Portland (Oregon) CBD and Urban Area Commuting Profile: 2000" (www.publicpurpose.com/ut-cprof-por.htm).

49. Dueker and Bianco (1999).

50. Knaap (1985).

the value of land between inner and outer growth boundaries varied between the two counties. Knaap concluded that the inner growth boundary was perceived to be a genuine and binding constraint on development in Washington County but less of a constraint in Clackamas County. Hence, land values differed signifi- cantly inside and outside the inner boundary in Washington County but not as much in Clackamas County. Fischel attributed the discrepancy to the fact that Clackamas County, which is more rural and less affluent, "may have been more readily forthcoming" in expanding the growth boundary.[51]

Downs compared increases in median home prices between 1980 and 2000 in the Portland PMSA to those in other U.S. metropolitan areas.[52] He found evi- dence that housing prices in Portland did increase significantly faster than those in some comparable U.S. metropolitan areas, but only between 1990 and 1994. Downs then used regression analysis to estimate the impact of the UGB, control- ling for twenty-five key variables that could be expected to affect housing price increases (for example, crime rate, population in poverty, population density, and numerical increase in housing units). He estimated models using different time period intervals between 1990 and 2000. He did not find conclusive evidence that the UGB played a significant role in raising Portland's housing prices, mainly because the analysis was unable to disentangle the effect of the UGB from the effects of other policy interventions. He attributed the rise in housing prices between 1990 and 1994 to Portland's robust economic growth, which led to a significant rise in local employment and wage rates and thereby increased hous- ing demand and prices, rather than to any scarcity created by the UGB.

Portland's urban density remains significantly below the planned density of six to ten dwelling units per net acre of residential land within the UGB. Some estimates place the prevailing densities to be one-third lower than planned density.[53] One key reason is that municipalities have continued to zone for lower overall densities. Although the UGB is jointly enforced by the state and the local governments, local governments enforce land use regula- tions inside the UGB, which include certain minimum density requirements. There have been marked differences in implementation of the same require- ments across jurisdictions.[54]

IMPACTS ON REGIONAL SPATIAL TRENDS. Evidence about regional spatial trends in the Portland metropolitan area is mixed. Some researchers argue that Portland's growth management policies have indeed reduced urban sprawl and

51. Fischel (1990, p. 23).
52. Downs (2002).
53. Staley, Edgens, and Mildner (1999).
54. Fischel (1990).

increased density.[55] Others argue that Portland's development trends are not very different from those of other U.S. metropolitan areas.[56]

Using census data from 1980 and 2000, Jun traced jobs and housing development patterns for the four major counties in the Portland PMSA.[57] He found that the number of commuters working in Multnomah County, the core county of the PMSA, increased by only 22 percent while there was an increase of 50 to 121 percent in the outer counties. That is clear evidence of decentralization of employment. The share of the total PMSA population living in Multnomah County dropped from 41.3 percent in 1990 to 36.9 percent in 2000. Furthermore, between 1990 and 2000, the total population of Multnomah County increased by approximately 13 percent, while that of Clackamas, Washington, and Clark counties increased by 21 percent, 43 percent, and 45 percent, respectively—that is, there was higher population growth in suburban areas.[58] Cross-commuting between Clark County, Washington (outside the UGB), and the three Oregon counties (Multnomah, Clackamas, and Washington) increased, resulting in an increased average commute length. However, a separate study by Jun comparing Portland with seventeen other metropolitan areas in the United States found that "Portland has experienced a moderately higher increase in population density, a significant reduction in automobile dependence, and a rapid increase in public transit use relative to other metropolitan areas."[59] The author attributed the changes to Portland's smart growth policies and better transit accessibility in Portland.

The evidence from Portland indicates the following. First, investment in transit, together with other supportive policies, has resulted in increased transit mode share. Second, access to transit may lead to some premium capitalized in residential properties, but there has not been sufficient research to demonstrate it. Third, there is some evidence that the UGB has resulted in increased densities within the UGB. Finally, overall spatial trends are similar to those of other metropolitan areas, with continued decentralization of population and employment.

The First "New Generation" Rail System: The San Francisco Bay Area Rapid Transit System

The Bay Area Rapid Transit System (BART) was the first of the "new generation" rail systems of the 1970s. The BART Authority was established in 1957, and both approval of the initial plan and funding were secured in 1962—before federal transit funds became available. The BART system began operation in

---

55. See, for example, Patterson (1999); Nelson and Moore (1993).

56. For example, Los Angeles (Richardson and Gordon 2004), Atlanta (Cox 2001), and several other comparable U.S. metropolitan areas (Jun 2004).

57. Jun (2004).

58. U.S. censuses for 1990 and 2000.

59. Jun (2008, p. 102).

Figure 6-4. *BART Transit System*

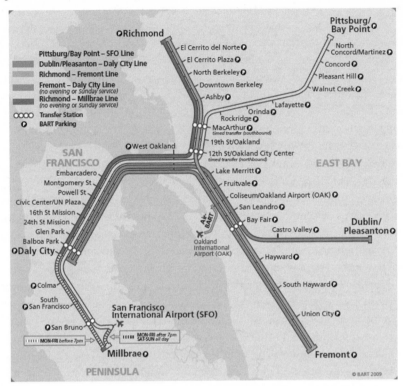

Source: San Francisco Bay Area Rapid Transit District (www.bart.gov/stations/index.aspx).

1972, and the seventy-two-mile system was completed in 1974. Additional lines were added in 1997 (along the I-580 corridor) and in 2003 (to San Francisco International Airport) (see figure 6-4).[60] BART was promoted as a way to reduce congestion and private vehicle use and to attract auto users back to transit by offering a high-speed commute alternative. As figure 6-4 shows, the geography of the San Francisco Bay area limits access to San Francisco. BART would, therefore, greatly increase labor force access to San Francisco.

BART was the subject of intense study during its construction and immediately after its opening. Its design incorporated what was leading-edge technology at the time—for example, an automated fare collection system and computerized train controls. The price of using new technology, however, was years of

60. Giuliano (2004).

operating problems. Early assessments of BART were not positive. Actual rider-ship in 1976 was only 51 percent of what was initially forecast, and BART reduced the number of automobile vehicle trips on highways by less than one-third of the amount forecast (44,000 actual versus 157,000 forecast).[61] One could argue, however, that the early years of BART were not a good indication of impacts for all the reasons discussed previously, such as the long time period required for land use markets to respond.

TRANSIT USE. Thirty years later, BART is an integral part of the bay area's transportation system. It ranks fifth in passenger trips and third in passenger miles among U.S. heavy-rail transit systems.[62] The San Francisco Bay area has the highest transit commute share (9.5 percent) of California's metro areas. The tran-sit mode share for commuters to downtown San Francisco is 50 percent, and those commuters account for just over 50 percent of the entire region's transit commuters. Downtown San Francisco has about 11 percent of the region's em-ployment. In contrast, the transit mode share for Oakland's downtown (with just 2 percent of regional employment) is 25 percent.[63] Although we have no specific evidence on the impact of BART on transit use more generally, BART offers a significant travel time benefit to San Francisco, consistent with the observed high transit mode share in San Francisco.

LAND VALUES AND LAND USE. The U.S. Department of Transportation funded a comprehensive study of BART and the Atlanta and Miami transit sys-tems after twenty years of operation.[64] Table 6-3 summarizes the results. BART impacts varied dramatically across the system. The greatest impact of the system was on the growth of downtown San Francisco, where BART improved labor force access substantially. The already vibrant downtown also benefited from favorable zoning and the availability of properties for redevelopment. The study estimated that about half of the 40 million square feet of office space con-structed between 1975 and 1992 was located within one to two blocks of the Embarcadero BART station.

In contrast to development in downtown San Francisco, in downtown Oak-land most of the development that occurred subsequent to BART's opening was either public or heavily subsidized, despite supportive public policies intended

61. Webber (1976).

62. American Public Transportation Association (2008).

63. Wendell Cox Consultancy, "San Francisco Bay Area CBD and Urban Area Commuting Profile: 2000" (www.publicpurpose.com/ut-cprof-sf.htm).

64. Cervero and Landis (1997).

Table 6-3. *Summary of BART Impact Study Results*

Comparison	Results
County business patterns data (1981–90); shift-share analysis of difference in job growth between ZIP codes with BART stations and ZIP codes without BART stations	Job growth in ZIP codes with BART stations was greater (57 percent of all job growth), but not known whether results were due to job growth in downtown San Francisco; all other BART station ZIP codes had less job growth than non-BART ZIP codes.
Employment density, census tract level (1980 and 1990); data from CTPP	Employment density increases in San Francisco CBD, Oakland CBD, and Concord Line and Fremont Line corridors but also in several highway corridors.
Office space in various locations before BART (1962); 1963–74; 1975–92	Downtown San Francisco: about two-thirds of new of-fice space built in the 1963–74 period and about three-quarters of new office space built in the 1975–92 period was within one-quarter mile of a BART station. Downtown Oakland: less than 10 percent of new East Bay office space over the entire period was built near a BART station; most new office space was built away from BART stations.
Matched pair comparisons of nine BART stations and similar freeway interchanges	More multifamily housing was built near BART sta-tions and slightly more nonresidential units were built near BART stations over the 1979–92 period.

Source: Genevieve Giuliano, "Land Use Impacts of Transportation Investments: Highway and Transit," in *The Geography of Urban Transportation*, 3rd ed., edited by Susan Hanson and Genevieve Giuliano (New York: Guilford Press, 2004), p. 266. Reprinted with permission of Guilford Press.

to promote development without direct subsidies. Giuliano notes that down-town Oakland is the most accessible node in the BART system, so theoretically it should have benefited the most.[65] Local conditions have mediated develop-ment patterns around other BART stations, along the Concord and Fremont lines. For example, the Walnut Creek and Pleasant Hill stations have experi-enced significant commercial and residential development, while other stations have not. The Fremont station area has experienced extensive development of moderate- to high-density housing, spearheaded by ambitious local zoning and municipal support, and there is some evidence that nearby apartment dwellers are paying a premium for access to the BART station. In Berkeley, public resis-tance to high-density redevelopment has deterred change around stations whereas in Richmond a poor local economy and a high crime rate have discour-aged development in areas around stations.

65. Giuliano (2004).

Landis and others found evidence that proximity to a BART station was capitalized in home prices (see also table 6-2).[66] Using 1990 home sales data from Alameda County and Contra Costa County, they found that proximity to the nearest BART station drew a price premium for single-family homes. However, contrary to conventional wisdom, access to a BART station was not capitalized in commercial property values. After differences in lot size, building size, and so forth were controlled for, buildings closer to BART stations did not sell at a premium in comparison with similar buildings located further away.

Evidence from BART illustrates how impacts of even a very large heavy-rail system vary. There is evidence of access capitalized in land values for residential property, but not for commercial property. Less direct proxies—employment and office space—show that impacts were large for downtown San Francisco, but modest to nonexistent in other locations. Local conditions, including zoning and land use policy, also have affected outcomes.

Rail Transit in the Sprawled Metropolis: The Metropolitan Atlanta Rapid Transit Authority

The Metropolitan Atlanta Rapid Transit Authority (MARTA) was established in 1965 to develop a regional transit system for Atlanta. Included in the plan was a two-line heavy-rail system focused on central Atlanta. Like BART, the rail system was intended to be a high-tech alternative to the automobile, providing high-speed access to downtown Atlanta. Unlike BART, however, MARTA was being built in one of the most sprawling and fastest-growing metropolitan areas in the United States. Between 1960 and 1970, the urbanized area population grew more than 50 percent, to about 1.1 million. As of 2000, the urbanized area population had reached 3.5 million, and the metropolitan statistical area (MSA) population reached 4.1 million.[67] Most of the population growth (80 percent) occurred in the suburban and exurban counties, while the central county added only 20 percent more residents.[68] With no geographic or topographic constraints, Atlanta's growth has spread outward. The 2000 urban area population density was 1,783 persons per square mile; comparable figures for Los Angeles and San Francisco–San Jose were 7,068 and 6,127 respectively.[69]

Between 1965 and 1979, MARTA provided only bus service in the region. The first rail line of the system, the East Line connecting the Avondale and

---

66. Landis and others (1995).

67. Wendell Cox Consultancy, "High-Income World Urban Areas: Growth and Population Density" (http://demographia.com/db-econ-uaintl.htm).

68. Federal Highway Administration (2003).

69. Wendell Cox Consultancy, "High-Income World Urban Areas: Growth and Population Density" (http://demographia.com/db-econ-uaintl.htm).

Figure 6-5. *MARTA Transit System*

Source: Metropolitan Atlanta Rapid Transit Authority (www.itsmarta.com/uploadedFiles/Schedules
_And_Maps/Rail_Map/Rail-Map-0302010.pdf).

Georgia State stations, began operating in 1979. MARTA's rail system consists
of two major spines: the East-West Line and the North-South Line, crossing at
Five Points station in downtown Atlanta (see figure 6-5). Presently, MARTA
operates 48.1 miles of rail transit providing service to thirty-eight stations.

TRANSIT USE. Atlanta represents a case in which the basic urban structure is
inconsistent with transit use. Downtown Atlanta accounts for just 7.3 percent of

Table 6-4. *Mode Split of Commute Trips, Atlanta MSA*
Percent

Mode	1990	2000
Drive alone	77.9	77.0
Carpool	13.0	13.6
Bus/streetcar transit	3.4	2.4
Rail/subway transit	1.0	1.1
Others	4.7	5.9

Source: Federal Highway Administration (2003).

urban area employment, with most employment dispersed throughout the area. With few large concentrations of population or employment, conventional transit is a poor fit with travel patterns. It is therefore not surprising that even the central business district (CBD) has a comparatively low transit commuting mode share (14.3 percent) despite its location at the center of the rail system and that the metropolitan area commuting mode share is 4.2 percent. In addition, the private vehicle commute share to the CBD is 83.7 percent, not much different from that of the entire metropolitan area, 89.7 percent.

MARTA reports nearly half a million average weekday passenger boardings on its transit system (including rail and bus service). Between 2001 and 2006, ridership steadily declined; however, since 2006, the number of passengers on the system has increased slightly. Between 1990 and 2000, the share of transit declined from 4.4 percent to 3.7 percent. The decline in transit share came from a drop in bus transit's share; rail transit's share remained mostly unchanged (see table 6-4.)

LAND VALUES AND LAND USE. The U.S. Department of Transportation also funded extensive studies of MARTA. Bollinger and Ilhanfeldt studied MARTA's impacts on population and employment growth between 1980 and 1990.[70] Using census data from 1980 and 1990, they estimated simultaneous models of population and employment growth. They modeled employment growth as a function of proximity to MARTA, employment in the previous decade, labor force access in the previous decade, change in labor force access, and other control variables. Population growth was modeled as a function of employment access, level of employment in the previous decade, proximity to MARTA, and other control variables. The study focused on the twenty-nine rail stations where MARTA provided services in 1990, and the study area was limited to a quarter-mile radius from each station.

70. Bollinger and Ilhanfeldt (1997).

Results showed no evidence of either positive or negative impacts of MARTA on total population or employment in station areas. There was some evidence that MARTA had altered the composition of employment in favor of public sector employment, but only near stations with high levels of commercial activity (as opposed to residential neighborhoods). The authors attributed the findings to MARTA's limited impact on accessibility, the absence of significant increase in transit use, and the fact that public policy efforts were limited to rezoning.

Bowes and Ihlanfeldt also studied the relationship between residential property values and proximity to MARTA's rapid-rail transit stations.[71] The authors used a standard hedonic pricing model to estimate the direct effects of station proximity.[72] In addition to direct effects, which include both transit access and external costs such as exposure to noise and pollution, the authors also examined indirect effects, which include increased crime in the neighborhood and increased retail activity in the neighborhood. The authors used 1991–94 single-family residential sales data from the city of Atlanta and DeKalb County.

In the hedonic pricing model, the authors controlled for various housing characteristics and neighborhood quality measures. Access measures included distance categories for nearest freeway on-ramp (less than one-half mile, one-half to one mile, one to two miles, or two to three miles) and linear distance categories to the nearest MARTA station (less than one-fourth mile, one-fourth to one-half mile, one half to one mile, one to two miles, or two to three miles). The results show that the properties within one-fourth of a mile of a rail station sold for 19 percent less than properties more than three miles away from a station. However, properties between one and three miles from a station were 3.5 percent more expensive than those further away.

The authors interpreted their findings to be the result of the combined effects of crime rate (higher near rail stations close to the CBD) and retail activity (higher near stations further from the CBD). Rail stations that were close to the CBD and had a parking lot tended to attract more crime and to depress property values. Rail stations that were further from the CBD and had retail activity tended to raise property values. With no increase in transit market share, those results are reasonable. Effects correlated with station areas were influencing property values. Higher property values within one to three miles reflected the retail amenities near stations, which were accessed primarily by private vehicle.

---

71. Bowes and Ihlanfeldt (2001).

72. They also used two auxiliary regression equations to estimate the effects of retail trade and crime on property values.

To encourage development around rail stations, the city of Atlanta created special public interest districts (SPID) located around select MARTA rail stations in the downtown, Midtown, and Buckhead areas in 1989. The city waived minimum parking, height, and FAR requirements in SPIDs to encourage higher-density commercial development at those locations. In 1996, the zoning changes for SPIDs in the Buckhead area were supplemented by requirements for a certain percentage of residential development to be constructed concurrently with any new office project greater than 100,000 square feet.

Nelson studied the influence of rail station proximity and the role of SPID policies on office/commercial property values in the three SPIDs in Midtown.[73] Midtown is located about 0.6 miles north of the edge of downtown Atlanta and is served by three MARTA stations. Each Midtown SPID has a radius of about 0.2 miles and an area of approximately 101 acres. The author found that both proximity to rail stations and SPID policies raised commercial property values. Those findings are questionable for several reasons. First, the author estimates the model using only thirty observations, the entire universe of office/commercial building sales transactions between 1980 and 1994. Second, the study does not control for building age, quality, or site amenities. Third, the model does not test for the fixed effect of SPID zoning. As noted earlier in this chapter, it is more likely that the SPID zoning, not the presence of the rail station, created incentives for new development.

Conclusions from Case Studies

Our case studies reveal three very different efforts to use transit investment to influence metropolitan structure. Portland represents an ambitious, integrated transport and land use plan that has resulted in more transit use and possibly higher densities within the UGB. There is also evidence of growth spreading beyond the UGB, and the overall structure of the metro area is similar to that of other areas of its size. Given that land use change occurs slowly, we might expect Portland to become increasingly different from its peers as the UGB becomes more of a constraint. (Washington state has now instituted growth controls, which will limit the spread of growth in that direction.) Portland has benefited from both state and metropolitan land use controls, a unique circumstance in the United States.

The BART system was the result of a consensus agreement among several counties in the San Francisco Bay area. It was built in a mature, relatively dense metropolitan area with a challenging geography that already had a high level of

73. Nelson (1999).

transit use. Unlike the Portland system, BART was not part of a comprehensive land use plan, although it was advocated as a means for limiting sprawl. It is not surprising then that BART outcomes have varied across the system. BART's accessibility benefits and its land use impacts were greatest for San Francisco. Other factors affected outcomes in other areas—crime and depressed local economic conditions in Oakland and Richmond, development incentives in Walnut Creek and Fremont.

The MARTA system had neither geographic nor policy advantages. Metropolitan Atlanta's urban form was and is dispersed and low density and therefore largely incompatible with conventional urban public transit. As would be expected under such circumstances, the rail system had no impact on accessibility and consequently no impact on land values or land use. Observed changes near rail stations are more likely a response to favorable zoning.

Conclusion

Our review of the evidence on accessibility and land use impacts, together with our brief case studies, suggests that rail transit does not consistently lead to significant land use changes. There are examples in which higher-density development has followed at some rail transit station locations, most often through land use policies that make development in those locations less costly and more profitable than development in similar locations. In those cases, it is not the rail investment but the land use policies that have generated the outcome. There are fewer examples of rail investment itself generating changes in land values and thereby more intensive development, and the literature suggests that the changes have been of small magnitude. If rail transit investments do not have consistent or predictable impacts, it follows that such investments are not consistently effective as growth management tools. We now address two questions: why transit investments have limited impacts on metropolitan areas and under what circumstances transit investments are most likely to be effective.

There are many reasons for the limited land use impacts of most transit investments, as discussed earlier. They include the dominance of the private vehicle and highway networks, decentralized metropolitan spatial structure, the durability of the capital stock, declining importance of transport costs in the location choices of households and firms, and public policies that support such macro trends. At the metropolitan scale, even large transit investments have little impact on accessibility because transit constitutes such a small share of both the transportation network and metropolitan travel. To provide access to rail transit at a level comparable to street network access would be prohibitively expensive. Atlanta provides an extreme example: it would take an additional 2,125 miles of rail line and 2,800 new MARTA stations to permit at least 60 percent of Atlanta residents to walk to a transit station.[74] If we assume capital costs of about $60 million per mile, such a system would cost around $127 billion. At the submetropolitan level, local conditions play a role. Rail transit investment may be ineffective because of unique neighborhood characteristics, resistance to higher-density development, lack of transit demand, limited transit connectivity, plentiful parking, and so forth.

With regard to the conditions for effective transit investment, the observations originally made by Knight and Trygg regarding ideal conditions for transit investments and subsequently adapted by many others continue to be appropriate.[75] We offer a somewhat expanded list. Rail transit investments are most likely to have some influence on local land use when

—public transit offers a substantial accessibility improvement, which is readily observed in shorter travel times than with other modes.

—the existing transportation network (including the freeway network) is heavily congested.

—the metropolitan area is experiencing growth and the rail corridor has significant growth and development potential.

—supportive land use and transport policies are in place within the corridor, including development incentives around transit stations and stringent parking management policies.

Why Transit Investment?

We have not considered the costs and benefits of using transit investment as a growth management strategy, but given the uncertain effects of the investments, it is worth considering why urban planners and policymakers continue to advocate transit as an effective growth management tool. A number of arguments have been advanced. The first is based on transit investment as a second-best option. Given that the best option for dealing with the external costs associated with the automobile—pricing—is politically infeasible, we must invest in transit so that it can compete effectively with the private vehicle. Once the investments are made, it only makes sense to encourage development around rail nodes to attract residents and workers, thereby creating a market for the transit service and achieving compact development goals. Unfortunately, as long as the private vehicle remains underpriced, transit investment is a very costly and largely ineffective means for increasing transit mode share and influencing residential and job location choice.

Other arguments deal with fairness. Decades of investment in the highway system contributed to the demise of public transit and to urban sprawl. Highways have effectively been subsidized because highway users have not paid for

74. Bertaud and Richardson (2004).
75. Knight and Trygg (1977).

their negative impacts. It is therefore only fair to subsidize transit and to invest in revitalizing and expanding transit systems. However, it is inefficient to offset the effects of one form of subsidy with another. Also, fairness arguments are based only on sunk costs. The issue, however, is not whether past investments should be compensated but rather what policies would be most effective in solving existing problems.

A related fairness argument is based on the geography of public investments and economic opportunities. Suburbanization, supported by highway investments and housing policies, has been selective, leaving cities with fewer employment opportunities and more dependent populations. Federal and state public transit subsidies are a means of directing resources to cities and contributing to urban revitalization. However, such investments may lead to higher local public costs. The risk in making transit investments for local economic development is the potential burden of operating subsidies, which are largely funded by local sources.

There is also a fairness argument on the land use side. Public policies have distorted the market by subsidizing homeownership through, for example, the mortgage interest tax deduction and zoning that restricts higher-density or mixed-use development. Because those policies have restricted the supply of higher-density location options, using transit investment as a way to increase the supply is justified. This argument hinges on housing preferences and assumes that there is a scarcity of high-density housing options. If that is the case, then eliminating zoning and other restrictions should lead to more of this type of development, with or without any transit investment.

A third argument rests on long-term indirect benefits. Smart growth is a policy goal because of expected long-term benefits in congestion reduction, energy savings, greenhouse gas reduction, formation of neighborhood social ties, and so forth. Because transit investment is one mechanism for promoting smart growth, it is justified. Investments and subsidies now will lead to benefits in the future.

Given the record to date, one might ask why these long-term benefits continue to be part of the justification for rail transit investment. Responses include the following. First, land use change is a very slow process, so the effects of today's investments will be seen decades into the future. Second, changes in general economic conditions such as higher-than-expected per capita income and lower fuel prices make it even more important to invest heavily in rail transit in order to provide a level of service more competitive with that of the automobile. Finally, lack of impacts is due primarily to local conditions, including insufficiently supportive local policies. Because it is not possible to predict the future, we cannot say whether the impacts of sustained transit investment will differ in the future from investment impacts in the past. However, if public policies toward private vehicles do not change, it is unlikely that the future will be greatly different from the past.

There are other political economy explanations for the continued promotion of transit as a growth management tool. First, from a local perspective, transit investment is a bargain, because capital costs are subsidized up to 80 cents on the dollar. Local policymakers make their decisions on the basis of the discounted price, which may be very attractive given the large economic multiplier effects predicted for such projects. State and federal funding is a powerful incentive, as indicated by the fact that there are no examples of rail transit capital investments that are fully funded by local governments—and there is a list of proposed projects that far exceed available subsidy funds.

Second, extensive transit investment is a political imperative stemming from the fragmentation of local decisionmaking. Political support for transit investments is often contingent on different jurisdictions receiving their "fair share," even when such investments are difficult to justify.[76] Just as metropolitan areas across the country compete for federal funds, local city council members compete for projects within their neighborhoods. This creates pressure to allocate investments on the basis of political efficacy rather than project effectiveness.

Together, the availability of outside funds and competition among jurisdictions create more demand for transit projects. State and federal governments must be convinced to provide more funds. Long-term indirect benefits (energy savings, congestion reduction, climate change mitigation) provide an effective justification. Because those benefits are widely valued and they are promised for sometime in the future, today's political leaders gain public support by promoting them while minimizing the risk of being held accountable if the benefits do not materialize.

Finally, a political economy perspective explains why transit investment is widely promoted and advocated while pricing to address the external costs is not. Increasing the price of using private vehicles would impose additional direct costs on users but the benefits would be dispersed. In contrast, transit costs are indirect and spread across the population, while the benefits are concentrated.[77] A political economy perspective is consistent with widespread and growing support for transit as a metropolitan growth management strategy, despite the record.

76. Giuliano (2007).
77. Dunn (1998).

Closing Thoughts

This chapter begins by noting that a major goal of urban policy over more than half a century has been to try to reverse spatial trends and reduce urban sprawl. Despite various policy interventions, however, decentralization of population and employment has continued, suggesting that the interventions have at best slowed the rate of decentralization.[78] Urban sprawl is of concern because of external costs associated with it. The number of concerns has grown over time, and they now include public health and global climate change in addition to congestion, environmental pollution, energy consumption, social segmentation, and unequal job opportunities. Assuming that those problems are in fact associated with urban sprawl, it is important that effective policies for reducing sprawl be identified. More generally, there are any number of reasons why metropolitan growth might be better managed.

Our review of the literature provides little evidence that transit investment has had significant impacts on urban structure. More than three decades of research provides some reasonable indicators of conditions under which transit investment does contribute to changes in the spatial structure of metropolitan areas; those conditions, however, exist in relatively few places. Transit investment therefore is typically not an effective strategy for achieving changes in urban structure. One important reason for the limited impact of transit investments is the underpricing of the private vehicle. Without changing our policies regarding private vehicles, transit investment will remain an inefficient strategy for influencing travel behavior and thereby location choices.

Are there any second-best options that would be more effective than rail transit investment? We suggest more reliance on land use policy itself. Eliminating regulations that discourage or prevent higher-density or mixed-use development will be effective in places where demand is sufficient to support such development. Providing incentives in the form of density offsets, flexible parking requirements, or reduced fees will promote higher-density development. And using smart growth principles in the design of new communities is a direct way of influencing urban structure.

Although properly pricing the use of private vehicles is politically difficult, parking policy is both feasible and effective. Donald Shoup's exhaustive research has shown that charging for parking significantly affects travel behavior; reducing travel demand promotes carpooling and transit and allows for higher-density development.[79] We also suggest more serious consideration of bus transit. In most

---

78. Kim (2007); Lee, Seo, and Webster (2006); Giuliano and others (2007); Lee (2007).
79. Shoup (2005).

parts of most U.S. metropolitan areas, development densities will not reach levels that require rail mass transit without a major change in energy prices or regulatory policies. High-quality bus transit can easily serve moderate-density areas, and busways give buses the same travel time advantage as rail, typically at far less cost. Moving U.S. metropolitan areas to more sustainable spatial organization requires understanding how households and businesses make residence and business location choices and how those choices can be effectively and efficiently influenced.

References

Agarwal, Ajay. 2009. "Do Local Governments Influence Metropolitan Spatial Structure? Evidence from the Los Angeles Region." Paper presented at the 2009 Western Regional Science Association Conference, Napa, California, February 22–25, 2009.

Alonso, William. 1964. *Location and Land Use.* Harvard University Press.

American Public Transportation Association. 2008. *Public Transportation Fact Book*, 59th ed. Washington.

Anas, Alex, Richard Arnott, and Kenneth Small. 1998. "Urban Spatial Structure." *Journal of Economic Literature* 36, no. 3: 1426–64.

Bertaud, Allain, and Harry W. Richardson. 2004. "Transit and Density: Atlanta, the United States, and Western Europe." In *Urban Sprawl in Western Europe and the United States*, edited by Harry W. Richardson and Chang-Hee Bae, pp. 293–310. Burlington, Vt.: Ashgate Publishing Company.

Boarnet, Marlon G., and William T. Bogart. 1996. "Enterprise Zones and Employment: Evidence from New Jersey." *Journal of Urban Economics* 40, no. 2: 198–215.

Bollinger, Christopher R., and Keith R. Ihlanfeldt. 1997. "The Impact of Rail Rapid Transit on Economic Development: The Case of Atlanta's MARTA." *Journal of Urban Economics* 42, no. 2: 179–204.

Bowes, David R., and Keith R. Ihlanfeldt. 2001. "Identifying the Impacts of Rail Transit Stations on Residential Property Values." *Journal of Urban Economics* 50, no. 1: 1–25.

Brunori, David. 2004. *Local Tax Policy: A Federalist Perspective.* Washington: Urban Institute.

Castells, Manuel, and Peter Hall. 1994. *Technopoles of the World: The Making of Twenty-First Century Industrial Complexes.* London and New York: Routledge.

Cervero, Robert. 1997. "Transit-Induced Accessibility and Agglomeration Benefits: A Land Market Evaluation." Working Paper 691, Institute of Urban and Regional Development, University of California, Berkeley.

Cervero, Robert, and Michael Duncan. 2002. "Transit's Value-Added Effects: Light and Commuter Rail Services and Commercial Land Values." *Transportation Research Record* 1805: 8–15.

Cervero, Robert, and John Landis. 1997. "Twenty Years of the Bay Area Rapid Transit System: Land Use and Development Impacts." *Transportation Research A* 31, no. 4: 309–33.

Cervero, Robert, and Kang Li Wu. 1997. "Polycentrism, Commuting, and Residential Location in the San Francisco Bay Area." *Environment and Planning A* 29, no. 5: 865–86.

Chinitz, Benjamin. 1991. "A Framework for Speculating about Future Urban Growth Patterns in the U.S." *Urban Studies* 28, no. 6: 939–59.

City of Portland. 1988. *Central City Plan.*
———. 2006. *Central City District Plan.*
Cox, Wendell. 2001. "American Dream Boundaries: Urban Containment and Its Consequences." Atlanta: Georgia Public Policy Foundation.
Crane, Robert. 1996. "The Influence of Uncertain Job Location on Urban Form and the Journey to Work." *Journal of Urban Economics* 39, no. 3: 342–58.
Damm, David, and others. 1980. "Response of Urban Real Estate Values in Anticipation of the Washington Metro." *Journal of Transport Economics and Policy* 14, no. 30: 20–30.
Downs, Anthony. 2002. "Have Housing Prices Risen Faster in Portland than Elsewhere?" *Housing Policy Debate* 13, no. 1: 7–31.
Dueker, Kenneth J., and Martha J. Bianco. 1999. "Light-Rail Transit Impacts in Portland: The First Ten Years." *Transportation Research Record* 1685, 171–80.
Dunn, James A. 1998. *Driving Forces: The Automobile, Its Enemies, and the Politics of Mobility.* Brookings.
Ewing, Reid, Rolf Pendall, and Don Chen. 2002. *Measuring Sprawl and Its Impact: The Character and Consequences of Metropolitan Expansion.* Washington: Smart Growth America.
Federal Highway Administration. 2003. *Journey to Work Trends in the United States and Its Major Metropolitan Areas 1960–2000.*
Fischel, William. 1990. "Do Growth Controls Matter? A Review of Empirical Evidence on the Effectiveness and Efficiency of Local Government Land Use Regulation." Working Paper 87-9. Cambridge, Mass.: Lincoln Institute of Land Policy.
———. 2004. "An Economic History of Zoning and a Cure for Its Exclusionary Effects." *Urban Studies* 41, no. 2: 317–40.
———. 2001. *The Homevoter Hypothesis.* Harvard University Press.
Florida, Richard. 2002. *The Creative Class.* New York: Basic.
Galster, George, and others. 2001. "Wrestling Sprawl to the Ground: Defining and Measuring an Elusive Concept." *Housing Policy Debate* 12, no. 4: 681–717.
Gatzlaff, Dean H., and Marc T. Smith. 1993. "The Impact of the Miami Metrorail on the Values of Residences near Station Locations." *Land Economics* 69, no. 1: 54–66.
Giuliano, Genevieve. 2007. "The Changing Landscape of Transportation Decision Making." *Transportation Research Record* 2036: 5–12.
———. 2004. "Land Use Impacts of Transportation Investments: Highway and Transit." In *The Geography of Urban Transportation*, 3rd ed., edited by Susan Hanson and Genevieve Giuliano, pp. 237–73. New York: Guilford Press.
Giuliano, Genevieve, Ajay Agarwal, and Christian Redfearn. 2009. *Metropolitan Spatial Trends in Employment and Housing: Literature Review.* Special Report 298. Washington: Transportation Research Board.
Giuliano, Genevieve, and Kenneth Small. 1991. "Subcenters in the Los Angeles Region." *Regional Science and Urban Economics* 21, no. 2: 163–82.
Giuliano, Genevieve, and others. 2007. "Employment Concentrations in Los Angeles, 1980–2000." *Environment and Planning A* 39, no. 12: 2935–57.
Glaeser, Edward L., and Matthew E. Kahn. 2003. "Sprawl and Urban Growth." Discussion Paper 2004. Harvard Institute of Economic Research.
Gordon, Peter, and Harry W. Richardson. 1996. "Beyond Polycentricity: The Dispersed Metropolis, Los Angeles, 1970–1980." *Journal of the American Planning Association* 62, no. 3: 289–95.

Gottlieb, Paul D. 1995. "Residential Amenities, Firm Location, and Economic Development." *Urban Studies* 32, no. 9: 1413–36.

Graham, Stephen, and Simon Marvin. 1996. *Telecommunications and the City: Electronic Spaces, Urban Places*. London: Routledge.

Hanushek, Eric A., and John M. Quigley. 1990. "Commercial Land Use Regulation and Local Government Finance." *American Economic Review* 80, no. 2: 176–80.

Hess, Daniel B., and Tangerine M. Almeida. 2007. "Impact of Proximity to Light-Rail Rapid Transit on Station-Area Property Values in Buffalo, New York." *Urban Studies* 44, no. 5–6: 1041–68.

Hu, Pat S., and Timothy R. Reuscher. 2004. "Summary of Travel Trends: 2001 National Household Survey." U.S. Department of Transportation.

Ihlanfeldt, Keith R. 2004. "Exclusionary Land Use Regulations within Suburban Communities: A Review of the Evidence and Policy Prescriptions." *Urban Studies* 41, no. 2: 261–83.

Jackson, Kenneth T. 1985. *Crabgrass Frontier: The Suburbanization of the United States*. Oxford University Press.

Jacobs, Jane. 1961. *The Death and Life of Great American Cities*. New York: Random House.

Jun, Myung-Jin. 2004. "The Effects of Portland's Urban Growth Boundary on Urban Development Patterns and Commuting." *Urban Studies* 41, no. 7: 1333–48.

———. 2008. "Are Portland's Smart Growth Policies Related to Reduced Automobile Dependence?" *Journal of Planning Education and Research* 28, no. 1: 100–07.

Kim, Sukkoo. 2007. "Changes in the Nature of Urban Spatial Structure in the United States, 1890–2000." *Journal of Regional Science* 47, no. 2: 273–87.

Knaap, Gerrit. 1985. "The Price Effects of Urban Growth Boundaries in Metropolitan Portland, Oregon." *Land Economics* 61, no. 1: 26–35

Knaap, Gerrit, and Arthur Nelson. 1992. *The Regulated Landscape: Lessons on State Land Use Planning from Oregon*. Cambridge, Mass.: Lincoln Institute of Land Policy.

Knaap, Gerrit, Chengr Ding, and Lewis D. Hopkins. 2001. "Do Plans Matter? The Effect of Light-Rail Stations on Land Values in Station Areas." *Journal of Planning Education and Research* 21, no. 1: 31–39.

Knight, R., and L. Trygg. 1977. "Land Use Impacts of Rapid Transit: Implications of Recent Experiences." Final Report No. DOT-TPI-10-77-29 U.S.DOT. San Francisco: De Leuw Cather and Company.

Landis, John, and others. 1995. *Rail Transit Investments, Real Estate Values, and Land Use Changes: A Comparative Analysis of Five California Rail Transit Systems*. Institute of Urban and Regional Development, University of California, Berkeley.

Lee, Bumsoo. 2007. "Edge or Edgeless Cities? Urban Spatial Structure in U.S. Metropolitan Areas, 1980 to 2000." *Journal of Regional Science* 47, no. 3: 479–515.

Lee, Shin, Jong Gook Seo, and Chris Webster. 2006. "The Decentralizing Metropolis: Economic Diversity and Commuting in the U.S. Suburbs." *Urban Studies* 43, no. 13: 2525–49.

McMillen, Daniel P., and John F. MacDonald. 1998. "Suburban Subcenters and Employment Density in Metropolitan Chicago." *Journal of Urban Economics* 43, no. 2: 157–80.

———. 2004. "Reaction of House Prices to a New Rapid Transit Line: Chicago's Midway Transit Line, 1983–99." *Real Estate Economics* 32, no. 3: 463–86.

Mieszkowski, Peter, and Edwin S. Mills. 1993. "The Causes of Metropolitan Suburbanization." *Journal of Economic Perspectives* 7, no. 3: 135–47.

Mills, Edwin S. 1972. *Studies in the Nature of Urban Economy*. Johns Hopkins University Press.

Muller, Peter O. 2004. "Transportation and Urban Form: Stages in the Spatial Evolution of the American Metropolis." In *The Geography of Urban Transportation*, 3rd edition, edited by Susan Hanson and Genevieve Giuliano, pp. 59–85. New York: Guilford Press.

Muth, Robert F. 1969. *Cities and Housing*. University of Chicago Press.

Nelson, Arthur C. 1999. "Transit Stations and Commercial Property Values: A Case Study with Policy and Land Use Implications." *Journal of Public Transportation* 2, no. 3: 77–95.

Nelson, Arthur C., and Terry Moore. 1993. "Assessing Urban Growth Management: The Case of Portland, Oregon, the USA's Largest Urban Growth Boundary." *Land Use Policy* 10, no. 4: 293–302.

Pagano, Michael A. 2003. "City Fiscal Structures and Land Development." Brookings.

Patterson, John. 1999. "Urban Growth Boundary Impacts on Sprawl and Redevelopment in Portland Oregon." Working Paper, Department of Geography and Geology, University of Wisconsin, Whitewater.

Peterson, Paul E. 1981. *City Limits*. University of Chicago Press.

Redfearn, Christian L. 2007. "The Topography of Metropolitan Employment: Identifying Centers of Employment in a Polycentric Urban Area." *Journal of Urban Economics* 61, no. 3: 519–41.

———. 2009. "How Informative Are Average Effects? Hedonic Regression and Amenity Capitalization in Complex Urban Housing Markets." *Regional Science and Urban Economics* 39, no. 3: 297–306.

Richardson, Harry, and Peter Gordon. 2004. "Sustainable Portland? A Critique and the Los Angeles Counterpoint." In *Towards Sustainable Cities: East Asian, North American, and European Perspective on Managing Urban Regions*, edited by Andre Sorensen, Peter J. Marcotuillio, and Jill Grant, pp. 132–46. Burlington, Vt.: Ashgate.

Ryan, Sherry. 1999. "Property Values and Transportation Facilities: Finding the Transportation–Land Use Connection." *Journal of Planning Literature* 13, no. 4: 412–27

Shoup, Donald C. 2005. *The High Cost of Free Parking*. Chicago: Planners Press.

Staley, Samuel, Jefferson Edgens, and Gerard Mildner. 1999. "A Line in the Land: Urban Growth Boundaries, Smart Growth, and Housing Affordability." Policy Study 263. Los Angeles: Reason Public Policy Institute.

TriMet. 2009. "Facts about TriMet." Portland, Ore.

Warner, Sam Bass. 1978. *Streetcar Suburbs*, 2nd edition. Harvard University Press.

Wassmer, Robert. 1994. "Can Local Incentives Alter a Metropolitan City's Economic Development?" *Urban Studies* 31, no. 8: 1251-1278.

Webber, Melvin M. 1976. "The BART Experience: What Have We Learned?" *Public Interest* 45 (Fall 1976), pp. 79–108.

Index